THE ULTIMATE BEGINNER'S GUIDE FOR MINECRAFTERS

THE ULTIMATE BEGINNER'S GUIDE FOR MINECRAFTERS

UNOFFICIAL TIPS AND TRICKS TO SURVIVE AND THRIVE IN THE OVERWORLD!

MEGAN MILLER

NEW YORK TIMES BESTSELLING AUTHOR

Sky Pony Press
New York, NY

NOT OFFICIAL MINECRAFT PRODUCT.
NOT APPROVED BY OR ASSOCIATED WITH MOJANG.

Copyright © 2025 Megan Miller

All rights reserved. No part of this book may be reproduced in any manner without the express written consent of the publisher, except in the case of brief excerpts in critical reviews or articles. All inquiries should be addressed to Sky Pony Press, 307 West 36th Street, 11th Floor, New York, NY 10018.

Sky Pony Press books may be purchased in bulk at special discounts for sales promotion, corporate gifts, fund-raising, or educational purposes. Special editions can also be created to specifications. For details, contact the Special Sales Department, Sky Pony Press, 307 West 36th Street, 11th Floor, New York, NY 10018 or info@skyhorsepublishing.com.

Sky Pony® is a registered trademark of Skyhorse Publishing, Inc.®, a Delaware corporation. Visit our website at www.skyponypress.com.

10 9 8 7 6 5 4 3 2 1

Library of Congress Cataloging-in-Publication Data is available on file.

Cover design by Kai Texel
Cover and interior photographs by Megan Miller

ISBN: 978-1-5107-8121-4
Ebook ISBN: 978-1-5107-8440-6

Printed in China

AUTHOR'S NOTE

This guide is based on the Java Edition of Minecraft, release 1.20.4. Minecraft updates the game about every year, so new content (new mobs, blocks, buildings, etc.) are always being added, and may have been added since publication; however, the principles of gameplay will be the same. The Bedrock Edition of Minecraft is increasingly similar to the Java Edition; any differences remaining are typically quite small and are described in the Minecraft wiki at https://minecraft.wiki.

CONTENTS

Introduction: What You Do When You Play Minecraft   xi

1. Starting Your World   1
2. Surviving Your First Day   13
3. Surviving Your First Week: Staying Safe   29
4. Food and Farming   42
5. Mining and Caving   61
6. The Natural World   75
7. Places to Go   95
8. Stuff and Things   112
9. Weapons, Armor, and Tools   128
10. Moo! Oink! The Passive Mobs   142
11. Grrr! Mobs That Attack   154
12. Villages and Villagers   173
13. Technology: Redstone and Rails   188
14. Surviving the Nether   213
15. Magic: Enchanting and Potions   229
16. The End Game: Dragons and Withers   244

Appendix A Game Settings   260
Appendix B Customizing Minecraft   270
Appendix C Beyond Survival: Other Ways to Play Minecraft   274
Index   279

THE ULTIMATE BEGINNER'S GUIDE FOR MINECRAFTERS

INTRODUCTION
WHAT YOU DO WHEN YOU PLAY MINECRAFT

Minecraft is an open world sandbox game. *Open world* means that the size of the world is essentially limitless, and *sandbox* means you can do pretty much whatever you want. That said, gameplay in Minecraft doesn't include solving a mystery, racing cars, or building an army, but rather mining, crafting, exploring, building, farming, gathering, and battling in-game entities, known as *mobs*.

EVERY MINECRAFT WORLD—THE TERRAIN, WATERWAYS, AND GEOGRAPHY—IS PROCEDURALLY GENERATED FROM A RANDOM NUMBER (A *SEED*) ISSUED WHEN YOU CREATE A WORLD. THIS MEANS EACH NEW WORLD IS UNIQUE, ALTHOUGH IT WILL CONTAIN ALL THE COMMON FEATURES AND STRUCTURES, LIKE DESERT TEMPLES AND VILLAGES.

Because there is no storyline or set of tasks to accomplish, there's no real winning or losing. Some players lead a peaceful life of farming, crafting, and mining. Others like to explore the endless terrain, from desert oases to forested mountains, or feel driven to protect villages from zombies. Maybe you'll choose to focus on engineering contraptions that automatically kill monsters or produce iron ingots, or building huge structures, like hobbit holes, mansions, and spaceships. Nothing is stopping you from doing it all!

Let's look at what playing Minecraft is all about.

What You Do

Minecraft is a game in which you appear in a new, blocky world and you can walk and interact with pretty much everything in the world—the blocks, the animals, the people, everything! Mostly you'll be doing the following.

BREAK, DESTROY, AND PLACE BLOCKS

Almost every part of your landscape is made of blocks. A *block* is a cube made of wood, stone, or other materials that's one meter (about 3.3 feet) cubed. Some items take up the space of a block, but are not cubes, like a flower or patch of grass. You can break many blocks by punching them with a tool or your hand. Breaking a block often drops an item you can use. For example, destroying a patch of growing grass drops wheat seeds you can farm, and breaking a tree trunk drops wood you can use for building shelters or tools. Sometimes you'll need a tool like an axe or a pickaxe to break some blocks, like a wooden fence or a block of ore.

YOU USE LEFT-CLICK TO BREAK BLOCKS, LIKE THE LOG BLOCKS THAT MAKE UP A TREE.

EXPLORE

Minecraft worlds are immense and unique, with randomly spawned deserts, forests, plains, mountains, swamps, rivers, oceans, caves, hidden fortresses and dungeons, villages, animals, and monsters. You can travel by foot as you explore, but you can also craft boats to sail rivers and oceans (Chapter 2) or tame a horse and equip it with a saddle to travel far distances (Chapter 9).

EXPLORE YOUR WORLD TO FIND VILLAGES, TRAIL RUINS, SHIPWRECKS, AND MUCH MORE.

BUILD

Use the many blocks in Minecraft (planks, logs, mud bricks, terracotta, stone, and more) to build whatever you like, from prairie cottages to underground Dwarven mines or airplanes hovering in the sky.

CRAFT

Use your resources and recipes to make new objects and goods by assembling them in a crafting table. Use a furnace to smelt ores and cobblestone, cook food, or dry kelp and sponges.

TO MAKE MORE STUFF, YOU'LL NEED A CRAFTING TABLE.

MINE AND CAVE
Explore the underground caves of your world to find rare geodes, valuable ores, lush caves, aquifers, and essential resources.

BATTLE
Use weapons like swords, axes, and crossbows to attack and kill monsters; most will drop useful items upon death.

FARM
Get more resources for food and crafting by farming, gathering plants, chopping wood, fishing, and breeding and killing animals.

TRADE
In villages, many inhabitants will gladly trade you some of their goods for precious emeralds (see Chapter 12). You will also encounter wandering traders traveling the land, ready to trade a few precious items.

LOOT
Find cool, rare, or valuable goodies by looting chests in villages, sunken ships, dungeons, fortresses, and other structures.

LOOTING (GETTING STUFF FROM CHESTS FOR FREE) IS NOT CHEATING!

ENCHANT
The Minecraft world also includes magic. Craft an enchanting table to imbue tools, weapons, and armor with special powers (see Chapter 15).

BREW POTIONS
Craft a brewing stand to make potions you can drink for special abilities or hurl at enemies to damage them (see Chapter 15).

ENGINEER

Collect a special ore, called redstone, and craft engineering components to harness the game's special electric power. You can use redstone to open and close doors, move blocks with pistons, light lamps, and more (see Chapter 13).

There's much more you can do too, including swimming, flying around with special wings called Elytra, collecting rare animals, and taming wolves and cats to be your pets. I like protecting and enhancing villages and building roads that connect different points of interest in my world (something many people would find incredibly dull)!

> ONE OF MY FAVORITE THINGS TO DO IN MINECRAFT IS TO EXPLORE AND FIND VILLAGES TO DEFEND AND CONNECT THEM TO OTHER VILLAGES WITH ROADS.

Unavoidable Activities

You'll also have to do some somewhat less exciting but mandatory activities to keep yourself alive and achieve new things.

EAT

Everyone needs to eat. Your hunger bar goes down as you expend energy, and up as you eat. Hunger is tied to health, and you must eat to heal if you are hurt. You can get food from numerous sources, such as killing animals and cooking their meat (though raw meat might make you sick!), farming or finding fruits and vegetables, and crafting more complex recipes.

SLEEP

At night, all sorts of monsters, like zombies and spiders, appear and, if they see you, they try to attack you. Craft a bed or find one in a village to sleep in to make it through the perilous night.

GAIN EXPERIENCE

As you perform certain activities—breeding animals, fishing, killing mobs (excluding baby animals and villagers), mining, smelting, and trading—you'll get experience points (XP), visualized as green orbs that float toward you. Make sure you collect these, as you'll need experience points to accomplish tasks later on.

THOSE LITTLE GREEN SPHERES CONTAIN VALUABLE EXPERIENCE POINTS.

DIE
It's going to happen, and happen a lot, especially if you like fighting mobs. But it's not really dying—it's more like a reset. You have 20 points of health, and damaging activities like falling, fighting, and drowning will deduct points. If your health falls to 0, you'll get a dramatic screen announcement of your death; click **Respawn** to bring your character back to life. You'll respawn where you last slept, or if that bed is unavailable, at your *world spawn*, which is where you started out when you first entered your world. Your inventory will be scattered on the ground where you died, but if you remember where you died and get there within about five minutes, you can often recover it. You will lose your accumulated experience points.

An Ever-Changing Game
Minecraft's developers, Mojang, update it almost yearly with new mobs, features, and activities. You can even play experimental prereleases of the game to see what's coming. Mojang regularly posts on their social media with their progress and ideas, and presents updates at a yearly online event, Minecraft Live. There's also a robust modding community that develops all kinds of mods (modifications) you can add to your game, from adding dinosaurs and zoo animals to expanding available ores and processing capabilities (see Appendix B).

Up Next
Now that you have an idea what you've signed up for, let's start a world!

1
STARTING YOUR WORLD

To start playing Minecraft, you'll need to generate and name a new world and adjust a few settings. In this chapter, we'll look at the fastest way of jumping into gameplay using most of the default settings. (For a more detailed look at global options and world settings, see *Appendix A*.) We'll look at the user interface, controlling your character, and navigating your world. In the next chapter, we'll guide you through your first day and some important tasks that will help you survive overnight!

But first, before you even create your world, you'll want to decide the difficulty level and game mode.

Game Mode

There are five game modes to choose from for your world. This book focuses on Survival mode, although general information is still applicable to the Creative and Hardcore modes.

In Survival mode, you're playing as someone who has to eat, sleep, and defend themselves against the environment (*PvE*, or *player vs. environment*). Creative mode is perfect for players who want to build; all survival qualities are stripped, so you don't need to worry about fighting or dying. In Creative, you can fly around the world and have unlimited access to the entire inventory of Minecraft blocks and items. Hardcore mode is an unforgiving Survival mode in which dying will boot you out of your world. You can't return to it again—your world is deleted upon death.

There are two other modes primarily for playing in Minecraft worlds (*maps*) that other creators have built: In Adventure mode, you can't break any blocks unless the programmer has allowed it. In Spectator mode, you can't touch any blocks, but you can float through blocks and the landscape to see everything. This mode is often used in customized games to allow defeated players to easily watch the rest of the game play out without affecting anything and it can be useful for finding underground structures. You can access these modes yourself within the game if you have enabled cheats. See the paragraphs below on Switching Modes and Levels.

Difficulty Levels: There are four difficulty levels to choose from: Peaceful, Easy, Normal, and Hard.

On Peaceful difficulty, no hostile mobs will spawn, except for some in the Nether and End. Your health regenerates quickly, and you can't die from starvation because your hunger bar never depletes. On the other hand, because no hostile mobs spawn, you won't be able to retrieve any rare items they might drop.

On Easy difficulty, hostile mobs do less damage than in Normal. Effects such as Poison and Wither don't affect the player (unless you meet a wither skeleton). Skeletons and zombies don't wear full armor, and zombies cannot break through doors or turn villagers into zombie villagers.

On Normal difficulty, zombies have a 50 percent chance of transforming a villager into a zombie villager, though they still can't break through doors. Hostile mobs deliver standard damage, and your health bar gradually depletes.

On Hard difficulty, hostile mobs deal more damage and skeletons and zombies can wear full armor. Spiders have a chance of spawning with special effects, like invisibility or strength. Zombies break down doors, can spawn reinforcements, and will turn villagers into zombie villager's 100 percent of the time. You receive much better loot from killing hostile mobs.

SWITCHING MODES AND LEVELS

If you're uncertain about which difficulty or game mode to choose, you can grant yourself the ability to change these at any time by turning **Cheats On** when creating your world. With Cheats On, you could play in Peaceful mode and change to Easy or Normal when you're ready to start killing hostile mobs. You change the game mode by pressing **T** to open chat, typing **/gamemode**, and entering a space. The chat dialogue will show you a menu of modes; select a mode and press **Enter** to confirm. Similarly, change your difficulty level by pressing **T**, typing **/difficulty**, and selecting from the displayed menu of options.

Setting Up Your World

Your first task is to generate and name a new world and adjust a few settings. In this chapter we'll set up a world using the default settings, which is the quick and easy

STARTING YOUR WORLD

option—for a detailed look at options and settings, see Appendix A. We'll then look at controlling your character and navigating your world. In the next chapter, we'll go over some tasks that will help you survive your first day.

1. Start Minecraft to open the Minecraft launcher screen. This allows you to select the version of Minecraft and other global settings, like your *skin* (character's appearance). Make sure the version of Minecraft reads "Latest Release" at the bottom left.

THE MINECRAFT LAUNCHER SCREEN

1. **MEGANFMILLER**—User account
2. **MINECRAFT: JAVA EDITION**—The game we're playing; available for Windows, Mac, and Linux
3. **MINECRAFT: FOR WINDOWS**—Bedrock Edition; available only on Windows
4. **MINECRAFT DUNGEONS AND LEGENDS**—These are two entirely different games based on combat and conquest
5. **WHAT'S NEW AND SETTINGS**—These apply to the Minecraft Launcher and not the Minecraft game
6. **LATEST RELEASE**—Selected game version
7. **INSTALLATIONS**—Here you can choose different Java edition releases to play Minecraft in (for experienced players)
8. **REALMS:** Lease a private Minecraft server
9. **SKINS**—Choose the look of your avatar
10. **PATCH NOTES**—Find out what new features were added in the current and past releases of Minecraft Java edition
11. **TOP RIGHT ICONS**—Quick Start menu for selecting a saved world to play in

CHAPTER 1

2. Click the **Skins** tab on the top menu, and on the next screen, select one of the characters shown. There are only aesthetic differences—arm size and outfits—between the avatars. See Appendix B for details on custom skins.
3. Select the **Play** tab and click **Play** to start the game.
4. On the main menu screen, click **Options** to change game options, such as volume or controls.

THE MAIN MENU, WHERE YOU CLICK OPTIONS TO ACCESS YOUR GAME SETTINGS, AND START OR QUIT MINECRAFT.

I recommend changing two settings. The default brightness setting is pretty dark, so under Video Settings, make sure Brightness is set to **Bright**. Under Controls, make sure Auto-jump is set to **Off**. Auto-jump moves you automatically up single blocks in front of you, which often places you in unexpected predicaments. Without Auto-jump, you'll press **W** and the space bar to climb blocks, and you'll avoid inadvertently falling into a lava pool or ravine. (See Appendix A for details on other available game options and settings.)

5. Click **Done** to return to the main menu and click **Singleplayer**.
6. This opens the Select World screen. Here, click **Create New World**.

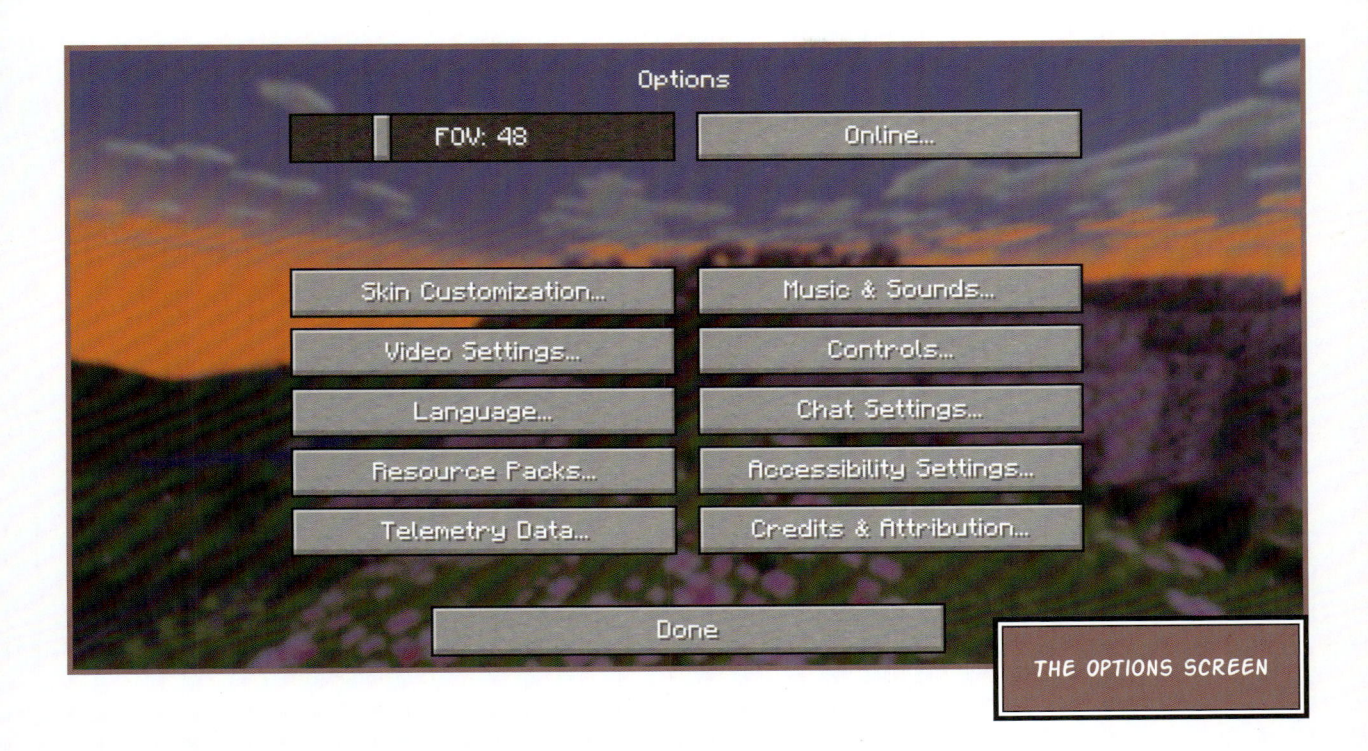

STARTING YOUR WORLD

THE OPTIONS SCREEN

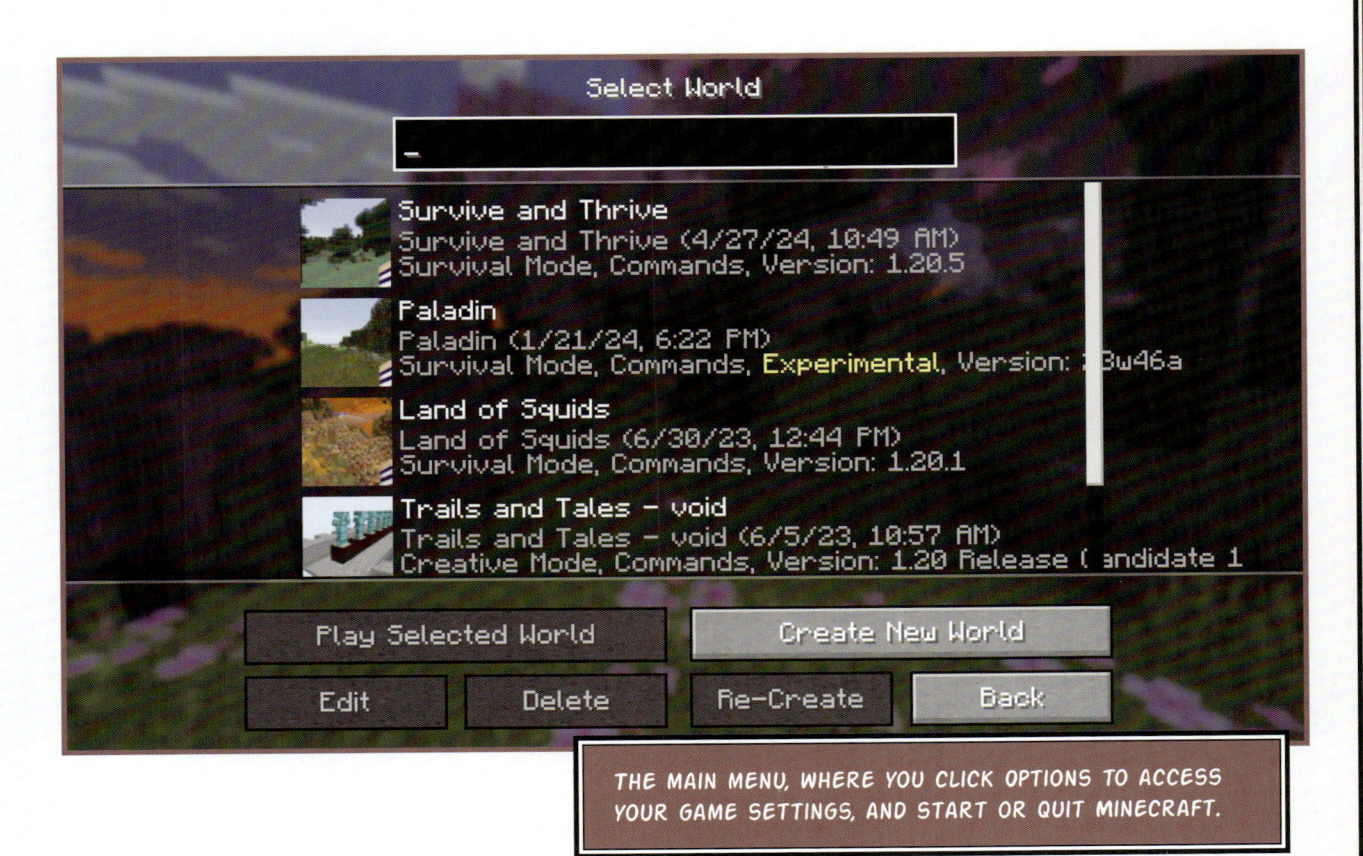

THE MAIN MENU, WHERE YOU CLICK OPTIONS TO ACCESS YOUR GAME SETTINGS, AND START OR QUIT MINECRAFT.

The Select World screen lets you choose between playing previous worlds you've created and creating a brand-new world.

7. On the Create New World screen, type in the name of your new world. Here is where you select your gameplay mode, difficulty level, and whether you want cheats on or not. For regular gameplay, leave the default settings on this page. (See Appendix A for details on World Settings and Appendix B on customizing Minecraft.)
8. Click the **Create New World** button at the bottom of the Create New World screen. In a few moments, you'll be plopped into your vast, randomly generated world.

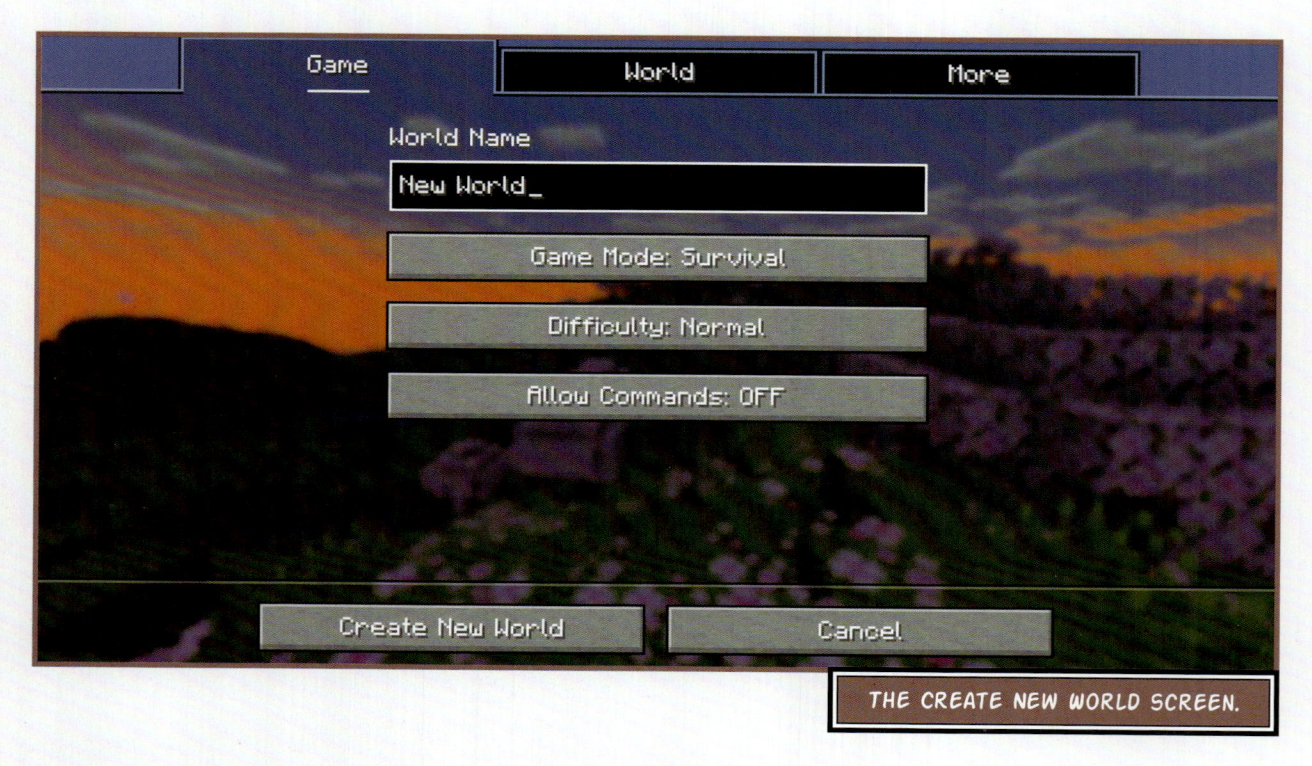

THE CREATE NEW WORLD SCREEN.

Spawning into Your World

The place your character is initially located is called the *world spawn*, and it could be in any environment: desert, forest, mountains, even the ocean.

You'll spawn into your world in the morning. A full day lasts twenty minutes, with half of it being nighttime, so you have ten minutes until dusk. Your first-day goals are to find shelter, food, and if possible, sleep in a bed by dusk, when it becomes dark enough for monsters to spawn. Sleeping skips past the night, waking you in the morning.

We'll go over how to make it through your first day in Chapter 2; right now, let's make sure we know where we are.

NOTE:
IF YOU SPAWN IN A LAKE OR OCEAN, PRESS THE SPACE BAR TO MOVE UP TO THE SURFACE, LOOK AROUND FOR LAND, AND SWIM TO SHORE.

The User Interface

These next sections will get you comfortable with the Minecraft GUI (graphical user interface) and main controls.

HEADS-UP DISPLAY

The *heads-up display (HUD)* refers to the information displayed on your screen that isn't part of the world, including the bar at the bottom of your screen. The HUD displays your hotbar inventory and the item you're holding, as well as the levels of your health, armor, hunger, and experience. If you're underwater, your oxygen level will appear above the Hunger Bar as blue bubbles. You can hide and reopen the HUD by toggling **F1**.

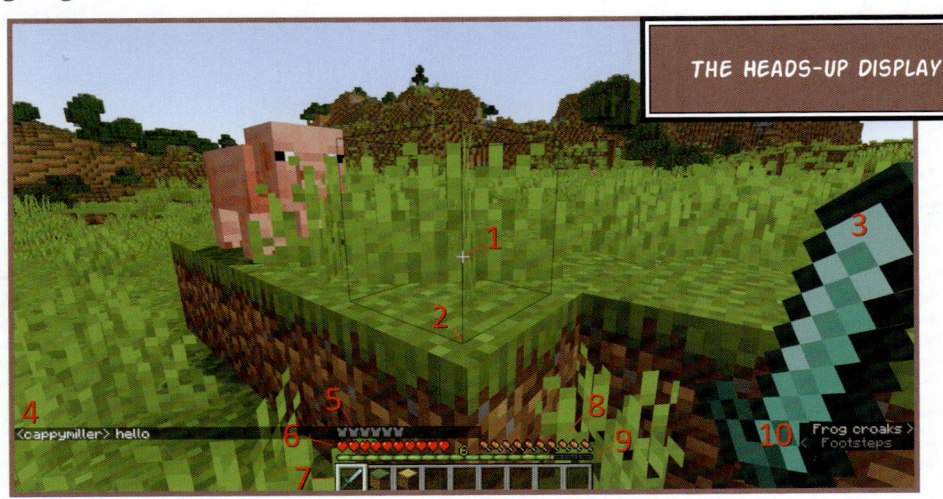

THE HEADS-UP DISPLAY

1. Cursor
2. Hitbox
3. Item in hand
4. Chat
5. Armor
6. Health
7. Hotbar
8. Hunger
9. Experience
10. Subtitles

Keep a close watch on your health and hunger bars. If you're on Hard difficulty, you'll start taking damage and starve to death when your hunger reaches 0. The hungrier you are, the slower your health replenishes; when you reach three drumsticks (also known as *haunches*) or six hunger points, you won't be able to sprint.

The HUD includes the following:

Cursor: Crosshairs show you the block where your fist, weapon, or tool will interact.

Hitbox: When your cursor rolls over a block, the block's *hitbox* displays. A hitbox shows the exact 3D area that you must click or right-click to interact with that block or entity.

Chat: The chat box shows game notifications as well as chat and commands from players; it's most useful in a multiplayer game. Press T to view the chat screen; it will fade after a few moments if it's not in use.

Subtitles: Subtitles describe the noises around you. You can turn them on and off in Options>Accessibility Settings.

Armor bar: Each piece of armor you wear adds to your armor bar, reducing the damage you take from hostile mobs and other sources like fire. Each chestplate icon in the armor bar represents 2 armor defense points, adding to a total of 20. See Chapter 9 for more on armor.

Hunger bar: Each drumstick is 2 hunger points; different foods will restore different amounts of hunger points. See Chapter 4 for more on food.

Health bar: Each heart is 2 health points (HP), and different sources of damage will take away different amounts of HP. If your hunger bar is around 10, you'll regenerate hearts automatically. Otherwise, you need to eat to restore HP.

Oxygen bar: Not shown here, the oxygen bar appears above the hunger bar when you're underwater. When it runs out, you begin taking damage.

Experience bar: This will fill up as you perform specific activities, like killing adult mobs, breeding animals, and smelting ore. Each successive level of experience requires more experience than previous levels. You'll need experience for enchanting (Chapter 15).

Hotbar: Your hotbar holds nine slots of inventory. Scroll with your mouse wheel or press 1 through 9 to highlight a slot and place the slot's item in your hand. Your highlighted item is shown on the right as being held in your hand.

STARTING YOUR WORLD

Hand: The image of your HUD, above, shows a sword held in the main hand. By default, the main hand is your right hand, but you can change this to be your left hand in Options>Skin Customization.

Off hand: Your other hand can hold items in the off-hand slot in the inventory screen (press **E**)—the slot is found to the right of your character and contains an outline of a shield, as players typically use the off hand to hold a shield. Press **F** on an inventory slot to toggle an item to the off hand. This will be discussed in more detail at the end of the chapter.

To get used to your inventory and hotbar, punch trees and grass or dirt to see the blocks break, fall, and move to your inventory when you are close.

YOUR INVENTORY SCREEN

Press **E** to open your inventory screen, where you have thirty-six inventory slots in addition to the nine in your hotbar. At the bottom is the hotbar displayed in your HUD. On the left of your character are four slots for your armor; on the right is your off-hand slot, a mini crafting grid, and your recipe book.

1. ARMOR SLOTS FOR HELMET, CHESTPLATE, LEGGINGS, AND BOOTS
2. 2x2 CRAFTING GRID
3. CRAFTING OUTPUT SLOT
4. OFF-HAND SLOT
5. CLICK TO OPEN RECIPE BOOK
6. MAIN INVENTORY
7. HOTBAR

PRESS E TO OPEN (AND CLOSE) YOUR INVENTORY SCREEN.

To move an item from your inventory into your hotbar, click and drag it into one of the nine slots. You can also hover your cursor over an inventory item and press the hotbar slot number (1–9) to move the item(s) directly to that slot. If there's an item already in that hotbar slot, this will swap the two items. Pressing **Shift** and clicking an inventory slot moves its contents into the leftmost empty hotbar slot.

To move items around in your inventory, drag and drop between slots. You can typically store up to sixty-four of one item in a slot, though some items are restricted to sixteen in a stack, and other special items, like a sword, won't stack at all.

> NOTE:
> BROKEN BLOCKS AND ITEMS THAT FLOAT ON THE GROUND WILL BE SUCKED UP INTO YOUR INVENTORY IF YOU HAVE SLOTS OPEN.

Click the green book icon to open the Recipe book. This will show you crafting recipes based on the resources you've come into contact with so far. Items highlighted in red are ones that you don't have the materials to craft; items highlighted in white are ones you can craft now. The recipe book won't show all recipes and resources available in the game from the get-go; to unlock a recipe, you have to discover the materials it uses. In this book, I'll mention resources needed for crafting specific items whenever possible.

THE RECIPE BOOK: THE TABS ON THE LEFT, FROM TOP TO BOTTOM, ARE AS FOLLOWS: ALL RECIPES, WEAPONS AND TOOLS, BUILDING MATERIALS, FOOD AND MISCELLANEOUS, AND REDSTONE.

1. ALL AVAILABLE RECIPES
2. WEAPON AND TOOLS RECIPES
3. BLOCK RECIPES
4. FOOD AND MISCELLANEOUS RECIPES
5. REDSTONE COMPONENT RECIPES
6. SEARCH FOR A CRAFTING RECIPE HERE
7. LIMIT TO SHOW ONLY RECIPES YOU HAVE MATERIALS FOR
8. RED OUTLINES ON THE RECIPES FOR WHICH YOU DON'T HAVE THE MATERIALS
9. CLICK THROUGH ADDITIONAL PAGES

CONTROLS

Now, let's get moving! Here are the main controls for moving around—you can change which buttons or commands are assigned to these actions under Options>Controls according to your own comfort. For example, I usually change the Sprint key to Caps Lock because I can easily reach it with my left pinky.

Walk: Use the WASD keys: Press **W** to move forward, **A** for left, **D** for right, and **S** for backward.

Sprint: Double tap and hold **W** or press the left **Ctrl** key to start sprinting.

Jump: Press the space bar to jump. If you're flying or swimming, jumping raises your position or keeps you afloat.

Jump-Sprint: Press the space bar while you're sprinting to jump-sprint and move faster. This will use up more energy, so watch your hunger bar.

Sneak: Press **Shift** to sneak. Sneaking places you in a crouch, which slows your movement and prevents you from falling off the block you are on. It's very easy to fall, especially when building! If you're swimming or flying, pressing Shift will cause you to sink.

SNEAK TO STOP YOURSELF FROM ACCIDENTALLY FALLING OFF A BLOCK.

Break blocks and use tools and weapons: Hold the left mouse button down to break blocks. Left-click to attack a mob with a weapon when the weapon is equipped in your hand, or with a tool like a shovel or axe to break blocks.

Place blocks and use items: If you have a block in your hand, right-click the mouse (also called using) to place it. (If you have a stack of blocks in your hand, you can keep placing those blocks until you run out.) Right-click, or use, other functional items, blocks, and entities to perform the action associated. For example, right-click food to eat, right-click chests and doors to open, right-click to attach an equipped lead to an animal, right-click to cast an equipped fishing rod, and right-click villagers to trade.

Drop items in front of you: Press **Q** with the item in hand or selected in your inventory or drag and drop out of your inventory.

Up Next

Now that you've created your world and know how to move about, it's time to survive your first day. You have ten minutes until the sun falls, and Chapter 2 has a plan to get you to safety in the easiest and fastest way possible.

2
SURVIVING YOUR FIRST DAY

The Minecraft day lasts twenty minutes (daylight lasts ten), which goes by fast! It's important to gear up while it's light out to make sure you're safe throughout the night, because darkness brings monsters.

The best way to avoid evening mobs is to find or craft a bed and sleep in it until morning, bypassing the dark hours. You'll also need food, tools, and weapons to become more comfortable staying awake through the night.

If your world spawn is in an area with very few resources, like a desert or snowy landscape, your very first task will be to find a better environment. See the end of this chapter for some advice on how to get started in inhospitable biomes.

First Up: Save Your World Spawn

Before you start exploring, record where you spawned. When you die without a bed, you'll sometimes respawn at your world spawn, so it's a good idea to build a safe place here once you gather some materials (see Chapter 4 for building structures). Initially, you'll have no tools or materials, so your best option for marking your spawn is to take a screenshot of it or write down your coordinates.

Every block in your world has an assigned coordinate along the X (east-west), Z (north-south), and Y (up-down) axes. Keeping track of these is a foolproof way to avoid getting lost.[1] To find the coordinates of block you're on, press F3 to open the Debug screen, below. Listed in the left column in the second block of stats is your current XYZ position. Write your spawn location down or take a

> **NOTE:**
> TO FIND MINECRAFT SCREENSHOTS QUICKLY, PRESS **ESCAPE** TO GET TO YOUR GAME MENU. CLICK **OPTIONS>RESOURCE PACKS>OPEN PACK FOLDER**. THIS WILL OPEN UP THE RESOURCE PACKS FOLDER INSIDE YOUR MINECRAFT GAME FOLDER. FIND THE MINECRAFT GAMES DIRECTORY WITHIN THE FOLDER TREE AND LOCATE THE SCREENSHOTS FOLDER.

---

[1] In Bedrock Edition, you can enable a map that helps you get around; this isn't available in Java.

screenshot by pressing **F2**. Your world spawn position is usually fairly close to X-0 and Z-0. (To close the Debug screen, press **F3** again.)

PRESS **F3** TO OPEN (AND CLOSE) THE DEBUG SCREEN

First-Day Tasks

The quickest way to get started on your first day and make sure you can survive the night is to:

1. Gather wood and make a crafting table.
2. Craft a wood pickaxe.
3. Mine stone and craft stone tools.
4. Gather resources and eat.
5. Gather wood and wool to make a bed.
6. Hunker down and sleep.

We'll work through each of these tasks, step by step.

GATHER WOOD AND MAKE A CRAFTING TABLE

As in many survival games, your first task is to gather one of the main crafting resources—wood—and craft basic tools, which in turn will allow you to craft better tools. The crafting table will be your main way to turn resources like wood, stone, and iron into items like armor and weapons. To make your crafting table, you'll first need to gather wood by punching trees.

1. Walk up to a tree and continuously punch (left-click and hold) one of its wooden log blocks. If leaves are in your way, punch those to get rid of them—they might drop a stick, or an apple if it's an oak tree!

   As you punch, you should see that wooden log block cracking, and after a few seconds the block will drop. If the block doesn't pop into your hotbar, it should be on the ground nearby. Move close to the block so that it pops into your inventory.

Floating Leaves

If you don't break all of the log blocks in a tree, whatever logs and attached leaf blocks are left will remain in your world as a kind of green UFO. On multiplayer servers, leaving half-broken trees is usually a no-no for aesthetic reasons, so it's a good idea to get in the habit of completely breaking down any tree you harvest wood from. Once all the logs are broken, the remaining leaf blocks will decay over time.

2. Continue punching trees until you have four blocks of wood logs.
3. Press **E** to open your inventory.
4. Place three logs into one slot of your crafting grid. One log makes four planks, shown in the output slot to the right of the arrow.
5. Click the output slot three times to craft three sets of four planks. Alternatively, shift-click to craft all of the logs you have into as many planks as they can make.

> **NOTE:**
> SHAPELESS RECIPES ARE ONES IN WHICH YOU CAN PLACE THE MATERIALS IN ANY SLOT; FOR EXAMPLE, TO CRAFT PLANKS, YOU CAN PLACE THE LOGS IN ANY INVENTORY SLOT. IN SHAPED RECIPES, THE MATERIALS MUST BE PLACED IN SPECIFIC SLOTS. THE STICKS RECIPE—WHICH WE'LL SEE SHORTLY—IS SHAPED, AS YOU HAVE TO PLACE TWO PLANKS VERTICALLY.

Now we'll build the crafting table, which requires four planks, one in each crafting slot. Most recipes that use wood planks allow you to use different kinds of wood. Recipes that require a specific type of wood will typically have the wood's name in the recipe name, like *spruce door*.

CHAPTER 2

YOUR INVENTORY CRAFTING GRID. HERE YOU CAN ALSO CLICK THE RECIPE FOR PLANKS ON THE LEFT TO POPULATE YOUR CRAFTING GRID WITH THE NECESSARY MATERIALS. IF YOU SHIFT-CLICK ON A RECIPE, YOU'LL POPULATE YOUR CRAFTING GRID WITH THE MAXIMUM MATERIALS POSSIBLE.

6. Left-click the four plank blocks to pick them up. Hover them over the four squares of your crafting grid and right-click once in each square to deposit just one plank into each of the slots. Put any remaining plank blocks in an inventory slot.

Challenge: Inventory Management

In this challenge, you'll practice some key inventory management. Clicking and dragging a bunch of items over a few inventory slots places an equal amount of that block into each dragged-over slot. For example, dragging twenty-four oak blocks over four inventory (or crafting) slots will place six oak planks into each of those four slots. If you right-click while dragging, you'll place just one block into each new slot (the remainder stays with your cursor). To pick up half of a stack in your inventory, right-click that stack. To pick up all blocks of a certain type (up to sixty-four), double-click the blocks in just one inventory slot. Try each of these techniques with any number of blocks!

7. Click your crafting table in the output slot and drag it to a slot in your hotbar. Press **E** to exit your inventory.
8. Select the hotbar slot that your crafting table is in. This places it in your main hand, and it is shown on the right of the screen.
9. Right-click the ground to place the crafting table.

After placing your crafting table, right-click it to open its interface. You'll see its *crafting grid*, a 3x3 grid you place items in according to a recipe. This crafting grid has more spots than the 2x2 grid in your inventory and allows you to craft any recipe.

CRAFT A WOODEN PICKAXE

First, we're going to make a wooden pickaxe (or *pick*) so that we can mine stone to make a higher quality stone pickaxe. Wood tools are the first level of tools, so upgrading to more durable and stronger stone tools early on is super helpful. Follow the steps below to craft your own wooden pickaxe.

1. Right-click the crafting table to open its interface.
2. Place two plank blocks, one above the other, and craft four sticks. Place the sticks in your inventory.

STICK RECIPE

3. Now, right-click your wood planks three times across the top of the grid and place two sticks below this (or click the wood pickaxe recipe in your recipe book). Put your crafted wooden pickaxe in your hotbar.

THE RECIPE FOR A WOOD PICKAXE USES THREE PLANKS ACROSS THE TOP, WITH TWO STICKS CENTERED BELOW.

Challenge: Crafting With The Recipe Book

In your inventory, press the book icon to open the recipe book. The *recipe book* shows what you can craft with the resources in your inventory. If you have the resources, the recipe is bordered in white; if not, it's bordered in red. Click an available recipe to see how it will populate your crafting grid. Some recipes require the 3x3 crafting table, and some you can make in your 2x2 inventory grid.

Using the recipe book is a shortcut, so you don't have to drop the materials in the crafting grid in precisely the right configuration yourself—the book will do it for you. The recipe book is especially handy when you have to craft multiples of the same item, because you can just shift-click to populate your crafting grid with the maximum possible resources.

Now that we've crafted a wooden pickaxe, we can mine stone blocks so that we can craft the next level of tools: stone!

MINE STONE AND CRAFT STONE TOOLS

We'll create a stone pickaxe to help us mine more stone to make stone tools, including a stone pickaxe, a stone axe, a stone shovel, and a stone sword. (You can make these same tools using wood planks and sticks, but spending a little effort to make longer lasting and stronger stone tools is worth it.) The stone tools we want are a pick for better mining; an axe to

WARNING:
IF YOU HAVEN'T FINISHED THE FIRST DAY'S CHORES AND THE SUN IS SETTING, FIND A PLACE TO HUNKER DOWN. SEE THE SECTION "HUNKER DOWN AND SLEEP" BELOW, OR IN AN EMERGENCY, YOU CAN JUST DIG A HOLE THAT'S THREE BLOCKS DEEP, JUMP IN, AND PLACE A BLOCK ABOVE YOU. YOU'LL HAVE TO WAIT ABOUT TEN MINUTES TILL DAWN. YOU CAN USUALLY TELL IT'S DAWN BY THE SOUNDS OF ZOMBIES AND SKELETONS DYING IN THE SUNLIGHT.

chop trees; a shovel to dig dirt; and a sword for killing monsters. We'll also want to craft a furnace to cook food and smelt charcoal.

You can find stone a few blocks below grass and dirt or exposed in a cliff or shallow cave. If there's no immediate cave or cliff, dig out grass and dirt using a staircase pattern until you see gray stone blocks. You may need to dig out and around other stone variant blocks (like granite, andesite, or diorite) to find regular stone blocks.

To start mining, follow the instructions below:

1. Mine three stone blocks with your pick. Once stone is broken, it drops cobblestone, which you can use to build stone tools.
2. Return to your crafting table and craft a stone pick with three cobblestone blocks and two sticks.
3. Go back to your dugout and use your stone pick to mine out twenty or so more stone blocks: three for an axe, one for a shovel, two for a sword, eight for a furnace, and some more for extra resources.
4. Return to your crafting table and craft a stone shovel, a stone axe, a sword, and a furnace. Remember, you can use the recipe book to click the icon of an item and fill your crafting grid with the right materials. 
5. Place your stone tools in your hotbar so you have easy access to them.

6. Use the stone axe to break your crafting table and return it to your inventory so you can carry it around with you.
7. Throw away your wooden beginner's pickaxe, keep it for posterity, or use it as fuel. To throw it away, drag it out of your inventory and release it on the ground. Items dropped on the ground despawn after five minutes. You can also select the item and press **Q** to throw it.

Stone is the second level of materials for tools and weapons. Crafting weapons or tools from better materials makes them stronger, faster, and last longer. After stone, the next levels are iron and diamond. You can make gold tools and weapons as well, but these are both expensive and poor in durability.

GATHER WOOD AND WOOL TO MAKE A BED

Try to craft a bed, if you can, so that you can sleep on your first night. Sleeping changes the time immediately from evening to morning, completely bypassing the night and preventing a lot of mob spawning, so the sooner you right-click a bed, the safer you will be. You can only sleep once it is officially night, when the sun hits the horizon.

If you see a village nearby, you can find a bed in one of its houses—break the bed, get it in your inventory, and it's now yours to place and use. To craft a bed, you'll need three wood planks of any type and three wool blocks of the same color. (In your crafting grid, the three wood planks will go on the bottom row and the wool should be placed above them.) The hardest part is finding the wool. Sheep generate in grassy areas, although they can wander into woods. Keep your ears open to their bleating—sometimes you'll hear them before you see them. They're not going to be happy you're killing them; they'll race around after your first blow, but keep at it. Jumping and striking as you fall can deal a critical hit with more damage. If you can't find or make a bed, plan on making sure you have a safe shelter to stay in overnight, discussed later.

GATHER RESOURCES AND EAT

As you explore, you'll want to gather more logs from trees and find food. Ideally, you'll have the following before dusk: at least five food; ten wood logs (not planks); five coal (see below) or additional wood logs; and a bed. Avoid deserts, snowy areas,

SURVIVING YOUR FIRST DAY

and mountains (unless you spot a village) because of the low number of resources in these environments. You'll do best on grassy plains.

Keep track of the sun; when it starts to lower and the sky turns red, you need to find shelter. Until then, keep an eye out for villages, animals to kill for food, and other handy resources like the following.

Villages

A village will have everything you need: beds, food, loot, and usually some nearby trees to harvest. We'll discuss villages later in this chapter, and much more in depth in Chapter 12. If you come across a pillager outpost, stay away. Pillagers are gray-faced hostile villager-like mobs and will chase and kill you if you get too close.

AVOID PILLAGER OUTPOSTS LIKE THE PLAGUE UNTIL YOU HAVE THE RESOURCES TO FIGHT!

Cows, Chickens, Pigs, and Sheep

Attack animals with your stone sword. After striking, you'll need to pause a few moments for your sword to recharge—this keeps the sword's damage at its highest, requiring fewer strikes to kill. When an animal dies, they drop raw meat that

NOTE:
DON'T KILL EVERY FARM ANIMAL YOU SEE. THESE MOBS RESPAWN INFREQUENTLY. WHEREVER YOU SETTLE, YOU'LL WANT AT LEAST TWO OF EACH ANIMAL FOR BREEDING.

you can cook in a furnace. Cows also drop leather, chickens drop feathers, and sheep drop wool.

Exposed Coal and Iron

You can sometimes find veins of coal and iron (and copper) at the surface of exposed cliffs and in shallow caves. Mine it! Coal is essential in making torches to keep your base and environment lit, as well as cooking meat. You'll need iron for making armor, weapons and tools, and a shield. Copper is less essential.

ON THE LEFT, EXPOSED COAL (BLACK) AND COPPER (ORANGE AND TEAL); ON THE RIGHT, EXPOSED IRON. KEEP A LOOKOUT FOR THESE ORES AS YOU TRAVEL.

More Trees

Chop down trees so that you have a good supply of logs that can be made into tools or charcoal.

Your Hunger Bar

When your hunger bar drops down several drumsticks, place your furnace and add some raw meat to it. The top slot on the left is for the food item and the bottom slot is for fuel. You can use planks and most wooden objects, coal, and charcoal for fuel.

YOU SHOULD ALWAYS HAVE FOOD ON HAND TO TOP OFF YOUR HUNGER BAR!

You can eat raw meat to survive (raw chicken will give you a poison effect for a short while), but cooked meat is much more effective. If you have no meat, you can gather kelp in a nearby ocean and dry it out in a furnace; kill fish in a river; or find berries, fruits, or vegetables.

Shipwrecks

Along various shores, you might find the damaged remains of a ship. These can contain up to three chests with food and loot. You can also salvage them for wood. See Chapter 7 for more details about shipwrecks.

YOU CAN SOMETIMES FIND SHIPWRECKS ALONG THE SHORE, ALTHOUGH THEY'RE USUALLY SUBMERGED IN THE OCEAN.

Ravines

Ravines are pretty easy to fall into, and it's typically a long drop, so make sure to look at the ground ahead of you!

Sugar Cane

Sugar cane is necessary for making books and bookshelves, which you'll need for enchanting later in the game, and you will find it alongside rivers. If you come across sugar cane now, it's a good idea to pick some up.

When the sun starts going down in the west, and an orange sunset appears, it's time to stop gathering resources and start looking for where you'll spend the night.

HUNKER DOWN OR SLEEP

Once you have plenty of resources, you'll want to find a place to spend the night. Whether or not you've made a bed, you'll want to settle in a place that's protected from mobs.

Find Your Spot and Secure It

There are many ways to find a safe spot to rest. First, you want to keep away from shaded areas with trees and overhangs; these can create spaces dark enough for mobs to spawn. My usual preference is to just dig straight into a cliff or mountain at ground level and place blocks at the entryway. You can also find a shallow cave with a small entrance that you can block off.

If you feel confident in your building skills and have enough time before dusk, you can use some of your gathered wood to make a simple room big enough to fit your bed (we'll discuss base-building in more detail in Chapter 3). Regardless of where you choose to sleep, block off your spot so that mobs can't get in. If you're in a deeper cave, make sure to block off any entrances or openings so monsters won't spawn. If you have the time, craft a door with six planks of wood as your entrance/exit.

YOU CAN DIG STRAIGHT INTO THE SIDE OF A HILL TO MAKE YOUR FIRST OVERNIGHT HIDEY-HOLE.

Make and Place Torches

Mobs can't spawn with light around, so craft torches using coal or charcoal and sticks and place these torches every twenty blocks or so.

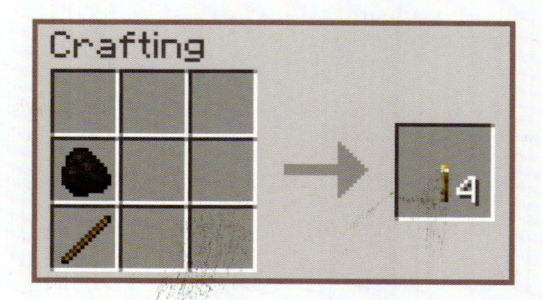

This should keep the light levels high enough to prevent hostile mobs from spawning nearby.

Make Charcoal

If you haven't found coal, make charcoal. Place your furnace and right-click it to open its interface. Place planks in the bottom left slot as fuel and logs in the top slot to burn. This will turn the logs into charcoal.

Cook Any Raw Meat You Have Left Over

Always keep a supply of food on hand, as food is the main way (besides potions and such) to heal yourself. Try to keep at least 5 quality food on you at all times, more if you are expending a lot of energy by, say, running around.

When It Turns Night, Sleep!

If you have a bed, place it and right-click it repeatedly when the sun starts reaching the horizon. Once it is officially night-time, you'll pop onto the bed, evening will change to morning, and you'll be popped out of bed again. Sleeping in a bed sets your spawn point to that bed, so if you die, you'll respawn beside the bed rather than at your world spawn.

If You Can't Sleep, Mine

If you haven't been able to find a bed in a village or enough wool to craft one, use the nighttime hours to mine. Dig out a descending staircase with your stone pickaxe, keeping it lit with torches, and gather any veins of ore you encounter (see Chapter 5 for more tips on mining and smelting ore).

Leave Your Hidey-Hole in the Morning

As the sky lightens, you'll hear the burning of zombies and skeletons in the sun. This doesn't mean you're safe—a monster could be hiding in the shade of a tree. When

> **CHALLENGE: Meet the phantoms**
>
> The only way to encounter a phantom—an undead, hostile, flying mob—is to avoid sleeping for three nights. If you're aboveground, you'll see them in the dark, swooping down to attack you. You can avoid them by hiding inside, and they will burn in daylight along with other undead mobs. If you continue to not sleep, the phantoms will be back the next night! To stop them from returning, all you have to do is sleep.
>
> If a phantom (or other hostile mob) is nearby when you try to sleep, you'll get a message saying, "You may not rest now, there are monsters nearby." This means a hostile mob is within eight blocks of your bed. To sleep, you'll need to either kill that mob or move your bed far enough away from it.

you're ready to leave, hold your axe and bum-rush the world outside, looking out for a place that's clear of monsters. For tips on killing hostile mobs, see Chapter 11.

Surviving through your first night is no small feat! Give yourself a quick pat on the back before heading back out into the world.

Emergency Escapes

If worse comes to worst, and you have no bed and nowhere to hide at night, you have two options. The first is to dig a three-block-deep hole in the ground, jump in, and place a dirt block above your head. Wait out the minutes or mine until daylight and then make a run for it, staying away from hostile mobs.

In an extreme situation, you can pillar up or hide on top of a tree. To pillar up, jump straight up while looking at the ground underneath you and place a block beneath your feet before you land. Place blocks until you are at least three blocks above the ground. At three blocks, most mobs won't be able to reach you, aside from skeletons, who can shoot arrows at you, and spiders, who can climb. Pillar higher for more safety. If you pillar up next to a tree, jump onto its canopy and create walls around yourself with any blocks you have on hand. When it's daylight, break the pillar blocks beneath you to return to ground level. Run away, being careful of any nearby mobs.

> **NOTE:**
> PILLARING UP (ALSO CALLED STACKING UP) CAN BE DANGEROUS IF YOU FALL. FALLING WILL DAMAGE YOU A HALF-HEART FOR EACH BLOCK FALLEN AFTER THE FIRST THREE BLOCKS—THIS MEANS DEATH IF YOU FALL TWENTY-FOUR BLOCKS. YOU CAN AVOID THIS BY FALLING INTO WATER, SO CONSIDER PILLARING UP NEAR A POND OR OTHER WATER. WHEN YOU'RE READY TO COME DOWN, YOU CAN JUMP INTO THE WATER INSTEAD OF BREAKING THE PILLAR BLOCKS BENEATH YOU.

Village Starts

If you find a village, you're in luck! It will have all the starting resources you'll need, unless it's a desert village, in which case you'll be stuck for wood. Most houses will have beds you can sleep in; if a villager gets to a bed first at dusk, just right-click the bed and the villager will jump off, allowing you to sleep. Punch (or craft and use a hoe) to break down hay bales, and use your crafting grid to turn hay bales into wheat, which you can then craft into bread. Loot the farms to find vegetables and seeds. Check houses for chests—they may contain tools, weapons, armor, food, and more. You might see an iron golem wandering around. It protects villagers and won't bother you unless you hit it or a villager.

If the village's buildings are decorated with cobwebs, it means the village is abandoned; proceed with caution and enter with a sword or axe. These abandoned villages are populated by zombie villagers, although they can die off before your arrival by burning up in the sun. Kill any remaining resident zombies before looting the place.

ABANDONED VILLAGES LIKELY HAVE ZOMBIE INHABITANTS.

Inhospitable Starts

While your world spawn will typically be in or near plains or a forest, it's possible to initially spawn in a pretty inhospitable area without trees or animals. Here are a few ways to get out of these areas, depending on which type you've landed in:

DESERTED ISLAND WITH FEW TREES

Chop trees to gather logs so you can craft planks and make a crafting table. Then craft a boat with five planks. If there are any animals for food, have no mercy. Kill them all and harvest their meat. When ready, right-click the water to place the boat, and right-click the boat to get in. Use the WASD keys to steer to greener pastures, literally: look for plains or woods. To get out of your boat at the shore, place your cursor on a solid block and press **Shift** to jump to that block.

OCEAN

Swim to the nearest land by jumping in the water; press **Shift** to lower into the water and press the Sprint key (default is left **Ctrl**) to move quickly underwater. Keep an eye on your oxygen levels, shown by a bar of bubbles above your hunger bar. You'll need to return to the surface before it runs out. If you see an island with trees, head there first to collect wood and make a boat so you can sail to the mainland.

DESERT OR SNOWY/ICY AREA

Head out of the area in any direction, looking for a forested or grassy area and collecting resources as you come across them.

Next Up

After making stone tools, gathering food and wood, and creating a safe space to survive overnight, you're ready to start settling down and improving your resources. In the next chapter, we'll look at the goals for your first week of survival, from building a small starter base to managing a potentially dangerous encounter with a group of pillagers.

3
SURVIVING YOUR FIRST WEEK: STAYING SAFE

Now that you've made it through your first day, it's time to settle down and collect resources. You're going to want a starter home—a base of operations that's bigger than your night one hidey-hole—as well as access to a steady source of food, a branch mine, maybe some tree and sugar cane farms. You also need to start collecting iron so you can upgrade your tools and weapons and make iron armor (see Chapter 5 for more on mining).

Storage

Before you can build a home, you're going to need somewhere to store all the resources you've gathered so far as well as your home's building materials.

CHESTS

A chest will hold twenty-seven stacks of items and can be crafted with your crafting table from eight blocks of wood planks of any type, which you can craft from wood logs. Right-click a chest to open it and drag or Shift-click stacks of items to move them between your inventory and the chest. Unfortunately, you can't transport a filled chest; you'll have to empty it before breaking it down. Note that chests can't open if there's a solid block above them, but a transparent or semisolid block (like glass or stairs, respectively) is okay.

USE SHIFT-RIGHT-CLICK TO PLACE CHESTS ON TOP OF EACH OTHER.

To make a double chest that holds fifty-four stacks of items, place two chests right next to each other. If you'd prefer to have two separate chests instead of a double, shift-right-click the ground next to your first chest with your second chest in hand. You can also shift-right-click the top of one chest, while holding the second chest, to place the second chest on top of it.

Building a Shelter

You're going to want a permanent shelter that acts as a safe space at night and somewhere to store your ever-increasing chests of goodies. You can continue to expand your hidey-hole, or you can build a stand-alone home. The aesthetics are up to you, though I don't recommend using wood for your entire build, as wood can catch fire and doesn't hold up well against creeper explosions. I recommend using stone or stone variants instead, as these blocks are stronger.

> IF YOU'RE ATTACHED TO THE HIDEY-HOLE YOU CREATED IN CHAPTER 2, FEEL FREE TO MAKE THIS YOUR MAIN SHELTER. YOU CAN SPRUCE IT UP WITH BEAM SUPPORTS, A COBBLESTONE WALL, AND OTHER DECORATIVE TOUCHES. HOME SWEET HOME!

Choose a location for your base that's relatively flat and free from mob-spawning areas (like Dark Forests, cave openings, and cliff overhangs). You'll want enough

SURVIVING YOUR FIRST WEEK: STAYING SAFE 31

space for your home, crop farms, and animal farms. Grassy, expansive plains are a great place to start out.

I'm going to show you how to build a sweet starter house with enough room for adding an attic floor at the top that you can use for extra storage.

COLLECT RESOURCES FOR YOUR STARTER HOME

To build this home, you'll need a 13x13-block flat area (clear it of grass and plants) and the following resources:

- 132 wood stairs: Craft from wood planks.
- 2 wood slabs: Craft from wood planks.
- 1 wood door: Craft from wood planks.
- 62 wood planks: Craft from wood logs.
- 38 cobblestones: Mine stone to create cobblestone.
- 137 stone bricks: Craft from stone created by smelting cobblestone blocks.
- 20 spruce or oak logs.
- 2 lanterns: Craft each lantern with eight iron nuggets (crafted from an iron ingot) and one torch, or use two torches instead.
- 3 cobblestone stairs: Craft from cobblestone blocks.
- 12 wood fences or glass panes: Craft fences from wood planks and sticks; craft glass panes from glass blocks created by smelting sand.

Once you've collected and crafted these resources, you're ready to start building!

BUILD YOUR HOME

Locate a 13x13-block flat area to build your home, and follow along:

1. Place the oak planks for the interior floor in a 6x9 rectangle. I've placed yellow and red wool blocks on the ground to help show the dimensions.

2. Find the center of whichever long side you'd like for your front door, and place four oak planks in a triangle.

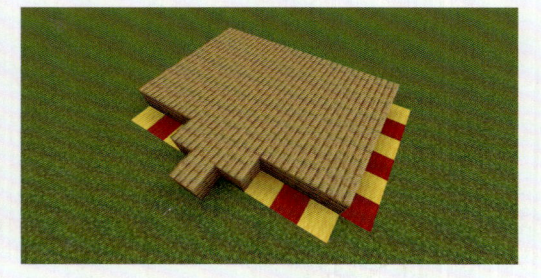

Creating space for the front door

3. Border the outside of the wood floor with rows of cobblestone, leaving a gap at the four main corners of the building.

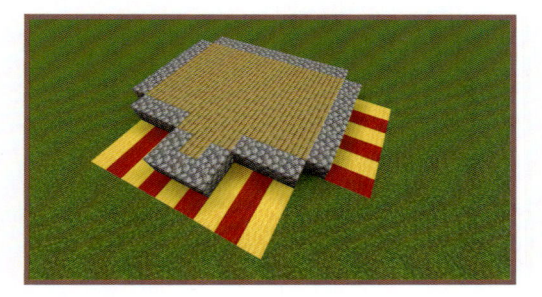

4. At each main corner, build a five-block-high column of wood logs. You can use the pillar up method to create a column (you'll take a bit of damage when jumping off, but not enough to kill you). Stand on the bottom block, then jump straight up and place another block below your feet.

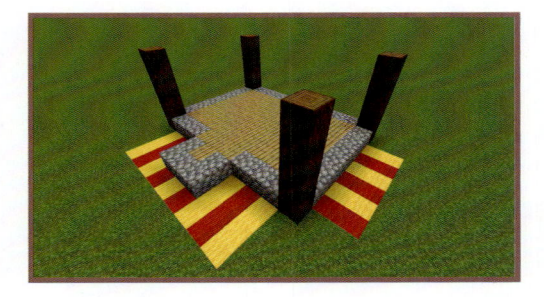

5. Build up each wall with stone bricks to the same level as the wood log beams. On the front of the building, leave a three-block-wide gap for the entryway. On the back wall, leave a gap for a 2x1 window, and on the side walls, leave a gap in the center for 2x2 windows.

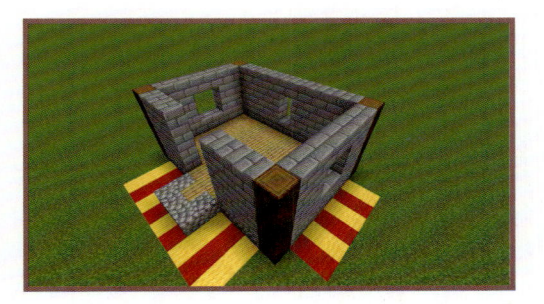

6. On the shorter sides' walls, build up three rows of stone bricks in a staggered triangle shape, with the bottom row six blocks wide, the middle row four blocks wide, and the top row two blocks wide.

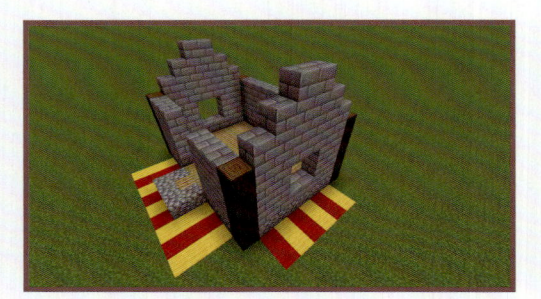

7. Build the roof by placing a row of stairs at the same level as the topmost wood logs, so that they stick out from the building one block. (Place the outer stairs last so that you can attach them more easily.) For the first row of the front side, leave a three-block gap over the door. Continue to place four more rows of stairs one block up and one block in from the bottom row, until you've reached the top with five rows of stairs.

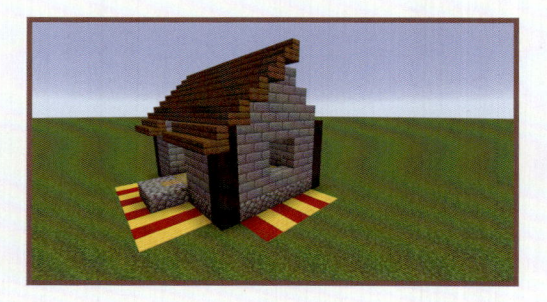

8. Do the same for the back side of the house, without a gap on the bottom row.

9. Build up 2×2 side walls of the entryway with stone bricks to make an entryway to the house.

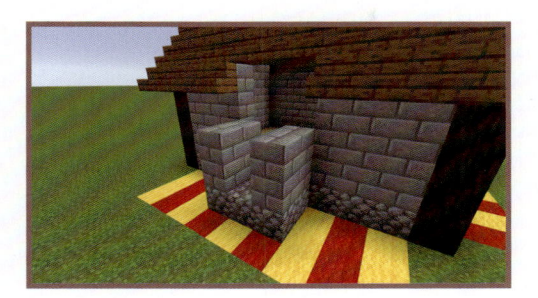

10. Add a 2×3 ceiling of stone bricks over the entryway.

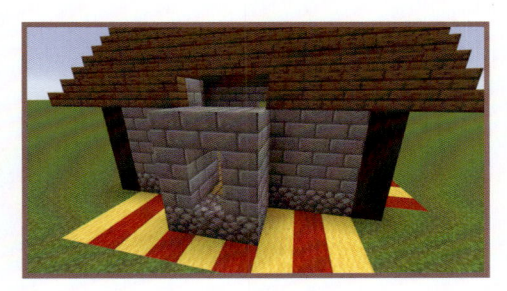

11. We'll build the roof of the entryway with planks. Along the center of the entryway roof, place two spruce planks.

12. In front of these planks, place three spruce slabs.

13. On each side, place two spruce stairs to connect to the rest of the roof and create a stair-like structure.

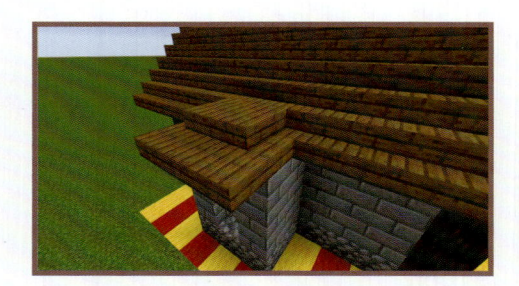

CHALLENGE: Building with Stairs

You can make stair blocks from all wood plank blocks and most stone variants, and you can use them not just for stairs and roofs but also to make patterns in walls and other structures. While holding a stair block, click the bottom of a block to place stairs right-side up against that block. Click the top of the block to place the stairs upside down.

Try to replicate these two walls built from stairs. You may need to place some temporary blocks to position the stair blocks.

PLACE TWO STAIRS AT RIGHT ANGLES AND JOIN THEM WITH A THIRD STAIR. THEIR STEPS WILL COMBINE TO FORM A CONTINUOUS RIDGE.

14. Place fences or glass panes in your windows.

15. Place your door in the entryway.

16. Place three cobblestone blocks and three cobblestone stairs at the front of your porch and two lanterns or torches on either side of your door (and any other finishing decorations).

Make sure to light up the interiors and roofs of any buildings you create to prevent mobs spawning there. In this build, your roof is fine because it uses stair blocks, and mobs don't spawn on stairs. Mobs also don't spawn on bottom slabs. Slabs are half-height blocks, made from planks or stones. Bottom slabs are slabs placed on the bottom half of a full block space. Mobs will spawn on top slabs placed on the top half of a full block space.

17. You can further embellish the house to your liking. Keep mobs away with a fence and plenty of torches or other lighting sources. To finish off the build, I've added fencing, exterior steps, bushes, and lights to my starter house.

Other Week One Activities

In addition to farming (Chapter 4) and mining (Chapter 5) there are a few other tasks you can attend to in your first week. For example, you'll likely want to make a bow and arrow, prepare for pillager patrols, and keep an eye out for wandering traders.

CRAFT A BOW AND ARROW

The bow is your primary ranged weapon, allowing you to fight hostile mobs from afar rather than rushing at them with an axe or sword. To get the string to make a bow, you'll need to fight spiders, which can drop up to two strings when killed. If you're not ready to take on spiders, you can find string later as you explore (typically in treasure chests, trail ruins, and mineshafts).

To make arrows, you'll need feathers and flint. You can gather feathers from

BOW RECIPE.

ARROW RECIPE.

killing chickens. To get flint, use a shovel to break gravel; flint has a 10 percent chance of dropping instead of gravel, so you'll need to break a lot of gravel to craft arrows! You can find gravel while mining, near water, and on some mountains.

PROTECT YOUR WORLD SPAWN AREA

It's a good idea to ensure that your world spawn point is a safe space, stocked up with tools, weapons, a bed, and extra resources like wood, armor, and food. You'll most likely end up in a situation where you've died and respawned at the world spawn area, especially if you're traveling. The rule is, if you die you'll spawn at the bed you most recently slept in,

> **NOTE:**
> IF YOUR MAIN BASE IS FAR FROM YOUR WORLD SPAWN, CONSIDER KEEPING AN EXTRA BOAT OR EVEN A HORSE HERE TO QUICKEN YOUR JOURNEY BACK.

SURVIVING YOUR FIRST WEEK: STAYING SAFE

if you haven't broken it. If you have, you'll respawn around your world spawn point. This may be less than ideal, but you can ease the situation by adding a shelter at world spawn and lighting the area up around it to prevent mobs from spawning there.

YOUR WORLD SPAWN'S SHELTER DOESN'T NEED TO BE ANYTHING FANCY, SO LONG AS THERE ARE PLENTY OF LIGHTS AROUND AND INSIDE IT!

MEET THE WANDERING TRADER

Within the first few days of playing, you'll probably come across a wandering trader leading two llamas. Right-click the trader to see what they're offering; they typically trade natural items like dripleaves, cactus, dyes, or nautilus shells for emeralds. To get emeralds, you'll either have to mine in a mountainous area or visit a village and trade with a villager for them (see Chapter 12 for more on villagers).

THE WANDERING TRADER SOMETIMES OFFERS RARE ITEMS, SO BE SURE TO ALWAYS KEEP A SUPPLY OF EMERALDS ON YOU!

Wandering traders leave (despawn) after a few days, but generally return every now and then. At sundown they may suddenly vanish in front of your eyes; traders drink an invisibility potion to avoid hostile mobs.

PUSH BACK THE PILLAGER PATROLS

After about five in-game days, you'll likely be confronted by a pillager patrol of two to five pillagers—villager-like people with a penchant for blood. They'll spawn within fifty blocks of you, and if they get within ten or so blocks, they'll attack you with crossbows. If pillagers are near a village, they'll also attack villagers.

Try drawing one pillager away from the rest at a time by approaching one side of the group slowly so that only the closest pillager notices and follows you. Watch out for the patrol captain wearing the giant banner on their head. If you kill the captain directly (by sword or arrow), you'll receive an ominous bottle, which you can use later to start pillager raids or ominous trials in trial chambers.

THE PILLAGER PATROL CAPTAIN HAS A GIANT BANNER ON THEIR HEAD; IF YOU KILL HIM, HE'LL DROP AN OMINOUS BOTTLE.

MAKE SOME ADVANCEMENTS

As you go about mining and crafting, you'll see notices appear at the top right of your screen, known as *advancements*. Advancement notices pop up when you complete specific activities—making your first crafting table, crafting your first iron pick, and so on. While you won't get any rewards for completing advancements, they can serve as a guide. Some later advancements are difficult enough to qualify for bragging rights.

Press L to open your advancement screen for an overview of the advancements you've achieved (highlighted in gold) and those upcoming (gray). Advancements

MOUSE OVER AN ADVANCEMENT'S ICON TO SEE ITS NAME AND DESCRIPTION.

work in a tree hierarchy, so you'll open up more branches as you complete them. Mouse over an advancement icon to see its name and description. In addition to the main area of advancements, there are four additional categories: the Nether (started by entering the Nether dimension); the End (started by entering the End); Adventure (started by killing an entity or being killed); and Husbandry (started by eating food).

Up Next

Now that you've survived your first week in Minecraft, settling into a new home, exploring the terrain, and perhaps meeting a few neighbors, it's time to really plant some roots—like potatoes and carrots—and get your food game going. Chapter 4 will show you the ins and outs of setting yourself up with an ongoing stream of tasty food and farm-grown supplies.

4
FOOD AND FARMING

Setting up a continuous supply of food is a top priority in the early game, as staying full allows you to quickly heal from damage. Crop plants and farm animals are easily renewable sources of food. In this chapter, we'll make a starter crop farm, a classic crop farm, and a chicken farm. You'll also learn to farm other resources, like certain trees and plants, for specific activities like crafting and enchanting.

Food and Hunger

Not all food in Minecraft is created equal. Some will fill more haunches in your hunger bar, and some will give more saturation points (a hidden feature). The more saturation points a food has, the slower your hunger bar diminishes. Of the most easily attained foods, the ones that provide the most saturation and hunger points are cooked meats, stews, soups, baked potatoes, and bread. Foods with the least saturation and hunger are sweets, berries, and uncooked meats.

KEEP A LOT OF HIGH-SATURATION FOOD ON HAND TO ENSURE YOU NEVER GO HUNGRY.

As mentioned, your hunger bar depletes quickly when performing high-energy activities like sprinting, jumping, fighting, and swimming. (When you are in a boat, your hunger won't deplete the hunger bar.) When you reach three haunches, you won't be able to sprint. Because your hunger level influences recovery time, it's a good idea to have a stockpile of quality food when entering into a dangerous situation or high-energy activity (one in which you'd rather spend your time holding your sword than a beetroot). Your health regenerates quickest when your hunger bar is full, and won't regenerate at all if your hunger points are 17 or less. On Normal difficulty, your hunger will deplete to 1 point, and on Easy, it will only deplete to

FOOD AND FARMING

43

10 points. However, on Hard difficulty, you will start taking damage when your hunger bar reaches 0 and starve to death when your health reaches 0.

FOODS AND THEIR SOURCES, SORTED BY HUNGER VALUE

Food	Icon	Source	Hunger Value
Rabbit stew		Craft from one cooked rabbit, one carrot, one baked potato, one brown mushroom, and one wooden bowl. Mushrooms can be gathered in forests, and they will drop from giant mushrooms in Dark Forests	10
Cooked porkchop		Smelt raw porkchop	8
Steak		Smelt raw beef	8
Pumpkin pie		Craft from one pumpkin, one sugar, and one egg	8
Cooked mutton		Smelt raw mutton	6
Cooked salmon		Smelt raw salmon	6
Beetroot soup		Craft from six beetroot and one wooden bowl	6
Cooked chicken		Smelt raw chicken	6
Honey bottle		Use a glass bottle on a beehive	6

(Continued on next page)

Food	Icon	Source	Hunger Value
Mushroom stew		Craft from one red mushroom, one brown mushroom, and one wooden bowl.	6
Baked potato		Smelt one potato	5
Bread		Craft from three wheat; wheat can be gathered from village farms, and village hay bales; wheat seeds can be gathered from village farms and by breaking grass	5
Cooked cod		Smelt raw cod	5
Cooked rabbit		Smelt raw rabbit	5
Apple		Apples drop from oak and dark oak leaves.	4
Carrot		Gather from village farms	3
Raw beef		Kill adult cows	3
Raw porkchop		Kill adult pigs	3
Raw rabbit		Kill adult rabbits	3

FOOD AND FARMING

Food	Icon	Source	Hunger Value
Cake (slice)		Craft from three buckets of milk, three wheat, two sugar, and one egg	2
Cookie		Craft from two wheat and one cocoa bean.	2
Glow berries		Gather by right-clicking cave vines in lush caves	2
Sweet berries		Gather by right-clicking sweet berry bushes in taiga forests	2
Melon slice		Chop grown melons; melons and melon seeds can be gathered in jungles	2
Raw chicken		Kill chickens	2
Raw cod		Kill in oceans	2
Raw mutton		Kill adult sheep	2
Raw salmon		Kill in rivers and colder oceans	2
Beetroot		Gather from village farms	1

(Continued on next page)

Food	Icon	Source	Hunger Value
Dried kelp		Smelt kelp gathered from oceans	1
Potato		Gather from village farms	1
Tropical fish		Catch from fishing or from killing in warm oceans	0.5

To cook stews and sweets, you'll need to unlock their crafting recipes, which you can do by gathering their ingredients. For example, stews and soups require a wooden bowl, which is crafted from three planks of wood. Mushroom stew uses a red and a brown mushroom; rabbit stew requires a cooked rabbit, a carrot, a baked potato, and a mushroom (brown or red); and beetroot soup is made with six beetroots.

MUSHROOM STEW RECIPE

COOKING

When you're cooking with a furnace, each piece of coal or charcoal will cook eight items. You can cook four food items at a time without using fuel on a campfire—craft one with a piece of charcoal or coal, three sticks, and three wood logs. The campfire will light automatically when you place it. Be careful: You'll take damage if you step on the fire. (FYI: placing a hay bale

TO EAT CAKE, PLACE IT ON THE GROUND OR ANOTHER SURFACE AND RIGHT-CLICK IT. YOU'LL EAT IT BY THE SLICE.

crafted from nine wheat beneath the campfire will make a smoke signal that rises twenty-four blocks instead of the default ten).

To cook with the campfire, right-click it with one or more cookable food items. The food will be arranged around the campfire, cook for about thirty seconds, and then pop off and onto the ground. You can extinguish a campfire with a shovel or water and relight it with a flint and steel (crafted with one flint and one iron ingot).

Challenge: Build a Campfire
Dig a hole, make a hay bale, and place it in the hole you've just created. Place a campfire on top of it to make a smoke signal. Then, cook four raw salmon into cooked salmon using the campfire.

FISHING

Fishing is a good, albeit slow, way to get food and valuable loot early in the game. Craft a rod from three sticks and two string. Cast your rod by right-clicking an open area of water; the bobber will bounce and splash a bit. Within thirty seconds (less if it's raining), you should see a trail of blue splashes approaching the bobber. When this trail reaches the bobber, the bobber will dip below the water. Right-click again to reel in your catch. It may be fish, junk, or more rarely, treasure (if you're fishing in open water). Treasure can include bows, fishing rods, enchanted books, saddles, name tags, and nautilus shells. Junk may actually also be helpful, and includes string, lily pads, bones, ink sacs, and leather. There are several enchantments you can cast on your rod to increase your chances of finding treasure and getting bites quickly (see Chapter 15 for more on enchantments).

Challenge: Fishing Away
Craft a fishing rod. Fish until you pull up thirty catches. You'll catch more fish quicker while it rains. This will give you good experience with your fishing technique and a good idea of what you can catch. Maybe you'll even pull up some treasure!

Other Types of Food

In addition to your standard steak-and potato types of food, there are a few edibles that can give you *status effects*. These may be *buffs* that give you positive effects, like fire resistance, or *debuffs* that negatively affect your character, like poison.

GOLDEN FOODS

Gold-encrusted foods—golden apples, enchanted golden apples, and golden carrots—provide superior hunger and saturation benefits, and a golden apple also gives you the status effects of Regeneration (regenerates health) and Absorption (adds extra, temporary health hearts). You can craft a golden apple using an apple and eight gold ingots, and a golden carrot from a carrot and eight gold nuggets. The extremely rare enchanted golden apple is not craftable; you can only find it in treasure chests. Eating the enchanted golden apple will imbue you with powerful, short-term buffs like Absorption, Fire Resistance (protects against fire), Resistance (protects against damage), and Regeneration that are especially useful in battles.

SUSPICIOUS STEW

You'll find suspicious stew within food chests in shipwrecks. Eating this stew will give you several seconds of a random buff or debuff, like night vision or blindness. Craft it yourself by crafting mushroom stew with a flower. The type of flower determines the effect.

SUSPICIOUS STEW FLOWERS AND EFFECTS

Flower	Icon	Effect
Allium		Fire resistance
Azure bluet		Blindness

FOOD AND FARMING

Blue orchid or dandelion		Saturation
Cornflower		Jump boost
Lily of the valley		Poison
Oxeye daisy		Regeneration
Poppy		Night vision
Tulip		Weakness
Wither rose		Wither

Challenge: Suspicious Stew

Craft a wooden bowl from three planks and gather the materials for a Cornflower Suspicious Stew. Craft the Suspicious Stew, eat it, and enjoy a few moments of the Jump Boost status effect.

TOXIC FOOD

Spider eyes and poisonous potatoes are toxic; these restore some hunger, but poison you for a short while, so they can be worth eating if your hunger is low and you have no other food. Similarly, you can eat pufferfish and rotten flesh dropped by slain zombies; neither are an optimal source of food, as they do more harm than good. Rotten flesh might give you the Hunger effect (quickly diminishes hunger points), and pufferfish will give you Nausea (warps your vision), Hunger, and Poison effects.

> **NOTE:**
> DRINKING A BUCKET OF MILK WILL REMOVE ANY POSITIVE OR NEGATIVE STATUS EFFECTS. TO GET A BUCKET OF MILK, RIGHT-CLICK A BUCKET CRAFTED FROM THREE IRON INGOTS ON A COW. DRINKING A BOTTLE OF HONEY WILL REMOVE ANY POISONOUS EFFECTS. WE'LL LEARN MORE ABOUT HONEY LATER IN THIS CHAPTER.

Crop Farming

One way to keep a supply of food at hand is by crop farming wheat, carrots, beetroot, and potatoes. For carrots and potatoes, plant the vegetable itself. You can get these from village farms. For wheat and beetroot, plant the seeds. You can get wheat and beetroot seeds by harvesting these plants in a village farm. You can also get wheat seeds by breaking grass (a percentage of grass drops wheat seeds). A harvest of potatoes often includes a poisonous potato or two that aren't really usable for anything other than last-ditch emergency food.

MAKE A SMALL STARTER FARM

The easiest way to start a farm is to grow seeds next to a river or pond. Once you've found the right location, follow the instructions below:

1. Gather your seeds and vegetables, craft a hoe (with two sticks and two cobblestone), and find some flat ground near a pond or river. The ground should be on the same level as the water.
2. Within four blocks of the water, right-click the hoe on the grass or dirt blocks to turn the blocks into farmland. The ground will turn brown and striped to indicate it is ready to be planted on. (Any farmland that is too far from a water source will revert back to dirt pretty quickly.) The water hydrates the farmland (up to four blocks) so you can plant your seeds.
3. Right-click your seeds on the blocks to plant the crops.
4. Wait. It can take several Minecraft days for a crop plant to mature.
5. Left-click to harvest mature crops. Wheat and beetroot crops will also drop seeds along with the crop plant.

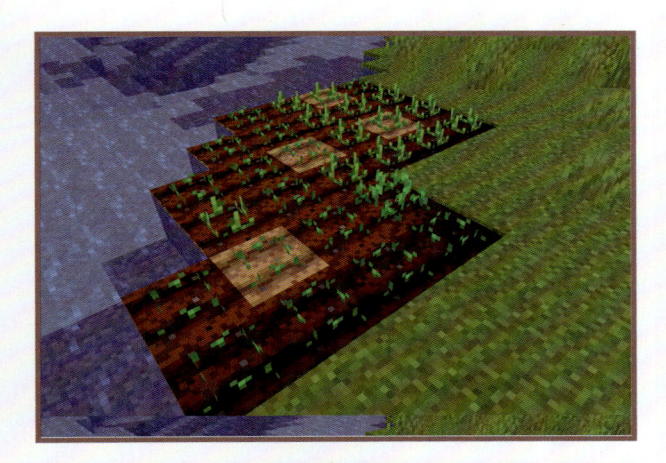

HOE YOUR FARMLAND AT THE SAME LEVEL AS YOUR WATER SOURCE.

FROM LEFT TO RIGHT, FULLY GROWN (TOP) AND STARTING SEEDLINGS (BOTTOM) FOR WHEAT, BEETROOT, CARROTS, AND POTATOES.

MAKE A CLASSIC FARM

Because water hydrates farmland up to four blocks away, a classic farm is 9x9 blocks with a single water source block placed into a hole in the middle. You'll need a flat area of grass or dirt that receives full sunlight, a bucket, a hoe, and your seeds.

1. Craft a bucket with three iron ingots.
2. Right-click your water bucket on a water block in a pond, river, or sea to fill it.
3. In the center of the 9x9 farm area, dig out one block.

4. Right-click the hole with your water bucket equipped to place the water.

5. Use your hoe to turn the rest of the blocks in the farm area into farmland.

6. Plant your seeds and wait till harvest. Here I've planted wheat and potatoes in rows, and used torches to light up the area.

Your crops will grow faster if they're planted in rows of distinct crops, if they receive light through the night if you're not sleeping, and if you remain relatively close by. Leaving the area of your farm by more than one hundred blocks will stop the plants from growing.

> **NOTE:**
> YOU CAN USE BONE MEAL AS A FERTILIZER TO SPEED UP GROWTH OF MOST PLANTS, EXCLUDING CACTI AND SUGAR CANE. CRAFT BONE MEAL FROM BONES (ONE BONE GIVES THREE BONE MEAL) DROPPED BY SKELETONS AND RIGHT-CLICK THE PLANT FOR A CHANCE TO GROW IT TO ITS NEXT STAGE.

PUMPKIN AND MELON FARMS

Farming melon and pumpkin works the same way as crop farming, though the matured crops are a bit different! You'll plant the pumpkin or melon seed (gather these by breaking the plant, typically found in villages), which eventually sprouts into a vine. Once the stem is fully grown, it will produce a mature fruit that sits on the ground beside it. Use an axe to harvest the melon or pumpkin. The stem will continue producing fruit, as long as there's an empty block of dirt or grass next to it.

Challenge: Crop Mastery

1. Create various farms for wheat and beetroots, carrots and potatoes, and pumpkins and melons.
2. Make beetroot soup from six beetroots and a wooden bowl.
3. Make a baked potato with a furnace or campfire.
4. Get three to seven melon slices by breaking a melon with your hand.

Animal Farming

To farm animals for food, you'll want at least a pair of sheep, cows, pigs, or chickens (any two will do, as Minecraft's mobs aren't gendered). The goal is to pen them into an area, breed them to produce many offspring, kill most of them for food and other drops, and begin again by breeding the remainder.

MAKE A CHICKEN FARM

To make a chicken farm, you'll need at least two wheat seeds, some nearby chickens, wood planks and sticks, and an open 7x7 patch of flat land.

1. Craft nineteen wood fences and one gate using thirty wood planks and eighteen sticks. You can use any type of wood for the planks, as long as they're all one type.

FENCE RECIPE.

GATE RECIPE.

2. Place the fence in a 6x6 square, leaving a space open on one side.

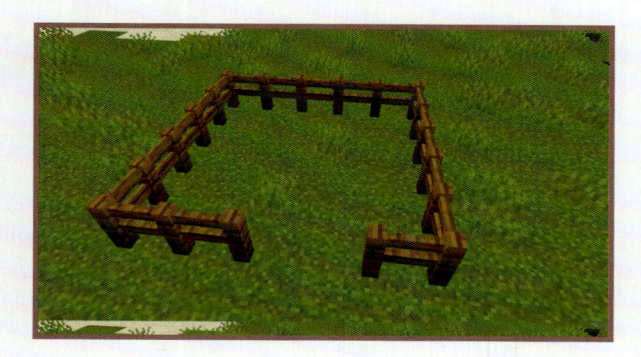

3. Place the wood gate in the gap. Animals can't open gates, so this is for you to enter and leave while keeping the animals in.

4. On the side of the pen that's closest to the roaming chickens, place one or two blocks, one block high, to act as a little stair that allows the chickens to climb over the fence and into the pen.

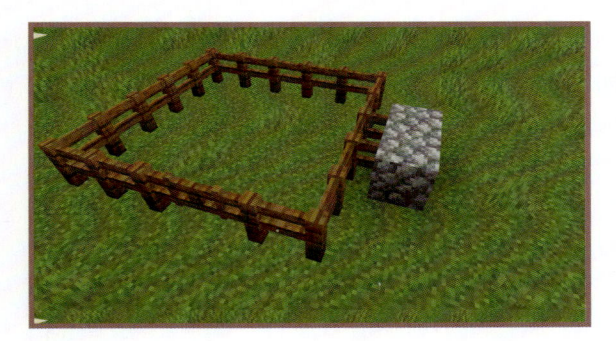

5. Place the seeds in your hand and go to the chickens. Seeds (wheat, melon, pumpkin, and beetroot) are their favorite food, so they should follow you. Be careful, though: if you go too fast or stop holding the seeds, they'll lose interest.

6. With the seeds still equipped, walk slowly to the block(s) by the pen. Walk backward or take a look behind you occasionally to make sure the chickens are still following you. Jump up onto the block for climbing the fence and then jump into the pen. The chickens will follow you.

7. Right-click two chickens with your seeds equipped. You'll see red hearts float above their heads. The two chickens should approach each other and in a few moments a baby chick should appear! You've bred your first animals.

Once bred, chickens have a five-minute cool down. During this time, using a seed on them has no effect. Chicks take twenty minutes to mature. You can speed up a chick's growth by feeding it seeds. The mature chickens will lay eggs every so often. These eggs don't hatch, but you can either throw the eggs on the ground for a 1/8 chance at spawning a new chick, or keep the eggs to make cake or pumpkin pie. When you have plenty of mature chickens, say ten or more, you can slay some with a sword or axe for meat and feathers—be sure to leave at least two, so they can continue breeding.

FARMING OTHER ANIMALS

You can pen other farm animals like sheep, pigs, and cows in the same way as your chickens. Create a fenced-in area with blocks to climb in and lure at least two of the same kind using their favorite food. For sheep and cows, this is wheat; pigs enjoy beetroots, carrots, and potatoes. Once you've penned your animals, breed them in the same way, by giving them food. Kill cows for leather (you'll need this to craft books for enchanting) and raw beef, sheep for wool and raw mutton, and pigs for raw porkchops. You can also right-click a cow with a bucket in your hand to get a bucket of milk.

Challenge: Husbandry Expert
Gather two of each farm animal: chicken, pig, sheep, and cow. Make separate pens and farms for each, and breed them to reach a population of ten for all four animal types.

Other Things to Farm

In addition to food, you'll also want to set up farms for other resources, such as trees for wood and sugar cane for paper. Here are a few of the most common resource farms to consider.

TREES

Wood is used in so many recipes and builds that you'll want to create an area for growing trees. If you enjoy building, you may also want to store a variety of saplings for growing trees with different-colored wood. When you chop down a tree, it drops saplings you can plant to grow a new tree of the same type. Your tree farm can be as simple as an open area with twenty or more saplings.

To grow, trees need a light level of 7 or above and about five blocks of space between trees to accommodate their foliage blocks. Saplings grow into trees randomly, but growth can be as quick as one every twenty seconds. Because trees provide shade for mobs to spawn, it's a good idea to keep this area well-lit with plenty of torches and lanterns.

SUGAR CANE

Start farming sugar cane early, as you'll need plenty to make paper to make books for enchanting. Sugar cane must be planted on grass, dirt, or sand next to (and on the same level as) a water block. If you don't have the time to set up a proper sugar cane farm, you can simply plant it along the edge of a river. You can also use paper to trade with librarian villagers.

Fully grown planted sugar cane is three blocks tall (while wild sugar cane can grow four blocks tall). Once it's fully grown, break the middle block to have both the middle and top block drop, leaving the bottom sugar cane to continue growing.

YOU CAN START GROWING SUGAR CANE QUICKLY BY PLANTING IT ALONGSIDE A RIVER OR LAKE.

ULTIMATELY, YOU MAY WANT A LARGER SUGAR CANE FARM, WHERE ONE ROW OF WATER HYDRATES TWO ROWS OF SUGAR CANE.

HONEY

If you see bees buzzing, there's a nest nearby you can farm for honey or honeycomb. You'll find nests beneath the foliage of an oak or birch tree in plains, forests, and meadows. Each naturally spawned bee nest will house three bees.

Bees will leave their nest during the day (as long as it's not raining) to collect pollen from nearby flowers. After five pollen deposits, the nest becomes full with honey. At this point, you can collect either honey or honeycomb. Honey bottles can be used to craft sugar for cooking or honey blocks that slow down mobs (and players) walking on them. Honeycomb is used to create candles, beehives, decorative honeycomb blocks, and to *wax* (right-click on or craft with) copper blocks, preventing them from oxidizing and turning green.

WHEN NESTS ARE FULL WITH HONEY, THE HONEY DRIPS OUT OF THEM! BEES WILL ALSO SHOW COLLECTED POLLEN ON THEIR BACKSIDES.

However, collecting honey or honeycomb will aggravate the bees, who will attack you. If they sting you, you'll be poisoned and the stinging bee will die within a minute. (You can drink a bucket of milk or a honey bottle to remove the Poison effect.) To calm the bees, place a campfire five blocks below the nest to smoke the nest and to prevent the bees from injuring themselves in the fire. Then right-click the nest with a glass bottle to collect the honey or with shears to collect honeycomb.

> NOTE:
> TO CRAFT GLASS BOTTLES, FIRST SMELT THREE SAND TO CREATE THREE GLASS BLOCKS. THEN CRAFT THE THREE GLASS BOTTLES FROM THE GLASS BLOCKS.

You can lure and breed bees with flowers (as you lured and bred chickens earlier). You can also craft new nests, called beehives, to house new bees. Beehives are crafted from six planks and three honeycomb. Neither nests nor beehives need to be placed on a tree to function. Note that you should only break a bee nest or beehive with a tool enchanted with Silk Touch; not doing so will anger the nest's residents and nearby bees.

Challenge: Bee Wizardry

Create your own apiary of six beehives protected by campfires and surrounded by flowers. Breed bees from natural nests and lure their offspring to your beehives.

CACTUS

Cactus is the only plant you can use to create green dye (see Chapter 8 for more on dyeing). To grow cactus, you'll first need to gather cactus blocks by breaking cactus in a desert. Then you can plant each single cactus block on sand, leaving one block of space between each plant. You can break the top blocks after the cactus has grown three blocks high, leaving the bottom block to continue growing.

COCOA BEANS

Cocoa beans are used to make brown dye and cookies and are found in jungles. To grow cocoa beans, plant the beans on the sides of jungle wood logs. They grow in three stages, from small green pods to large orange ones.

VINES

Vines are used decoratively and to craft mossy stone bricks and mossy cobblestone. (You can craft one mossy cobblestone or brick with one vine and one cobblestone or stone brick.) To grow vines, plant them on a raised beam of stone or other building blocks. As the vines grow down, use shears on the lower growth to gather the vines, leaving the top of the vines to continue growing.

Up Next

You should now have a few farms producing a steady stream of high-quality food. With your stash of food at hand, it's time to explore caving and mining! Chapter 5 will take you through the steps of mining safely and finding the minerals and ores you'll need for strong weapons and tools.

5

MINING AND CAVING

Once you've decided where to set up base, it's time to start mining and caving to get ores you can smelt into metals for better armor and tools. Mining involves creating tunnels belowground and excavating ores and minerals that you expose as you dig. Caving involves venturing into caves that generated as part of the terrain and mining the ore blocks exposed on the cave walls. Caving is often the fastest way to get ores, but is dangerous, given that monsters will be spawning in the cave's dark corners and crevasses.

Mining

Mining is slower but safer than caving, so before you have the necessary equipment to protect yourself, mining is the best way to harvest ores. Early on, your goal should be to get enough iron ore to set you up with full iron armor, tools, and weapons. Your second goal is to get diamonds. They're quite a bit rarer than iron, so expect more than a few mining sessions before you have enough for full diamond gear and tools.

Different ores appear at different levels in the world, listed below. *Levels* refers to the y value (or height) a block is at. Sea level is y=63; the top height at which you can place blocks is y=320; the bottom level is a layer of impenetrable bedrock at y= –64. At levels below y=0, ores are embedded in deepslate—a dark, tough stone—rather than stone. You can check your level in your Debug screen using **F3**.

Ores

Ore		Lowest Y Level	Highest Y Level	Highest Concentration
Coal		0	320	Around y=45
Copper		–16	112	Around y=43
Diamond		–64	–4	Increases with lower levels

(Continued on next page)

Ore		Lowest Y Level	Highest Y Level	Highest Concentration
Emerald*		−16	320	Increases with higher levels
Gold**		−64	32	Around y= −18
Iron		−64	320 (no iron between y=73 and y=79)	Around y=14 and at very high levels above y=144
Lapis lazuli		−64	64	Around y= −2
Redstone		−64	16	At y= −32 and below

*Found only in mountainous biomes
** In badlands biomes, gold also generates from y=32 to 256.

One of the best ways to begin mining is to set up a *branch mine*, where you dig parallel tunnels through the ground at levels where you'll find the most ores. When setting off to mine, you'll want to take a pickaxe, torches, and wood to craft more tools. You'll mine enough coal (at levels above y=0), iron, and cobblestone for additional crafting resources. (You may want to take or craft an extra furnace to smelt your mined iron ingots and make more pickaxes.) Wood is the one thing you don't want to run out of, as it is essential for tools and torches. Other items to take are a crafting table; basic tools (shovel, sword, axe); and for long stints, a bed. (You can also take a bucket of water to pour over pools of lava and turn them into walkable obsidian, but it's not necessary.) Aside from these items, keep your inventory open to store mined ores.

To start a branch mine:

1. First, build or dig out a safe location to place the entrance to the branch mine to prevent mobs from entering. I often use my first hidey-hole for this purpose.
2. Dig out a staircase four blocks high, going down one block at a time. Although you only need two blocks of space to fit in and descend, you'll bump your head on the way down unless you increase the height by at least one block. It's also a good idea to place stair blocks if you'll be using your mine repeatedly, and this needs an additional one-block space.

Adding stair blocks makes entering and leaving your mine much faster, and conserves hunger. (You can make stair blocks from all the cobblestone you'll be gathering while mining, and then place them in your stairwell while you return to ground level after mining.)

A FOUR-BLOCK-HIGH TUNNEL. (THIS IMAGE WAS TAKEN IN SPECTATOR MODE, WHICH ENABLES YOU TO SEE THROUGH STONE TO VIEW UNDERGROUND STRUCTURES AND FEATURES.)

Cardinal Rules for Digging

There are two main rules when mining: don't dig straight down, and don't dig straight up.

If you dig straight down, there is a good chance you'll fall straight into lava or a ravine and die. To avoid falling, stand in the center of two blocks and dig out both, one at a time. With each block you dig, you're left standing on the upper block so you can see what's coming below.

Digging straight up can cause sand and gravel to fall on your head and suffocate you, also ending in death. If you do need to dig straight up, you can avoid death by suffocation by placing a torch on the block you're standing on, as any falling gravel or sand will break into an item drop when it hits the torch. After digging out blocks above you, pillar up as far as you can go (see page 26 for how to pillar up). You'll need to remove the torch when pillaring up, so ensure you replace it when you start digging up again. The one thing the torch won't protect against is water (or lava); if water falls on you, dig sideways to escape it or swim up to the surface. You can tell if there's water or lava above a block by the water or lava drips coming from the block.

3. Dig your staircase down to a good iron level, such as y=15. As you go, place torches to keep the light level above 0 (about one every twenty blocks if you're mining horizontally and one every ten if you're staircasing). Of course, mine any ores you find along the way.
4. Once you reach y=15, dig out a room that's about 11x11 (it really can be any size you want, but it's easiest to start out small!). From this base room, you'll dig out mining tunnels, or branches, that are two blocks high and one block wide, on each side of the room. You can expand this room as you make more branches.

Warning

There's lava underground that can generate as a single block or spring, shallow pools, or even large pools that fill entire caves. If lava is nearby, you'll hear pops; this is a good clue that you need to be careful in proceeding. Lava overhead, one block above you, will show orange drips coming from the block. Once you expose lava that is at your level or higher, it will flow toward you. Block off the flow by placing stone or cobblestone on top of it or on the block directly in front of it. You can remove single-source lava by placing a torch or block in its place. If you encounter a lava pool, you can pour water over it to create obsidian or replace the lava with cobblestone or other blocks. You can pick up lava with an empty bucket to make a bucket of lava; this can be used to light enemies afire in combat.

5. Start digging your branches: along one side of the room, dig out a branch two blocks high and one block wide. Mine the ores you find, placing torches every fifteen blocks or so. Keep going until you reach a cave system or something dangerous you want to block off, such as a mineshaft (see Chapter 8) or lava flow.

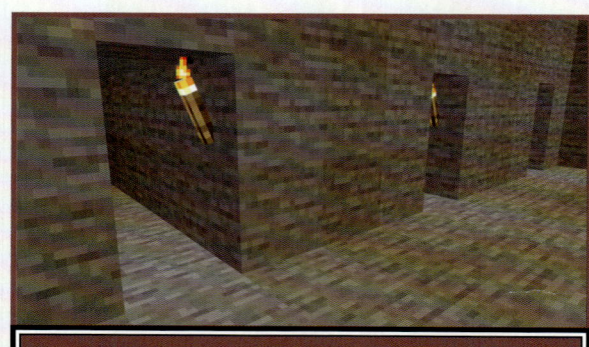

THESE BRANCH MINES ARE SPACED FOUR BLOCKS APART (THREE BLOCKS IN BETWEEN).

6. Continue digging out branches from your main starting room to access more ore. To uncover every single ore, you could make branches that are two blocks apart. However, ore rarely generates in veins that are only one block wide. Instead, ore clumps and veins are usually at least two blocks wide. You can cover more ground faster by making branches that are three blocks apart.

Use the same process to mine out other ores at levels they are most common. When you're ready to return to the surface, it may be worth setting down your bed and trying to sleep to ensure you don't reenter the surface world at night. When you can, place stair blocks up your staircase so that you can run up and down the stairs without jumping and expending a lot of energy.

> **NOTE:**
> TO OPEN UP INVENTORY SPACE, YOU CAN CRAFT NINE OF A SINGLE RAW ORE (AS WELL AS REDSTONE DUST, LAPIS, DIAMONDS, AND EMERALD ORE) INTO A BLOCK, AND CONVERT THE BLOCK BACK TO NINE ORE OR MINERALS ONCE YOU'VE MADE IT BACK HOME TO YOUR CHESTS.

Challenge: Mountaineering

Find a high mountain and climb it, looking on its slopes or cliffs for exposed ore and minerals. Collect coal, iron, copper, emerald, and any other ore you see!

Caving

Caving is simply mining inside caves and ravines. Because caves can be full of hostile mobs, you may want to wait to experience the dangerous art of caving until you've gathered and smelted enough iron or diamonds to make a full set of armor, a sword, and a shield. When you're going caving, you'll want to take the same resources as you did when mining, with the understanding that you'll be doing more fighting (so bring quite a few weapons and more than enough food!).

As you explore the aboveground terrain, you'll come across a number of various cave openings (holes in the ground or hills) and ravines. The dark, rocky ledges on ravine walls are prone to spawning mobs that will attack you unannounced. If you're nervous about mobs (as I am), try to find a cave that extends deep into the ground.

Mobs will spawn at light level 0, so it's important to quickly light up as much cave as possible with torches to prevent more mobs spawning. Once you've cleared and lit an area of caves, mine the ores you see on the cave walls. Caving can yield ore more efficiently than branch mining, but there's also a high chance of getting lost, which can really slow you down.

FINDING YOUR WAY

Here are some tactics you can use to avoid getting lost in the caves:

- In narrow caves, place torches along only the left or the right wall (as long as you're consistent) so you can retrace your steps.
- Mark areas where you can climb back upward with multiple torches, such as two torches placed one above the other.
- Mark off areas you've already explored with something identifiable, like a block of dirt with a torch on top.

As you explore more caves, you'll begin figuring out your own ways to keep track of where you are. If you're thoroughly lost, get as high up to ground level as possible (y=64) in the cave system, and then dig a staircase up and out.

CAVE TYPES

Caves come in all shapes and sizes, from small, surface openings to massive caverns deep in the world, and may be connected to other caves or stand alone. There are three main types of caves; the most dangerous are *cheese* caves (connected caves). These are groups of large, interconnected caves, reminiscent of Swiss cheese. With their messy layouts, it's easy to overlook a dark tunnel or overhang that may spawn mobs.

The other types of caves are known as spaghetti and noodle. *Spaghetti caves* are long, winding caves; *noodle caves* are thinner versions of spaghetti caves. These cave types can often lead you quickly down to lower levels, where rarer ores like diamond are found. When you reach the end of a long, tunnel-like cave, mine a few blocks of stone from the end wall to see if the cave tunnel continues.

MINING AND CAVING

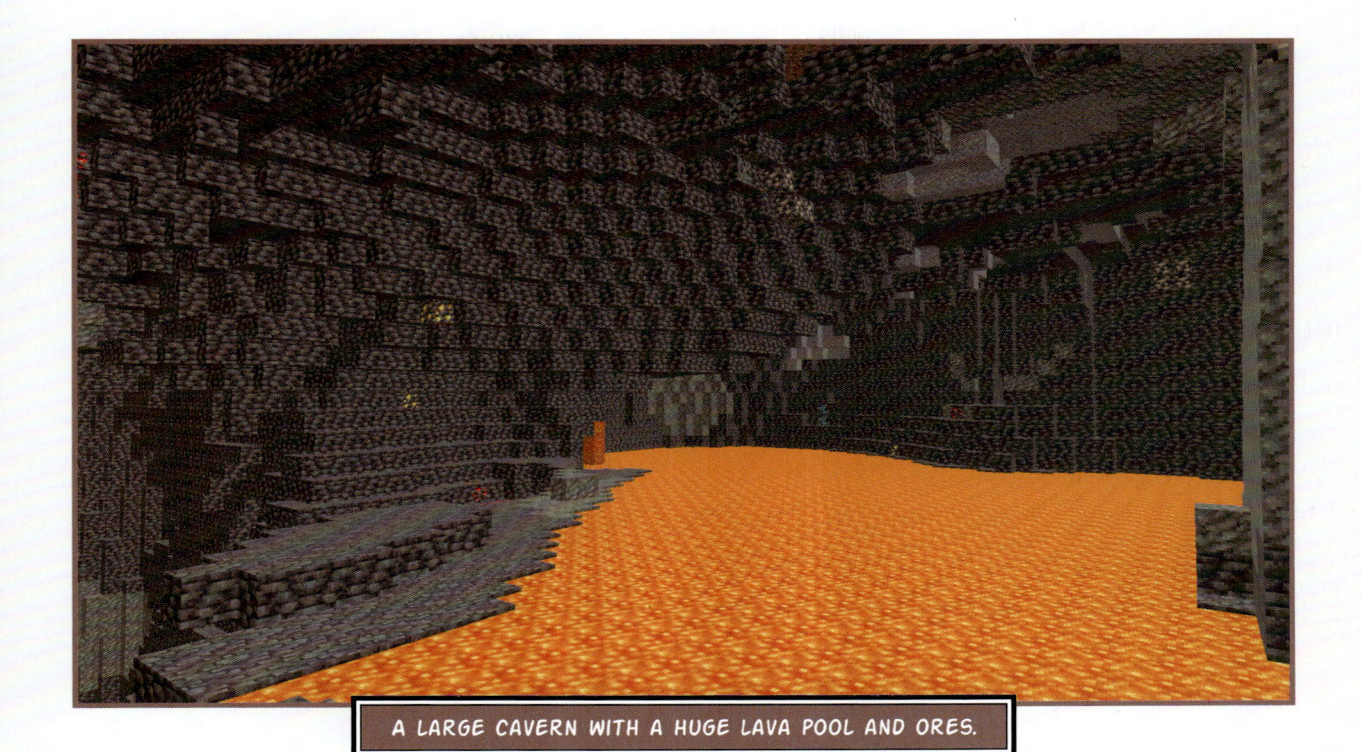

A LARGE CAVERN WITH A HUGE LAVA POOL AND ORES.

Occasionally, caves can be aquifers, either partially or fully waterlogged or lava-filled (see "Aquifers and Underground Lakes" for more information). There are also massive, cavernous caves with pillars of deepslate reaching fifty blocks to the ceiling.

CAVE BIOMES

Biomes are environmental habitats, like jungles or deserts, with unique plants, mobs, and terrain. While most biomes are aboveground, there are some unique underground biomes that apply only to caves. For example, lush caves. *Lush caves* are caves overgrown by vines, moss, and bushes, and are a good place to find clay. *Dripstone caves* contain hanging and standing columns of dripstone; copper ore generates more here.

Mining Resources

Let's take a look at the kind of resources you can expect to find in mines and caves. Stone and ore blocks need to be mined with a pickaxe, and some require a specific level of pickaxe (stone, iron, or diamond), or else they will not drop anything when mined. I've categorized these resources by the tool you'll need to break them.

WOOD OR BETTER PICKAXE

You can use a wood pickaxe to mine stone, stone-related blocks, and coal, though it's the least efficient pickaxe. Because it cannot mine most ores, has low durability, and mines slowly, you should upgrade to stone tools as soon as possible.

Stone, Stone Variants, and Rocks

When mining, the bulk of your collected materials will be various types of stone. Mining stone, for instance, drops cobblestone, which you can smelt back into stone. Both stone and cobblestone are used in many crafting recipes. The other stone variants are primarily used as decorative building blocks. At lower levels (about y=0), stone is replaced by deepslate, which drops cobbled deepslate when mined. You can smelt cobbled deepslate back into deepslate to use decoratively.

TOP ROW, FROM LEFT TO RIGHT: STONE, GRANITE, ANDESITE, AND DIORITE. BOTTOM ROW: DEEPSLATE, TUFF, CALCITE, AND SMOOTH BASALT.

If mining in mountainous biomes, you might come across a regular-looking stone (or deepslate) block that is actually infested. Infested stone contains silverfish, which are tiny but hostile (see Chapter 11 for more information). It's impossible to tell from the block's appearance that it's infested, although an infested stone block will break more quickly than a regular stone block.

Coal

Mining a coal ore block drops one piece of coal, used in crafting torches, blocks of coal, campfires, and fire charges.

STONE OR BETTER PICKAXE

To start mining common ores, you'll need to upgrade to a stone pickaxe.

Copper Ore

Mining copper ore drops raw copper, which you can smelt into copper ingots using a furnace and fuel like coal. Copper ingots are used in crafting lightning rods, spyglasses, and copper blocks—including stairs and slabs—which can be crafted into cut copper. Cut copper is a decorative block of square copper bricks. Copper and cut copper blocks weather over time, taking on a greenish, oxidized patina. You can use a honeycomb once (either by right-clicking the block with a honeycomb equipped or crafting) to "wax" the block and prevent further oxidization, keeping the copper at its current stage of oxidation. Right-clicking copper blocks once with an axe removes one stage of oxidation as well as any wax (and its protection).

Lapis Lazuli

A lapis lazuli ore block drops several pieces of ore, which you can craft into decorative blocks or blue dye. It's most useful in the enchanting process; you need one to three lapis for each item you enchant (see Chapter 15).

Iron Ore

Smelt raw iron ore into iron ingots. Iron is used to craft many functional blocks, like anvils, buckets, and rails, as well as weapons and tools.

IRON OR BETTER PICKAXE

An iron pickaxe mines significantly faster than a stone pickaxe and is necessary to harvest the rarest ores. Once you start branch mining, you should find enough iron to make additional pickaxes as you need them.

Redstone

Redstone ore blocks drop redstone dust, an essential ingredient for redstone components like observers, powered rails, and pistons used in building contraptions (see Chapter 13 for more information).

Diamonds

Diamond ore is so precious that if you come across a block you'll want to first mine out all blocks around it, (a) to make sure that you've found all the diamonds in the vein and (b) to ensure there's no lava pocket that the dropped diamonds may fall into. Diamonds are used for crafting the best weapons and armor, including netherite armor (see Chapter 14), enchanting tables, and jukeboxes.

Emeralds

Emerald ore is rarer than diamonds and is found only in mountainous biomes. Emeralds are used for trading with villagers and the wandering trader.

Gold

Gold ore blocks will drop raw gold, which you can smelt into gold ingots. Gold ore is especially plentiful in badlands biomes. Although it's not valuable in crafting armor and tools, it is essential for trading with piglins in the Nether (more on this in Chapter 14).

DIAMOND PICKAXE

Aim to get enough diamonds to create a diamond pickaxe. Although an iron pickaxe can mine almost all the same blocks as a diamond pickaxe, the latter has much higher durability and speed, and there are a few ores that only a diamond pickaxe can mine.

Obsidian

Obsidian is one of the hardest blocks in Minecraft. It takes over nine seconds to break with a diamond pickaxe, and is resistant to explosions. It forms underground when water streams over standing (nonmoving) lava. Right-click a bucket of water on a block adjacent to a lava pool to start a flow, turning it into obsidian you can walk over and mine. It's used to create portals and can also be found in ruined portals as well as in the End.

Obsidian generates naturally near lava, so mined obsidian can easily fall into lava and get destroyed. To avoid this, mine out a block adjacent to the obsidian and pour in a bucket of water. As you mine, the water will flow and turn any newly exposed lava into obsidian.

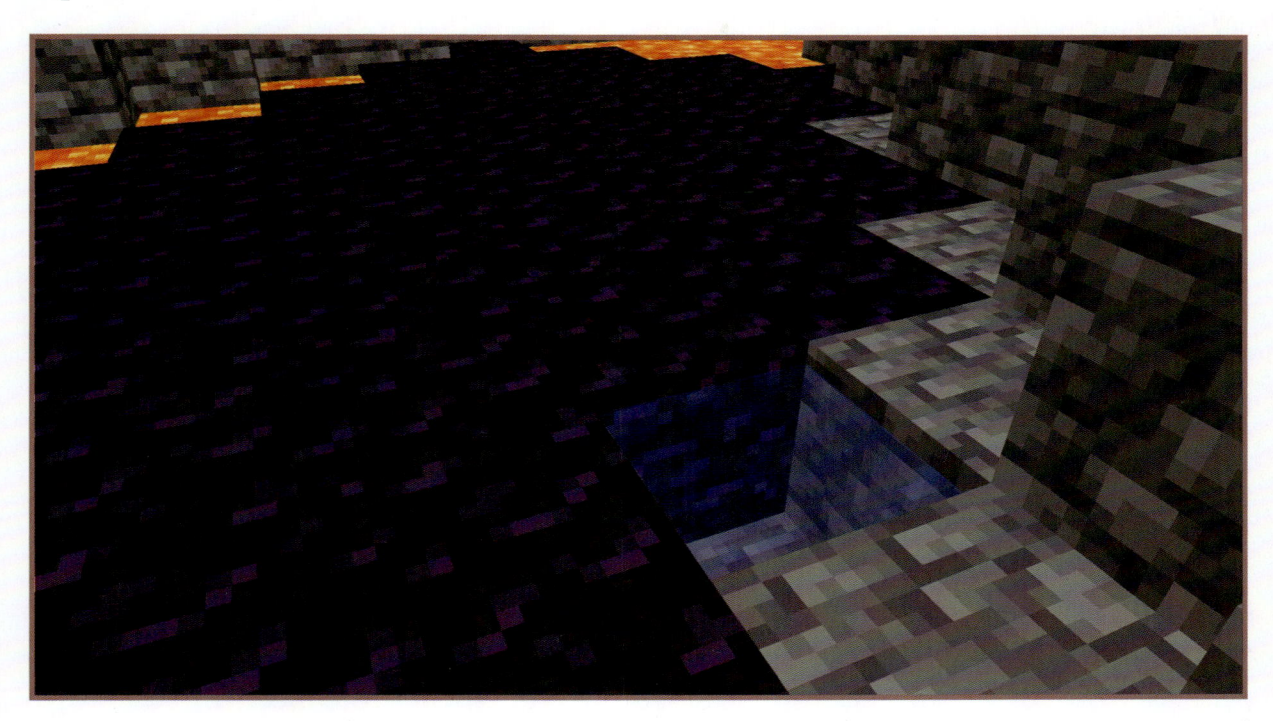

SHOVEL

You'll need a shovel of any type to mine the following blocks. As with all tools, a wood shovel will be the slowest and least durable and diamond will be the hardiest and most efficient.

Clay

Mined clay drops four clay balls, which can be smelted into bricks, or recrafted into clay blocks that you can smelt into decorative terracotta blocks.

Sand

Unlike most blocks, sand is gravity-affected; if you mine the block beneath it, the sand will fall down, landing on the next block it encounters. Sand can be smelted into glass and crafted into sandstone. You can also craft it with gunpowder to create TNT, or with gravel and dye to create blocks of concrete powder.

Dirt

Dirt is useful in landscaping or modifying terrain, and necessary when creating farmland and growing crops. You can dig out dirt or craft it with gravel to make coarse dirt, a dirt variant. When placed next to grass, dirt will convert into grass blocks; coarse dirt won't convert.

Gravel

Gravel is also gravity-affected, which can pose a suffocation risk if you're mining directly above your head and unwittingly unleash a column of gravel. Gravel is a crafting ingredient for coarse dirt and concrete powder.

Underground Features

As you explore below the surface, you're going to find a variety of unique features (and some creatures), whether you're caving or digging out your own mines. The vine-like glow lichen, for example, emits a soft light level of 7 and can be found on occasional solid blocks underground. (You'll need shears to collect it.) You'll also encounter bats, which just fly harmlessly about. In dark pools of underground water, you can find axolotls and glow squid (see Chapter 10). Here I'll detail a few main features besides ores to look out for.

ORE VEINS

Ore veins are very rare, but if you find one, you're in for uncovering a lot of ore—hundreds and potentially thousands of ore blocks. Above y=0, ore veins are composed of copper ore and granite blocks and an occasional block of raw copper. Below y=0, they're made of iron ore and tuff blocks with some blocks of raw iron. Blocks of raw iron, copper, and gold can be decrafted into nine ores; you can also craft them with nine ores.

AQUIFERS AND UNDERGROUND LAKES

There's plenty of water belowground, too, in aquifers or waterlogged caves, pools, and lakes. To explore waterlogged caves, you'll want to have armor enchanted for underwater breathing and mining (see Chapter 15). Magma blocks form on underwater lake beds occasionally, and emit bubble columns that can pull you down to them. You'll take damage if you stand on magma blocks, but you can sneak (shift) to avoid this.

AMETHYST GEODES

As you mine and cave, you're likely to come across amethyst geodes. These are crystalline formations you can find underground between y= –64 and y=30. Amethyst geodes are slightly elongated, empty spheroids about twenty blocks high and fifteen blocks wide and have three layers of rock or crystal around an empty interior. The outer layer is a dark stone called smooth basalt and the middle layer is a white stone, calcite. Underneath these two layers is a layer of amethyst crystal blocks (you can mine these with any pickaxe) and budding amethyst crystal blocks. Budding amethyst crystal blocks can't be mined; they'll drop nothing. You'll find some amethyst clusters of crystals growing on budding amethyst blocks (the crystals are only generated on these blocks). The clusters mature in four stages: they start as small, medium, and large amethyst buds and eventually grow into full-sized clusters. You can use any pickaxe to mine the fully grown clusters, which will drop amethyst shards. The shards are used in crafting spyglasses and tinted glass (see Chapter 9). If you use a pickaxe enchanted with Silk Touch, you can mine and gather the buds and clusters themselves (without Silk Touch, buds will drop nothing).

Challenge: Caving Mastery

Extract all the types of ores and find a geode from just exploring caves. You're looking for coal, copper, diamonds, emeralds, gold, iron, lapis lazuli, redstone, as well as amethyst shards from the geode.

FOSSILS

Fossils are very rare underground structures you can find in desert or swamp biomes between levels y= –50 and y=45. They are constructed to resemble the skeletons of large creatures who died long ago. They are made of bone blocks and reach up to thirteen blocks long, nine blocks wide, and five blocks high. Above y=0, some of their blocks may be replaced with coal ore; below y=0, some may be replaced with diamond ore. The easiest way to find them is to branch mine in desert and swamp biomes, leaving three blocks between branches (the narrowest skeleton is a spine, three blocks wide). Use any pickaxe to break bone blocks. You can either use bone blocks decoratively or craft them into bone meal to use as fertilizer. Bone meal is also a crafting ingredient for some dyes.

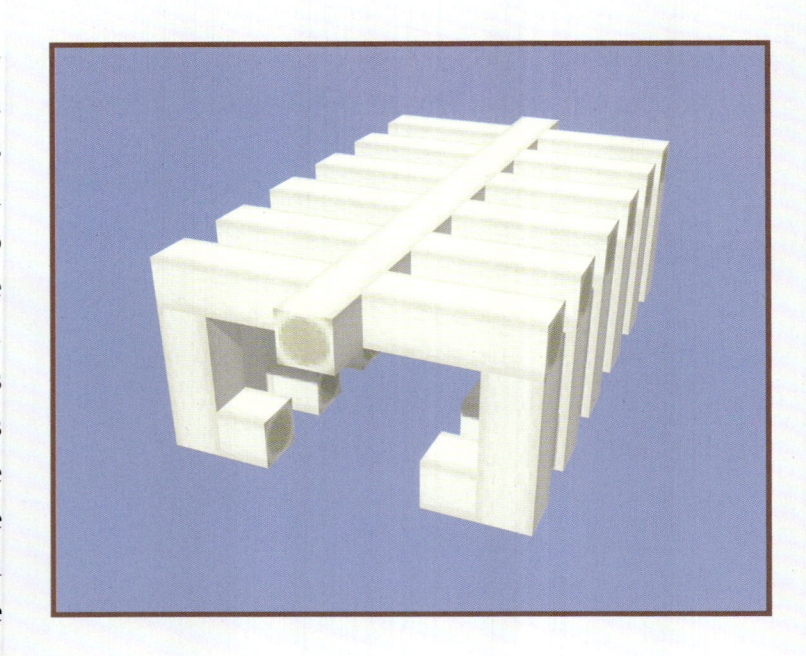

Up Next

In addition to geological features, you can find some structures underground, including mineshafts, dungeons, and very rarely, strongholds. We'll look at these in Chapter 8. In the meantime, now that you've acquired enough iron to make tools and armor, it's time to look aboveground at the biomes that create the differing landscapes of Minecraft and the resources they hold.

6

THE NATURAL WORLD

Now that you've gotten comfortable exploring underground, it's time to take a closer look aboveground at the world you're living in. In this chapter, we'll look at some natural features, like weather and light, as well as habitats and biomes. Biomes are environmental areas with distinctive climates, flora (plants), and fauna (animals). In the next chapter, we'll explore the structures you can find in some of these biomes, like desert pyramids and jungle temples.

Minecraft comprises three dimensions: the Overworld, which is the dimension you spawn in that resembles our world, and the Nether and End, which we'll discuss in Chapters 14 and 16, respectively. The Overworld is a lot like Earth, with landmasses small and large separated by oceans and topography including lakes, ponds, rivers, caves, ravines, hills, and mountains. Unlike Earth, the Overworld is approximately one-third ocean and two-thirds land. It also has islands floating in the sky, plentiful surface lava ponds, and tons of staggeringly deep ravines and massive cave openings.

The world stretches infinitely in horizontal x (east-west) and z (north-south) directions, but as we learned in Chapter 5, the world has upper and lower limits. The top building limit is y=320, though you can fly higher with Elytra (wings you can find in the End). Cloud layers move across the sky from east to west at y=192–195. Sea level is at y=63, and at y= –64, there is an unbreakable layer of bedrock that separates the Overworld from an empty space below called the Void.

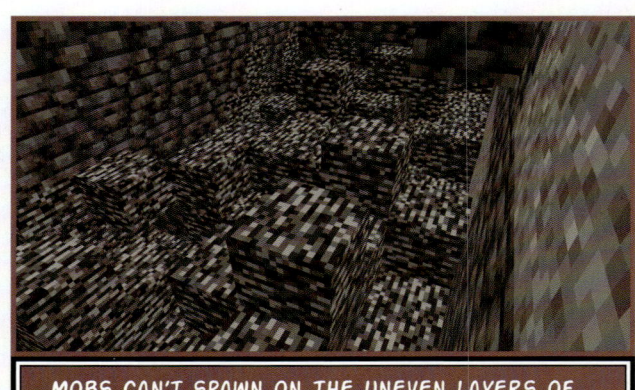

MOBS CAN'T SPAWN ON THE UNEVEN LAYERS OF BEDROCK, THOUGH THIS DOESN'T NECESSARILY MEAN YOU'RE SAFE! AT THE BOTTOM OF THE WORLD, A DARK CAVE IS NEVER TOO FAR AWAY.

Weather

There are three types of weather in Minecraft: clear, precipitation, and thunderstorms. Weather occurs at the same time everywhere in your world, though it might look different depending on the biome you're in. For example, in dry biomes like the desert and savannah, the sky will darken but you won't experience rainfall. In colder biomes, precipitation comes in the form of snow instead of rain.

During thunderstorms, the sky becomes dark enough for mobs to spawn during daytime. You'll hear thunder and see deadly lightning bolts that can kill or damage you and start fires. A lightning strike can also transform some mobs: villagers become witches, creepers turn into charged creepers, pigs become zombified piglins, and red mooshrooms change color (see Chapters 10 and 11 for more on these mobs). If you'd rather avoid thunderstorms, you can sleep during them and wake to a clear morning.

Light

Natural light comes from the square sun moving westward across the sky. At night, the sun is replaced with the moon, which can change in shape with lunar, and also provides a little light. Light also comes from light-emitting blocks, whether crafted, like torches, or natural, like glow berries found in caves. Most hostile mobs require a light level of 0 in order to spawn, so be sure to light up the dark spaces around you.

What Are Biomes?

As you explore, you'll encounter biomes that vary in trees, flowers, animals, grass and leaf color, terrain, and even sky color. Most land biomes include rivers, ponds, cave entrances, ravines, and the occasional lava pond. A biome can vary in size from a few dozen blocks wide to a several hundred or more in length, all in irregular shapes. Biomes typically extend from the bottom of the world to the top, though several cave biomes are only found belowground. Typically, biomes with similar temperatures are near each other, like dry desert and badlands. A smaller pocket of a biome might even be enclosed within another.

> **NOTE:**
> TO FIND OUT WHAT BIOME YOU ARE CURRENTLY IN, PRESS F3 TO OPEN THE DEBUG SCREEN. ON THE LEFT, MIDWAY THROUGH THE SECOND BLOCK OF TEXT, YOU'LL FIND THE BIOME LISTED.

Let's take a look at the Overworld biomes you'll see on your travels, including biome-specific features like blocks, plants, and mobs.

Land Biomes

This category includes the main aboveground biomes, not including mountainous biomes. However, some of the following biomes may have hilly or high-elevation terrain.

BADLANDS

The dramatic, dry badlands biome features stretches of red sand with red sandstone, and small mountains and plateaus striped with colorful terracotta (stained clay). Though you won't find passive mobs here, you'll find plenty of dead bushes that drop sticks if you break them and some cacti that you can break and smelt into green dye. The badlands is the place to go for gold: gold ore is more common in badlands than any other biome, as are exposed mineshafts, which generate at higher altitudes. Variants of the biome include eroded badlands, with hoodoos (spires) of terracotta, and wooded badlands plateau, with highlands of grass and oak trees.

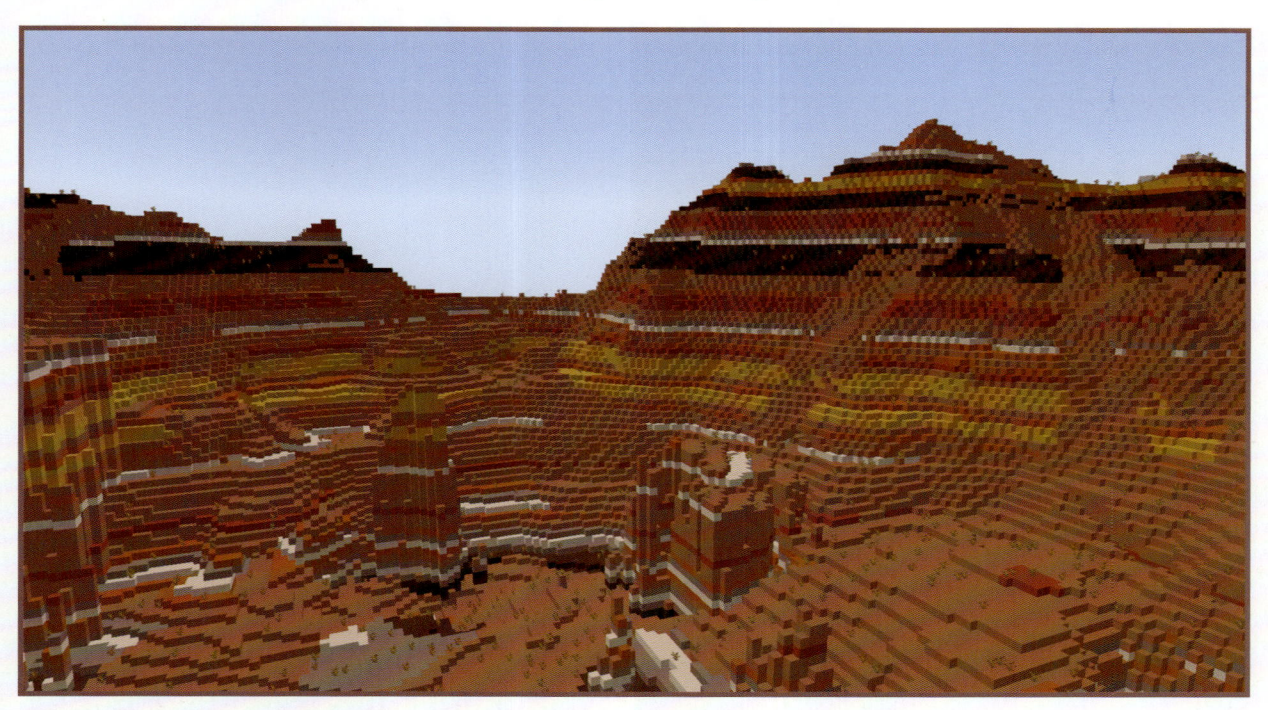

BEACH

The beach biome generates where land biomes meet the ocean. It's a sand-covered strip of land where turtles can spawn. Variants of the beach biome are the stone shore biome, which often occurs where mountain biomes reach the ocean, and the snowy beach, where the top layers of sand are covered in snow.

BIRCH FOREST

The birch forest biome is home to birch trees, bees, and flowers including the rose bush, peony, lilac, lily of the valley, dandelion, and poppy. While the standard forest biome is home to wolves, you won't find any in a birch forest. You may find cows, sheep, pigs, and chickens here (and in other grassy biomes). In the old-growth birch forest variant, the birch trees grow up to four blocks higher, and the ground is more rugged.

DARK FOREST

Dark forest biomes have dark oak trees, huge mushrooms, rose bushes, and small mushrooms, along with occasional oak and birch trees. The rare woodlands mansion (see Chapter 8) is found only in dark forests. The canopy in the dark forest is so thick that it's not uncommon for hostile mobs to spawn in the shadows during the day.

IT MIGHT BE SAFEST TO TRAVEL ON THE CANOPY ITSELF, RATHER THAN ON THE GROUND, WHEN TRAVERSING THE DARK FOREST BIOME.

DESERT

Desert biomes are vast stretches of sand with patches of sandstone. There are no trees here, only cactus, dead bushes, and golden desert rabbits. Desert wells can generate here, along with desert pyramids, villages, and pillager outposts (see Chapter 6 for more information on each of these structures). Husks (a zombie variant) will spawn here.

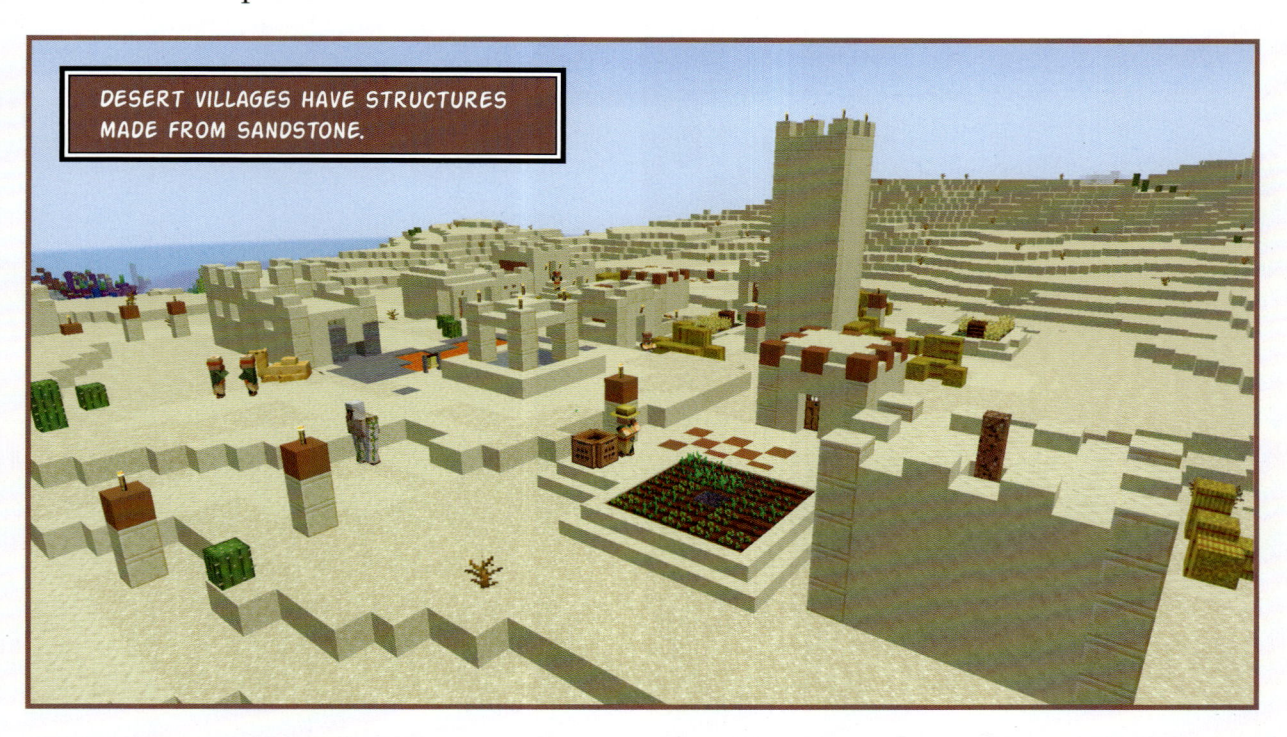

DESERT VILLAGES HAVE STRUCTURES MADE FROM SANDSTONE.

Falling Sand

Sand can sometimes generate as unsupported overhangs, often around chasms, cliffs, lava pools, or shores. If you cause the game to update any of the unsupported blocks (for example, by breaking one of the blocks), it and any nearby unsupported sand blocks will fall. If the sand falls on you, you may be covered and suffocated by it. This can also happen with gravel, but it's rarer. So watch out for sand (or gravel) blocks that don't have any solid supporting blocks beneath them!

FOREST

The common forest biome is made up of mostly oak and some birch trees and is home to wolves and bees. Because trees and their foliage create dark spaces, you'll encounter skeletons and more here at night. On a less dangerous note, you can find dandelions and poppies, and occasionally rose bushes, lilacs, peonies, and lilies of the valley. In the flower forest variant, you'll also find rarer flowers like allium and tulips.

THE FLOWER FOREST IS UNMISTAKABLE WITH ITS DENSE PATCHES OF FLOWERS.

Challenge: Flower Finesse

Create a flower garden that includes one of each of the sixteen Overworld flowers: allium, azure bluet, blue orchid, cornflower, dandelion, lilac, lily of the valley, oxeye daisy, peony, poppy, rose bush, sunflower, and four tulips (orange, white, pink, red), and the two ancient flowers, the pitcher plant and torchflower. See Chapter 10's section on the sniffer to see how to find and grow these ancient flowers.

JUNGLE

The *jungle* biome is dominated by huge jungle trees shrouded with vines, and rugged terrain covered in bushes. In this lush habitat, you'll find melons, bamboo, and cocoa pods, along with ocelots and parrots, and even jungle pyramids (see Chapter 7 for more on these). The bamboo jungle variant has dense thickets of bamboo growing on podzol (a dirt variant) and is home to pandas. The sparse jungle variant is grassy with jungle trees spread more sparsely.

THE JUNGLE IS ONE OF THE RARER BIOMES, WITH TREES THAT REACH UP TO THIRTY-ONE BLOCKS HIGH.

MUSHROOM FIELDS

The rare mushroom fields biome is found as an island or occasionally a peninsula. In place of grass, it's covered in *mycelium*, a fungus-like variant of dirt. The biome is dotted with giant red and brown mushrooms and has no other vegetation except small brown mushrooms. It's home to the rare *mooshroom*, a red and white cow with red mushrooms on its back. There is no regular hostile mob spawning in this biome, except for dungeon spawners belowground (see Chapter 7) and pillager patrols. A variant of this biome is the mushroom field shore, which borders the mushroom fields biome next to bodies of water.

THE MUSHROOM FIELDS BIOME, WITH ITS POPULATION OF MOOSHROOMS AND DEARTH OF MOB SPAWNING, IS ONE OF THE RAREST BIOMES IN MINECRAFT.

PLAINS

One of the most common biomes, plains are open grassy stretches spotted with oak trees. The plains biome is a great biome for your first headquarters, as you'll find farm animals here and open areas for building. You can find horses, donkeys, bees, villages, and pillager outposts here. The sunflower plains biome variant has large patches of sunflowers pointing east.

RIVER

The river biome follows the path of rivers winding through or separating biomes and extends several blocks beyond the rivers' edges. You can often find clay in riverbeds, sugar cane along the banks, and salmon and squid swimming in their waters. A variant is the frozen river biome, covered with ice and found in colder biomes.

SAVANNA

The dry savanna biome features acacia trees, occasional oak trees, and brown grass. You can find villages and pillager outposts here and llamas at higher elevations.

THE NATURAL WORLD

Pumpkins grow in savannas (as well as other grassy biomes). Variants of this biome include the windswept savanna, with extremely steep, high mountains, and plateaus, with wide, flattened highlands.

SNOWY PLAINS

The snowy plains biome is a snowy expanse occasionally spotted with oak and spruce trees. Igloos, villages, and pillager outposts generate here, alongside rabbits and polar bears. The ice spikes biome variation features dramatic spires of packed ice.

THE ICE SPIKES BIOME OFFERS VERY LITTLE TO SUSTAIN LIFE.

SWAMPLAND

In swampland biomes, oak trees grow wide canopies covered in hanging vines. Swamp oak trees generate only when the world is created; any new oaks you plant here will have normal foliage and no vines. The land is a darker grass broken up with shallow patches of water and ponds. Swamps are the only area where slime mobs spawn aboveground in low light. Witch huts, along with a witch and black cat familiar, can generate here as well. You'll find blue orchids, mushrooms, dead bushes, and sugar cane, as well as lily pads floating on the swamp water and seagrass on the bottom of ponds. Frogs will also spawn in swamps.

SWAMPLANDS CAN BE DIFFICULT TO TRAVERSE WITH THEIR BROKEN PATCHES OF LAND AND WATER.

A rarer variant of the swampland biome is the mangrove swamp, which features dense forests of mangrove trees and ground made of mud blocks. Mangrove trees are large and vine heavy and have exposed root blocks and muddy root blocks topped with moss. Instead of a sapling, the mangrove tree generates propagules which hang from its leaf blocks. The propagules can be planted just like saplings to grow mangrove trees.

FROM LEFT TO RIGHT, MUD, PACKED MUD, MUD BRICK.

Mud blocks, found naturally only in mangrove swamps, can also be created by using a water bottle on a block of dirt. You'll want a shovel to collect mud. You can craft muddy mangrove root blocks from a mud block and a mangrove root block, and you can craft a mud block and a wheat item to create packed mud. You can craft packed mud into mud bricks. Also, if you place mud blocks above a block above pointed dripstone, the mud will eventually convert into a clay block. Another useful feature of mud is that, if you place it on top of a hopper, the hopper is able to pick up any items dropped on the mud above it. This won't work with dirt.

TAIGA

The taiga biome is a spruce tree forest where you'll find wolves, foxes, rabbits, ferns, and sweet berry bushes. Villages and pillager outposts can also generate here. Variations of this biome include the old-growth giant spruce taiga and the old-growth pine taiga. In both variants, you'll find small outcrops of mossy cobblestone, podzol, and giant spruce trees. The snowy taiga variant has snow-covered ground and trees and the occasional igloo.

IN THE OLD-GROWTH GIANT SPRUCE TAIGA SHOWN HERE, THE FOLIAGE COVERS MOST OF THE TREE, WHEREAS IN THE OLD-GROWTH PINE TAIGA, THE LEAVES ARE MAINLY RESTRICTED TO THE TOP OF THE TREES.

Challenge: Tree Mastery

Collect eight saplings from each type of tree—acacia, birch, jungle, large jungle, oak, dark oak, spruce, and giant spruce—and grow one of each type. To grow the dark oak, giant spruce, and large jungle trees, you need to plant four saplings in a square. These trees require more space, as they have widths of 2x2 instead of 1x1.

Mountainous Biomes

There are two general categories of mountains: windswept hills and mountain peaks. Windswept hills are mostly stony and have lower altitudes, while most mountain peak biomes are snowy. Mountainous biomes are the only ones in which you can find emerald ore and stone infested with silverfish.

MOUNTAIN PEAKS

Mountain peaks form the highest mountain ranges. You can find pillager outposts in mountain peaks, as well as goats at higher elevations. Mountain peaks are formed from a combination of sub-biomes:

> MOUNTAINS OFTEN REACH CLOUD HEIGHT AND HIGHER, AND YOU MAY FIND GOATS ON THE HIGH PEAKS.

CHERRY GROVES

Cherry groves are found only in mountains. They are easily spotted because of the bright pink foliage of the cherry trees found only here. You'll see pink petals scattered around the cherry trees, and using bone meal on the grass in cherry groves will generate more pink petals.

FROZEN PEAKS

The *frozen peaks* biome is covered in snow blocks along with glacier formations of packed ice.

GROVES

These are small spruce tree forests on mountain peaks where you can find rabbits, foxes, and wolves.

JAGGED PEAKS

The tallest and most rugged of the mountain peaks biomes, jagged peaks generate on the tops of mountains. Goats can spawn here.

MEADOWS

In the meadow biome, you'll find gentle grassy slopes with patches of small flowers and occasional oak and birch trees. Bees, donkeys, rabbits, sheep, and villages spawn here.

SNOWY SLOPES

This biome has treeless slopes with layers of snow and powder snow. Goats and rabbits spawn here, as well as the occasional igloo.

STONY PEAKS

These are found in warmer biomes and typically lack snow.

In the grove and snowy slope biomes, you'll find treacherous powder snow. If you walk over powder snow, you'll fall into these blocks as deep as they're stacked. If you land in powder snow, try to break the snow so that you can walk to a solid block. If you're trapped, your screen will show an icy border, your body will begin to shiver, and you'll eventually start taking damage and freeze to death. You can protect against this by wearing leather boots (crafted from four leather), which allow you to walk on powder snow, and leather armor (you'll need twenty leather to craft the helmet, chestplate, and

IN THE CHERRY GROVE BIOME, PINK PARTICLES DRIFT DOWN FROM THE BLOSSOMS ON CHERRY TREES, AND THE GRASS IS SPOTTED WITH PINK PETALS.

leggings), which prevents you from freezing. Mobs are also susceptible to falling into powder snow, except for goats, who will avoid it, and the smallest mobs, like foxes and rabbits.

WINDSWEPT HILLS

The windswept hills biome includes rugged, stony highlands with mountains and patches of gravel. At high altitudes, snow will fall. You can find the occasional oak or spruce tree, areas of grass, and llamas. Variants of this biome include the windswept gravelly hills and the windswept forest. In the windswept gravelly hills, the stone slopes are mostly replaced with gravel, and far fewer trees grow. The windswept forest is similar to windswept hills, with more grass and oak and spruce trees.

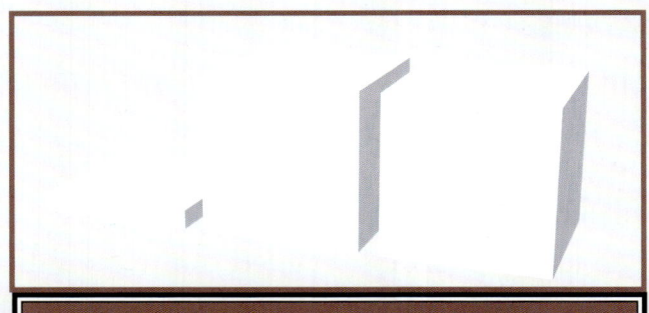

THE THREE TYPES OF SNOW, FROM LEFT TO RIGHT: SNOW (A LAYER OF SNOW THAT YOU CAN STACK AND THAT IS DEPOSITED BY FALLING SNOW), THE FULL SNOW BLOCK, AND THE POWDER SNOW BLOCK. POWDER SNOW BLOCKS HAVE A MORE JAGGED, DENSER PALE BLUE PATTERN ON THEM.

Cave Biomes

There are currently only a few cave biomes, but they can create some spectacular caves. These biomes are limited to underground areas—they don't stretch to world height or depth as regular biomes do. Once you're out of the cave biome, you'll be back in the biome assigned aboveground.

DEEP DARK

The Deep Dark is the scariest biome in Minecraft, because of the creepy warden it spawns and the treacherous Ancient City it can generate. You'll find this biome beneath mountains and savanna plateaus, and sometimes below badlands. You'll know you've reached the Deep Dark when you see dark turquoise blocks. You can find smaller Deep Dark caves as well as large, cavernous Deep Dark areas, and some massive areas will contain an Ancient City structure. The Deep Dark cave floors and walls are covered with large stretches of sculk blocks and sculk veins.

THE NATURAL WORLD

YOU'LL KNOW YOU'RE ENTERING THE *DEEP DARK* WHEN YOU BEGIN SEEING DARK TURQUOISE SCULK BLOCKS AND TURQUOISE SCULK VEINS.

You'll also find:

- **Sculk sensors**: These will sense vibrations within eight blocks (such as a player or mob moving, eating, placing and breaking blocks other than wool, dropping items, etc.) and activate nearby sculk shriekers (within eight blocks). To avoid detection by a nearby sculk sensor, you'll need to sneak by or place and walk on wool blocks or carpet. You can use wool blocks to completely cover the sensor on all sides, top and bottom, to prevent it from sensing vibrations from any angle.
- **Sculk shriekers**: Stand on a shrieker (or activate a sculk sensor within eight blocks of a shrieker) or activate it by sculk sensor four times, and it will emit an eerie wailing sound. The screech will activate nearby sculk sensors and can produce a darkness

effect, more or less blinding you. Much more dangerous, however, it can also cause the warden to spawn. The warden is a hulking mob that is blind but can follow you by sniffing you and sensing your vibrations. Read more about it in Chapter 11. The darkness effect and warden summoning are only produced by naturally generated shriekers, and not by shriekers placed by the player or generated by sculk catalysts.

- **Sculk catalysts**: These are blocks that will "bloom" when a nearby mob is killed, dropping experience orbs. The sculk catalyst bloom eats up those orbs and turns nearby blocks (in an amount relative to the experience dropped) into more sculk blocks, sculk veins, and rarely into sensors and shriekers.

The sculk blocks can be mined with any tool (a diamond hoe is fastest) but will only drop themselves when you mine them with a tool enchanted with Silk Touch.

The deep dark is the only place where wardens can spawn and the massive ancient cities can generate. Other mobs won't spawn within the deep dark, so if you can rid a deep dark cavern of sculk shriekers to stop wardens from spawning, the biome will be as peaceful as a mooshroom fields island.

DRIPSTONE CAVES

Stalactites made of dripstone and pointed dripstone blocks reach down from the ceiling of the dripstone cave biome; dripstone stalagmites grow up from the floor. Pointed dripstone is a gravity-affected block, meaning if the block it's attached to is broken, the pointed dripstone blocks will fall and cause damage to players and mobs directly below. Falling on pointed dripstone will harm you as well.

DRIPSTONE CAVES.

THE NATURAL WORLD

You'll sometimes find massive dripstone caves with columns of dripstone and pools of water. Copper ore generates more commonly in this biome.

LUSH CAVES

Lush caves are overgrown with carpets of moss and hanging cave vines fruiting with glow berries. You'll find patches of clay here, along with grass, vines, and spore blossoms. Dripleaf plants grow in shallow pools, and azalea bushes (both flowering and nonflowering) grow on moss blocks and moss carpet. If you see an azalea tree while you're traveling aboveground, that's a sign that a lush cave is below.

LUSH CAVES ARE A GREAT RESOURCE FOR A VARIETY OF PLANTS, INCLUDING MOSS, AZALEA BUSHES, CAVE VINES, DRIPLEAVES, AND GLOW BERRIES.

Ocean Biomes

There are five main ocean biomes, differentiated by their temperature. This is visualized by the color of the water, which ranges from an aqua in warm oceans to a dark purplish in frozen oceans. Sea level is at y=63, and the ocean floor is at approximately y=48. All oceans except for the warm biome have a deep variant that's about fifteen blocks deeper and generates ocean monuments: large templelike buildings infested with hostile guardian mobs. The ocean floor—typically gravel broken by patches of sand and dirt—rises and lowers into hills,

Challenge: Lush Foliage Finesse

The unique plants of lush caves can add a lot of character to your base.

1. Find a lush cave by exploring until you see an azalea tree growing aboveground.
2. Dig down in a circular staircase pattern, beneath the azalea tree, to find the cave. If you're lucky, the cave will have all types of lush plants: dripleaf, large dripleaf, cave vines with glow berries, moss blocks and carpets, azalea bushes, and spore blossoms.
3. Gather a few of each plant to bring home. Collect small dripleaf with shears; you can break the other plants with your hand. (Cave vines won't drop; you can just gather the berries.)
4. Plant a glow berry on the underside of a block to grow a new cave vine. As it grows, some of its blocks will be glow berries, but you can use bone meal on the vine to create new berries, which you can eat.
5. Place a spore blossom on the underside of a block, like the eaves of a roof, and they'll generate soft green particles floating in the air.
6. Place small dripleaves on clay or moss blocks (or any dirt variant if underwater.) You can use bone meal on a small dripleaf to create a big dripleaf plant.
7. Place a big dripleaf plant on any dirt variant or clay. Use bone meal (or another big dripleaf) on a big dripleaf to grow it one block taller. Spreading moss will turn dirt and stone variant blocks into moss blocks as well as create moss carpet, grass, and azalea bushes.
8. Place the moss in a grass or stone area you'd like to replace with moss, and use bone meal on it to spread the growth.
9. Place an azalea bush on the moss and grow the bush into a tree by using bone meal on it.

peaks, cliffs, underwater caves, and ravines. Low ravines may include magma blocks, causing bubble columns that can pull you downward. In all oceans you can find shipwrecks and underwater ruins (for more on these structures, see Chapter 7).

COLD OCEAN

The cold ocean biome has darker blue water, and cod, salmon, and dolphins. You'll find seagrass and kelp on the gravel ocean bed.

FROZEN OCEAN

The frozen ocean—the coldest of the ocean biomes—has dark, purplish water and houses salmon and polar bears. The seabed is mostly gravel, and the frozen ocean is covered with large stretches of ice, broken up by icebergs made of packed ice and blue ice.

THE FROZEN OCEAN IS DOMINATED BY TOWERING ICEBERGS AND STRETCHES OF FLOATING ICE.

There are three main types of ice: ice, packed ice, and blue ice. *Ice* is the most common, and if you break it with a regular pickaxe, it's replaced with a block of water. An ice block will also melt into water if you place a light source higher than 11 next to it. *Packed ice* is a denser ice block, craftable with nine ice blocks, and *blue ice* is an even denser ice that you can craft from nine packed ice blocks. Neither packed nor blue ice melt near light sources. To collect any of the three ice blocks, you'll need a pick with the Silk Touch enchantment.

FROM LEFT TO RIGHT, ICE, PACKED ICE, AND BLUE ICE.

LUKEWARM OCEAN

The lukewarm ocean has light blue waters and a mostly sand sea floor with patches of clay, dirt, gravel, seagrass, and kelp. You'll find tropical fish here, along with dolphin, cod, and pufferfish.

OCEAN

The ocean biome has medium blue waters and a gravel floor with kelp and seagrass. Dolphin and cod spawn here.

WARM OCEAN

Warm oceans have a distinctive aqua color and sandy bottom that grows seagrass. You can find coral reefs here, as well as light-emitting sea pickles, tropical fish, dolphins, and pufferfish. Coral reefs are made from variously colored coral blocks, coral, and coral fans. If you use a pick enchanted with Silk Touch, you can gather the coral live; otherwise you'll only gather a dead, gray version. Once you place coral blocks, they'll turn gray within moments unless one side is touching a water source block.

You'll find colorful coral reefs and tropical fish in the warm ocean biome.

Challenge: Biome Discovery

Explore the area around your starter home, keeping within a 750-block radius, and discover the biomes nearby. Collect any unique resources they may have, like cocoa pods from a jungle or acacia saplings from the savanna. Remember to take a bed with you so you can sleep every evening.

Up Next

You should now have a good idea of what kind of terrain, weather, and landscapes you'll encounter in future explorations, along with the unique resources they can provide you. In the next chapter, we'll take a look at some of the physical structures (temples, ruins, and more) you'll want to seek out on your explorations, from buried shipwrecks to woodland mansions.

7
PLACES TO GO

During your travels through the landscapes of Minecraft, you're bound to come across a variety of *generated structures*: randomly placed buildings that offer chests to loot, foes to battle, unique resources to gather, and even puzzles to solve. This chapter will describe each of these structures, where you might find them, and how to bypass any traps they may contain.

Generated structures can spawn aboveground, underground, and under the sea. In this chapter, we'll only discuss those structures that spawn within the Overworld; for Nether and End structures, see Chapters 14 and 16.

Aboveground Structures

Some aboveground structures are extremely rare, such as the Woodland Mansion, and some are fairly common, like ruined portals. Many spawn only in specific biomes.

DESERT PYRAMID

The desert pyramid is a structure found only in desert biomes and is comprised of two towers decorated with orange terracotta joined by a lower pyramid-shaped building. A pyramid will sometimes be partially submerged in the sand, so keep an eye out for the two towers. The entrance is in the lower building. As you enter, look out for mobs and light up any dark areas. Within the pyramid's main room, hidden below the floor, is a shaft that opens over a lower level containing four chests set into the shaft's walls, guarded by a stone pressure plate trap. To dismantle the trap, break it with a pickaxe. Be careful to not step on the pressure plate before breaking it; if you do, you'll trigger nine hidden TNT blocks. This will destroy all four chests and kill you. You can also find a hidden 5x5 room a few blocks below the pyramid's ground floor, either to the left or right at the back of the pyramid. It's filled with sand, some of which is suspicious sand that you can brush to find loot.

CHAPTER 7

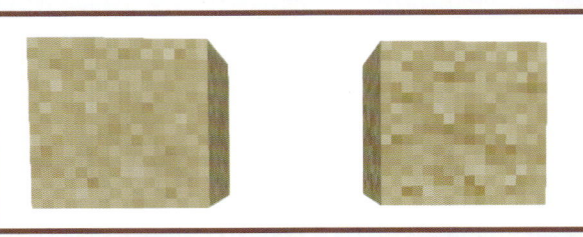

ON THE LEFT IS REGULAR SAND AND ON THE RIGHT, SUSPICIOUS SAND.

DESERT WELL

This small desert-biome well holds no loot, but it functions as an infinite source of water—a rare commodity in the desert—and can be useful as a landmark in the barren land. At the base of the well you may find blocks of suspicious sand, which you can brush to find loot.

While traversing the snowy plains, snowy taiga, or snowy slopes biomes, you might come across an igloo. Inside some igloos you'll find a carpet, under which you'll find a trapdoor and ladder that lead to an underground chamber. In this chamber,

PLACES TO GO

you'll find a loot chest, a potion brewing stand, and two prison cells containing a villager and a zombie villager. The igloo also has the resources for curing the zombie villager—a golden apple, a splash potion of Weakness, and a potion stand.

IGLOOS CAN BE QUITE HARD TO SPOT—LOOK FOR THE ICE BLOCK WINDOWS AND ENTRYWAY.

Challenge: Cure the zombie villager

Right-click the brewing stand to find and take the splash potion of Weakness. Look in the chest for the golden apple. Break the top block of iron bars holding the zombie villager and throw the splash potion of Weakness at it. Then right-click the golden apple on it. As the zombie converts back to a regular villager, it will shake and emit red particles. After a few minutes, the zombie villager should be cured. If this is your first time curing a villager, you'll get the advancement *Zombie Doctor*.

JUNGLE PYRAMID

The rare jungle pyramid generates in the jungle or bamboo jungle biomes, and like the desert pyramid it's booby-trapped. Directly inside its entrance is a staircase down to a lower level. On one side of the staircase, at the bottom, is a set of three levers that will reveal a loot chest when switched in the right order. The opening to the hidden chest is one level above, on the same side of the staircase. As you hear the sound of pistons moving blocks when you toggle levers, check upstairs to see if a hidden room is revealed.

THE LOWER FLOOR OF THE JUNGLE PYRAMID IS EXPOSED HERE; IT'S USUALLY HIDDEN UNDERGROUND WITH THE REST OF THE BUILDING SURROUNDED BY TALL JUNGLE TREES.

On the other side of the staircase is a booby-trapped corridor leading to a second loot chest. The booby traps are hard-to-spot trip wires that activate a dispenser that shoots arrows at you when you walk through them. You can disable the trap by breaking the string.

NOTE:
A *TRIP WIRE* IS A REDSTONE CONTRAPTION CREATED BY PLACING STRING BETWEEN TWO TRIP WIRE HOOKS.

PILLAGER OUTPOST

Pillager outposts are two-story towers with one or more disconnected outbuildings. You'll find them in the same biomes as villages (desert, plains, savanna, taiga, snowy plains, and meadows), along with mountain peaks biomes. It's generally best to avoid these outposts, as they're full of armed pillagers; however, the tower's top floor has a chest with loot, which may

TRIP WIRE HOOK.

include iron and enchanted books. If you run fast, you might make it out alive! Keep in mind that you can't capture or conquer a pillager outpost, because pillagers will continually spawn.

PILLAGER OUTPOST STRUCTURES CAN INCLUDE BUNDLES OF DARK OAK LOGS, TENTS, TARGET PRACTICES, AND CAGES (WHICH MAY CONTAIN IRON GOLEMS).

RUINED PORTALS

Ruined portals are broken vertical rectangles made of obsidian. They stand on an overgrowth of netherrack (a red block found in the Nether dimension), with little pits of lava and magma. These are nonworking Nether portals, which you'll read more about in Chapter 14. To fix these portals, you need to place blocks of obsidian to fill in the gaps in the rectangle and replace any non-obsidian blocks. You use a flint-and-steel (crafted with one flint and one iron ingot) on the portal's interior to activate it. Ruined portals usually have a loot chest and at least one block of gold to pilfer. They're also a good spot to gather some Nether-only blocks without going to the Nether, like netherrack and crying obsidian. Watch out for glowing magma blocks as these can damage you if you walk on them. Use Shift to sneak on them to avoid being hurt.

> RUINED PORTALS CAN ALSO BE FOUND UNDERWATER!

SWAMP HUT

Swamp huts (or witch huts) are found only in swamps, where they generate above the water on oak columns. These huts are home to a witch and a black cat. While the huts don't contain loot chests, witches drop some of the best loot in the game. However, witches are strong and hard to kill—they'll throw potions at you to poison and slow you while drinking healing potions themselves. It's best to steer clear unless you are prepared!

VILLAGE

Villages are great for collecting food, crops, loot chests, and more. You'll find them in desert, plains, savanna, taiga, and snowy plains biomes; they'll have unique architecture for each biome. Villages can be small or large and might be abandoned (as described in Chapter 2). If a village generates alongside a mountain, it might sprawl to the other side; be sure to check all sides of the mountain for buildings. We'll discuss villages and villagers in depth in Chapter 12.

THE SAVANNA VILLAGE USES A LOT OF THE LOCAL ACACIA TREE PLANKS FOR ITS BUILDINGS.

WOODLAND MANSION

Woodland mansions are very rare and found only in dark forests, often thousands of blocks from one's world spawn. They're one of the largest structures in Minecraft, with three floors of procedurally generated rooms. There's an entrance on one of the four sides of the building, at ground level or just above the cobblestone foundation. You can find some decent loot in a mansion, so check chests as you go exploring the rooms.

Two types of villagers (gray-faced, hostile villager types) live here—vindicators and evokers—as well as standard hostile mobs like

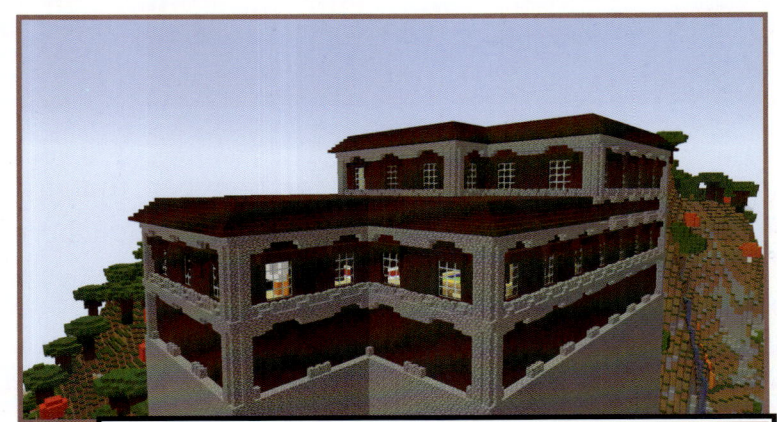

THE ROOMS IN A WOODLANDS MANSION ARE RANDOMLY GENERATED, SO EACH ONE IS SLIGHTLY DIFFERENT.

skeletons and creepers (see Chapter 11). You'll want high-quality, enchanted armor and weapons, and plenty of torches to light up the dark spaces as you go.

The number, type, and placement of rooms varies per mansion. A fair number of rooms are decorated to look like dining rooms, bedrooms, and conference rooms. Other rooms include jail cells, studies, and storage rooms. Some rooms are just plain bizarre, like the giant pillager statue room and the piles of blue wool room. Your mansion may also have secret rooms, hidden behind walls with no entryways. To access these, break open stretches of wall that don't have a door.

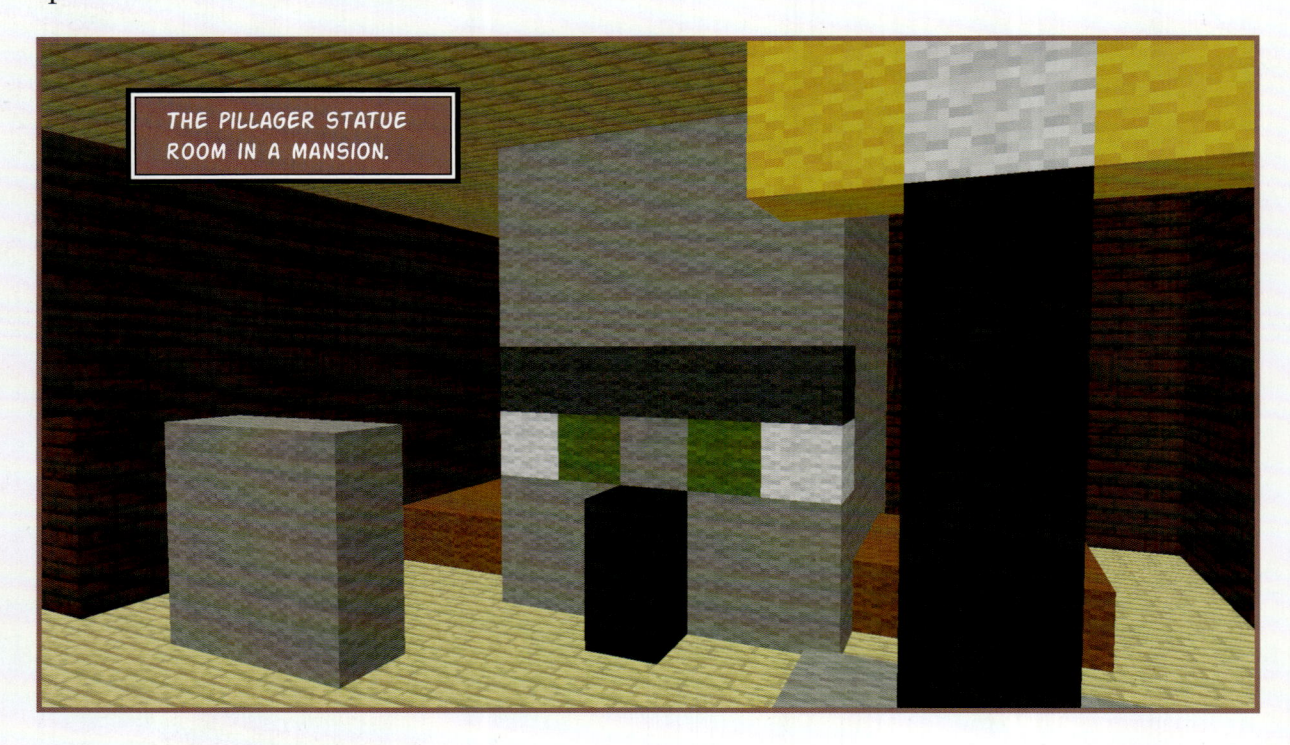

THE PILLAGER STATUE ROOM IN A MANSION.

Mansions are so few and far between that they're almost impossible to find without using a woodland explorer map, which you can buy from a cartographer villager (cartographers sport a gold monocle). To learn about trading with villagers, see Chapter 12.

Underground Structures

Some generated structures are underground, and a bit harder to find, but they're worth it for the loot!

ANCIENT CITY

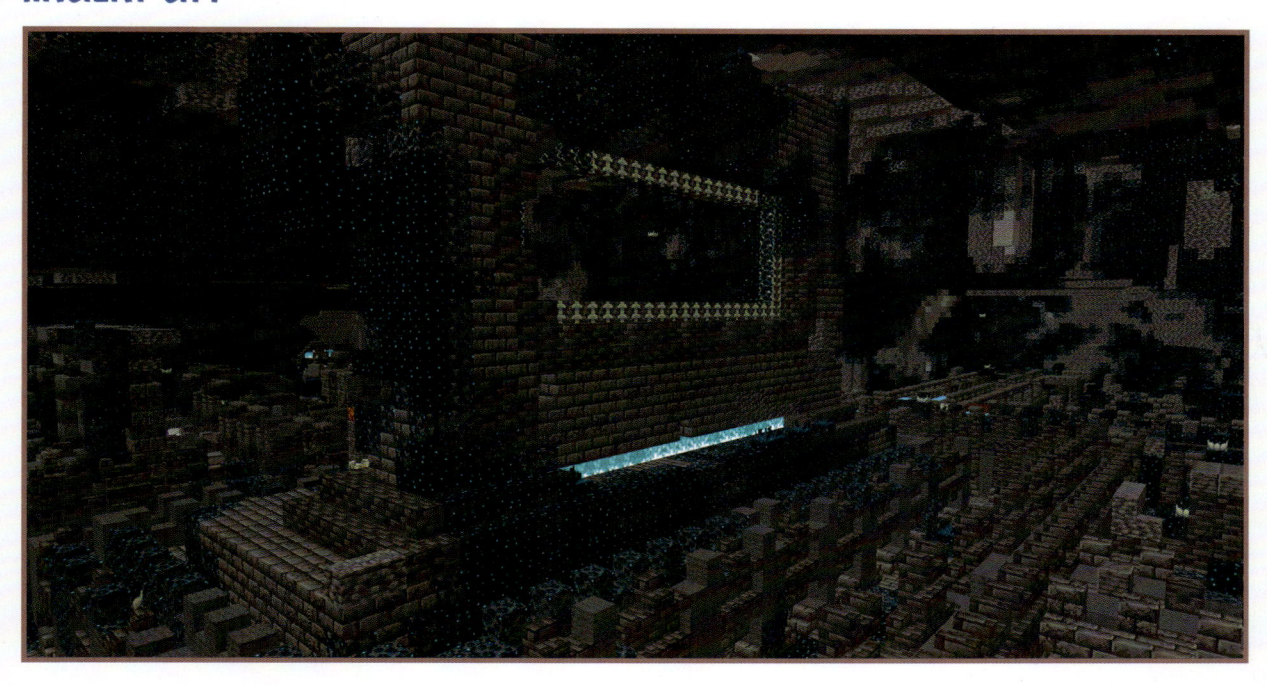

Ancient cities are generated in massive caverns in the deep dark biomes found below mountains at about y= –51. Be careful—only go here when you're prepared to manage the many sculk sensors and shriekers that will activate a warden spawning. You may want to delay your visit here until you have a top-tier bow and armor, and best, an Elytra so you can fly quickly away from any warden that spawns. See Chapter 6 and the section on the deep dark and Chapter 11 and the section on wardens to scope out what you are facing here.

At the center of the ancient city, you'll find a massive, portal-like frame. Dig beneath it to find redstone rooms that display examples of how to use redstone. There are ruined towers, buildings, and walkways—some partially covered in wool blocks or carpet—to explore here. The chests here contain goodies like armor, golden apples, unique smithing templates, disc fragments, echo shards, saddles, leads, enchanted books, and more. Most valuable may be a book enchanted with Swift Sneak—wearing leggings enchanted with this dramatically improves your speed as you sneak around the city. Additionally, you can craft nine disc fragments into a music disc and craft eight echo shards around one compass to create a recovery compass. You can use a recovery compass to direct you toward the place you last died.

BURIED TREASURE

Buried treasure is a single chest of quality loot like gold, emeralds, and diamonds buried on the coast beneath several layers of sand, gravel, or sometimes stone. You'll need a buried treasure map to find it, and you can find this map in the map chests of shipwrecks or ocean ruins. You'll want to follow the map so that your icon (the white pointer) is centered on the red X, and then dig down. You may need to dig around to find the chest; it might be submerged in water, but you'll usually find it next to sand blocks underground.

Using Maps

When you first hold a map, it may be empty and will show stripes for ocean areas. A red X for buried treasure will show you where to go. (Other maps, like woodland mansion maps and ocean monument maps, will have different icons.) The white marker shows your position. If it is a small square on the border, then you are not in the map area. You'll have to travel in the direction of the X icon. The map top is always north, and you can orient yourself by opening the Debug screen (press F3) to see what direction you are facing in. Orient yourself to the north, and then travel left (west), right (east), north (forward), or south (backward) to head toward the icon. Once you are inside of the range of the map, your white marker will change to a larger pointer to show where you are.

AN EMPTY MAP WILL SHOW OCEAN AREAS AS STRIPES. AS YOU GET CLOSER TO YOUR GOAL, THE MAP WILL START FILLING IN WITH COLORS.

DUNGEON

Dungeons are small, enclosed cobblestone rooms that generate underground, typically lower than y=0. They hold a couple of loot chests and a mob spawner block, which looks like a cage and will have a tiny replica of the mob it spawns (either a skeleton, spider, or zombie) at its center. The replica will start spinning when you're within sixteen blocks of it, indicating that it's activated. The block will spawn between one and four monsters every ten to thirty seconds but will stop when there are six mobs within four blocks of itself.

You can destroy the mob spawner block with a pickaxe, but I recommend turning off the spawner instead, as this gives you the option to create a mob farm. You can turn off the spawner by placing a torch on each side of the spawner and in each corner of the room.

Dungeons are always connected to a nearby cave or other open area, so if you notice an unusual number of monsters headed your way, investigate! If you find a dungeon, turn off the spawner and collect your loot quick!

> IF YOU COME ACROSS COBBLESTONE AS YOU'RE DIGGING, YOU'VE LIKELY UNCOVERED A DUNGEON. IF IT'S MOSSY COBBLESTONE, YOU'VE DISCOVERED A DUNGEON'S FLOOR. HAVE TORCHES AND WEAPONS AT THE READY!

> **NOTE:**
> BUILDING *MOB FARMS* ENTAILS TRAPPING SPAWNED MOBS BY ENCLOSING THE MOB SPAWNER BLOCK AND BLOCK AND LEAVING YOURSELF A TINY WINDOW TO STRIKE AT THE MOBS WITH.

MINESHAFT

Mineshafts are fairly common underground structures consisting of long, intertwined mining tunnels, with broken rail tracks, cobwebs, wooden supports and beams, and exposed ore. Bring torches and weapons, as mineshafts are only partially lit so you're likely to run across hostile mobs.

There are two features to look out for: minecarts that hold loot chests and collected masses of cobwebs, which hide cave spider spawners. The mineshaft is the only place you'll find cave spider spawners. Cave spiders will poison you as they attack, so have an escape plan or a bucket of milk on hand.

> CAVE SPIDER SPAWNERS OPERATE IN THE SAME WAY AS DUNGEON MOB SPAWNERS; TO AVOID ACTIVATING A SPAWNER, KEEP AT LEAST SIXTEEN BLOCKS AWAY FROM IT.

STRONGHOLD

A stronghold is an incredibly rare, massive underground stone-brick fortress. Up to 128 strongholds can spawn in a single world thousands of blocks from each other. Strongholds contain a portal room you can use to travel to the End dimension. See Chapter 16 for how to find a stronghold and use its portal room.

TRAIL RUINS

Trail ruins are underground archeological structures, seemingly villages of some kind of unknown, ancient origin. If you come across a few unexplainable terracotta blocks in a forest (taiga, snowy taiga, old-growth birch and taiga, or jungle), you are sure to have found the tip of the tower of a trail ruin. You can excavate a trail ruin by removing all the stone, dirt, coarse dirt, and gravel it is embedded in. You'll need a brush (crafted from a feather, copper ingot, and stick) to brush (right-click) on a block that looks very similar to gravel—suspicious gravel.

> EXAMINE THE FORESTS WITH TALLER TREES FOR TERRACOTTA BLOCKS, WHICH INDICATE A TRAIL RUIN IS BELOW.

Within several brushes of suspicious gravel, an item will begin to emerge and ultimately drop, as the suspicious gravel turns back into regular gravel. If you use a shovel or other tool on suspicious gravel, it will break with a clear glass-breaking sound and drop nothing. If you use a brush four or so times on regular gravel, nothing will emerge. Suspicious gravel is noticeably blotchier than gravel, but it can be easy to overlook it; using a brush on all gravel will eliminate mistakes.

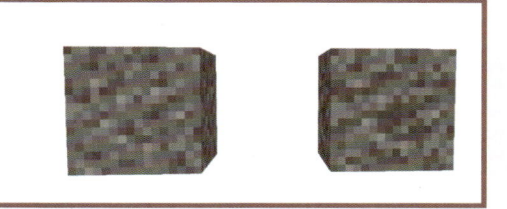

ON THE LEFT, REGULAR GRAVEL, AND ON THE RIGHT, SUSPICIOUS GRAVEL.

The items you can find by brushing suspicious gravel include diamonds, emeralds, leads, twenty types of pottery sherds, and four different smithing templates. If you have four sherds of the same type, you can craft a decorated pot, a pot with a decoration that reflects the design type of the sherd. For example, crafting four heart pottery sherds creates a pot decorated with a heart. The pot has a single inventory slot that you can store a stack of one type of block or item in. You can only retrieve those items by breaking the pot.

TRIAL CHAMBERS

Trial Spawner crackles

Trial chambers are underground structures made of a series of connected dungeons built with unique copper and tuff blocks, with specialized mob "trial spawners" throughout. When you approach a trial spawner, a number of mobs of the same kind (baby zombies, breezes, bogged, cave spiders, husks, silverfish, slimes, spiders, strays, skeletons, and zombies) will spawn nearby. The number of mobs spawned depends on the number of players in the trial chambers—a single player will generate the fewest number of mobs. Trial chambers are the only place that breezes spawn. You can find loot throughout in chests, barrels, dispensers, and pots. The goal is to defeat the mobs from each trial spawner—when you do, the spawner will eject some loot and a trial key (one for each player). You use the trial key to unlock a vault, a special container, for high-level loot. You can only open a vault once, but a vault can be opened by different players with their own keys. Once you defeat a trial spawner, it shuts down for thirty minutes.

A VAULT BLOCK IS PLACED ON A COPPER BLOCK PEDESTAL.

If you enter with the Bad Omen effect on (from drinking an ominous bottle dropped by Pillager captains or found in a trial vault), the Bad Omen effect turns into the Trial Omen effect. This in turn changes spawners and vaults into ominous spawners and ominous vaults, with harder-to-defeat mobs, ominous trial keys, and better loot. One specialty item you can only obtain from an ominous vault is the heavy core, an item that you use to craft the heavy-hitting mace weapon.

You can find Trial Chambers by trading with a village cartographer for a trial explorer map. You may need to trade with them to raise their trading level to have a chance of them offering a trial map.

Underwater Structures

Underwater structures can be the most difficult to access because of how easy it is to drown. You should bring enchanted gear and potions to help (See Chapter 15), and should carry a door as well, which works as an easy-to-place air pocket. When you place a door underwater, the block it takes up also becomes an air pocket that you can stand in to recover your breath.

Ocean Monument

Ocean monuments generate in deep oceans and are made of aqua prismarine blocks that are unique to this structure. You can trade with a cartographer villager for an ocean explorer map that will lead you to a monument. Ocean monuments house three hostile elder guardians—strong, fishlike mobs—in their upper floors. The entrance to the monument is located between the two front wings. Other similar mobs, called guardians, spawn in and around ocean monuments. (Learn more about these mobs in Chapter 11.)

Of interest here, besides the unique prismarine blocks and variants, is a hidden trove of eight gold blocks in the monument's center and a chance of one or more *sponge rooms*. These rooms contain a number of sponge blocks, which you can place in water to absorb water blocks up to seven blocks away. To find a sponge room, look for dark prismarine walls. After use, sponge blocks need to be dried in order to function again; you can dry them by placing them in a dry biome or heating them in a furnace.

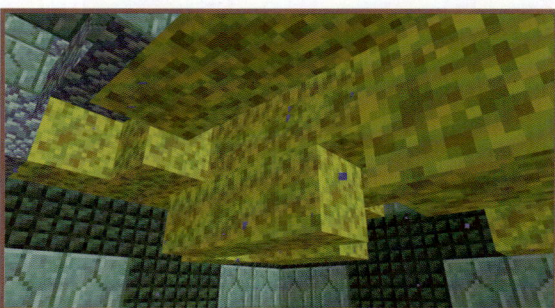

SPONGE BLOCKS ARE VERY HANDY IF YOU'RE BUILDING UNDERWATER, DRAINING A RIVER OR POND, OR CONVERTING AN OCEAN MONUMENT INTO YOUR HOME.

To loot an ocean monument, you'll need to kill the elder guardians. Elder guardians inflict a *Mining Fatigue* effect on nearby players, which makes it nearly impossible to break blocks. Bring buckets of milk to remove Mining Fatigue and use TNT to blast a hole in the roofs in order to get inside and kill the elder guardians as soon as possible. You can use blocks to create barriers between yourself and the guardians, blocking their line of sight and stopping their attacks. You'll need to wear armor that's been enchanted to help with breathing and moving underwater (see *Chapter 15*), and bring enchanted weapons. To create an air pocket that will allow you to breathe, bring a door to place on floors.

OCEAN RUINS

Ocean ruins are dilapidated buildings found on the ocean floor. They're built from stone bricks in regular and colder oceans, and sandstone in warmer oceans. Almost all ruins have a chest with potentially excellent loot, including a buried treasure map. Watch out for magma blocks on the ocean floor. They provide a column of air to breathe, but make sure to sneak (press **Shift**) when you stand on them to avoid damage. Also keep an eye out for *the drowned*—zombie variants that swim underwater. You can spot some ocean ruins by the light emitting from magma blocks and sea lanterns.

SHIPWRECK

Shipwrecks can be found anywhere in the ocean, from the seabed to the beach. They may be in a variety of conditions: upside down, sideways, right side up, fully intact, or missing huge chunks. You can find up to three chests inside, depending on how intact the shipwreck is. You should find a treasure chest in the top back of the ship that contains iron, emeralds, gold, diamonds, and more. A map chest, which contains a buried treasure map and other book- and navigation-related items, may be somewhere on the bottom deck. At the front of the ship, also on the bottom deck, you may find a supply chest that holds various food and supply items.

It's easy to lose track of time and air bubbles while exploring a shipwreck, so bring along a door that you can place to create an airspace to breathe in.

Challenge: Ocean Looting Genius

Go on an ocean looting spree. Find chests within shipwrecks and ocean ruins and collect buried treasure maps. Use the maps to find even better treasure. If you're having trouble finding loot, look for a dolphin and feed it one raw cod. (If it doesn't head off right away, keep feeding it.) Once fed, the dolphin should take you to the nearest treasure chest. Break the chests to "reset" the dolphin to find the next-nearest chest.

Up Next

You now know the basics of Minecraft: how to craft, mine, explore, loot, and survive. But your journey has only just begun. The next part of this book will take a closer look at the wealth of features in your world, from everything you can build and craft to the technical potentials of redstone engineering and the dangerous realms of the Nether and the End.

8
STUFF AND THINGS

Minecraft has so much to craft, collect, and loot that it's easy to miss some of its rarer features. This chapter gives an overview of some often-overlooked blocks and items you might find interesting for upping your game, from decorative versions of stone to fireworks and jukeboxes. We'll focus on blocks and features that you can acquire without visiting the End or the Nether; those will be covered in their respective chapters.

Building Blocks

While stone is one of the most common blocks in Minecraft's terrain, you can also find and craft a ton of other blocks to use for your builds, ranging from colorful concrete to intricately designed glazed terracotta. While blocks differ in their appearance, they also vary in their flammability and blast resistance. Wooden blocks, wool, and vegetation are flammable, while blocks made of harder stone material are the most resistant to blasts from creepers or other explosions. Blocks can also be transparent (letting some or all light through), like glass; or emit light, like sea lanterns; or be semisolid (not taking up a full block space) like a stair block. A few blocks are gravity-affected and will fall if there's not a block beneath them.

Bricks

You can smelt clay balls harvested from clay blocks (gathered in lush caves, riverbanks, lake beds, and coastlines) into brick items, which you can craft into brick blocks, and then into brick stairs, slabs, and walls. You can also craft stone variants into brick versions.

CONCRETE AND CONCRETE POWDER

Concrete has a unique crafting system: you first have to create concrete powder blocks from four sand, four gravel, and a dye of your choice (see page 119 for how to make dyes). You then place the concrete powder block into or next to water; the simplest way of adding water is to form a flat wall or layer of concrete powder and pour a bucket of water on the blocks. Concrete and concrete powder are both great for colorful builds, but concrete powder is used less often because it is gravity-affected and transforms when touched by water.

CUT COPPER

Copper blocks are crafted from nine copper ingots and can be crafted into cut copper, which forms a block in a bricklike design; from here, you can craft cut copper into cut copper slabs and stairs and anything else you use brick blocks for.

When you place a copper block in the world it will start to oxidize, which turns the copper into an aquamarine color in three stages: exposed, weathered, and fully oxidized. To halt the oxidization process, you can wax these blocks with honeycomb. To remove both wax and the layers of oxidation, right-click copper blocks with an axe.

GLASS

You can make a glass block by smelting one sand. You can then craft six glass blocks into sixteen thinner glass panes. You can use glass blocks to make transparent walls, roofs, floors, or windows; panes are used primarily for windows. Glass and glass panes can be dyed using the sixteen dyes. You can also make a dark glass that doesn't let light through, called tinted glass, by combining one glass block with four amethyst shards. Tinted glass is often used in mob farms, so that you can see the mobs spawn in darkness without letting light into their spawning area. You must use a pickaxe enchanted with Silk Touch to get back a glass block or pane that you break—tinted glass is the exception.

PRISMARINE

You can find prismarine blocks, including the variants dark prismarine and prismarine bricks, in ocean monuments and (rarely) ocean ruins. You can also craft prismarine blocks from prismarine shards and crystals, which are dropped from killing guardians and elder guardians. The regular prismarine blocks subtly shift colors from a bright aquamarine to a darker green. You can create slabs, walls, and stairs from prismarine and slabs and stairs from the dark and bricks variants. Prismarine is a harder, stonelike block, so you'll need to use a pickaxe to retrieve it.

Slabs, Stairs, and Walls or Fences

For many types of wood planks and stone-type blocks, you can create slabs, stairs, walls (for stone variants), and fences (for wood variants). Slabs are half-blocks that you can place in the upper or lower half of a block space and are often called top slabs or bottom slabs depending on how you place them. Mobs can't spawn on bottom slabs. You can place two slabs of the same type on top of each other, but not two of different types. Stairs allow you to climb up a block without having to jump, and walls and fences will stop most walking mobs except spiders (who can climb) from passing through. With wooden plank blocks you can also create fence gates to allow you to pass through.

STONE AND VARIANTS

You'll gather a lot of stone blocks, like granite, andesite, and sandstone, as you mine. What you may not know is that there are even more block types, beyond walls and stairs, that you can make by crafting or smelting these blocks. You can use a stonecutter, a functional block for making variations of stone blocks, to make many of these special blocks, or you can craft them.

Chiseled

Chiseled blocks are versions of stone blocks that display a distinctive design. You typically craft them from two slabs of a brick block or two slabs of sandstone.

Smooth

Stone, sandstone, and red sandstone blocks can be smelted to create smooth, or less textured, variants. The smooth stones can be further crafted into stairs and slabs and smooth stone can be crafted into smooth stone slabs.

Polished

You can craft polished versions of andesite, granite, diorite, and deepslate from four of the original block to make smoother and shinier building materials. You can craft each of these types of block into stairs and slabs and can make walls with polished deepslate.

> **NOTE:**
> IF YOU RUN OUT OF ANDESITE, DIORITE, AND GRANITE, AND DON'T HAVE TIME TO GO MINING, YOU CAN CRAFT THEM. CRAFT ANDESITE FROM DIORITE AND COBBLESTONE; DIORITE FROM COBBLESTONE AND NETHER QUARTZ FROM THE NETHER; AND GRANITE FROM NETHER QUARTZ AND DIORITE.

Mossy

Craft stone bricks and cobblestone with a moss block to create mossy stone bricks and mossy cobblestone; these in turn can make slabs, stairs, and walls for that abandoned, jungle-y look.

Cut

You can craft four blocks of sandstone and red sandstone into *cut* versions that bear engraved ridges. These can also be crafted into cut sandstone slabs.

Cracked

Stone bricks, deepslate bricks, and deepslate tiles (similar to bricks) can be smelted to create cracked versions, which have distress lines on their surfaces.

TERRACOTTA

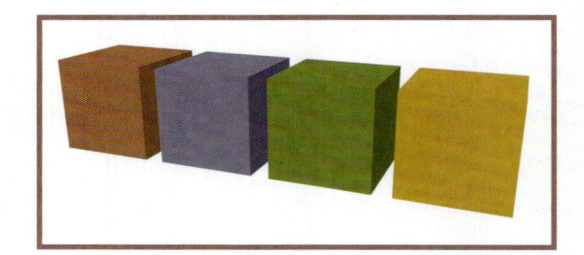

Terracotta is, by default, a reddish-brown type of baked clay made by smelting clay blocks. You can also dye the reddish-brown terracotta with any of sixteen dyes; the resulting color will be a combination of reddish-brown and the dye color.

GLAZED TERRACOTTA

You can go one step further in your terracotta adventures by smelting colored terracotta in a furnace. Smelting it results in glazed terracotta that sports a unique pattern; each color creates a larger 2x2 block pattern. As you place the glazed terracotta blocks, you can change the rotation of the pattern by rotating 90 degrees clockwise (or counterclockwise) four times as you place blocks in a square pattern. The pattern you make will be different depending on the direction you rotate and the order you place the blocks.

WOOD

By now, you know that the logs of the Overworld trees (acacia, birch, cherry, dark oak, jungle, mangrove, oak, and spruce, as well as bamboo) can be crafted into planks. These planks can also be crafted into stairs, slabs, fences, fence gates, doors, and trapdoors, with their own distinctive texture and color.

You can also create decorative versions of the log blocks themselves:

Wood blocks
Craft four log blocks to craft a wood block that has the log's bark texture on all sides.

Stripped log blocks
Right-click a log with an axe to strip the bark on four sides.

Stripped wood blocks
Craft four stripped blocks to create a wood block with all sides showing the stripped surface.

WOOL AND CARPETS

You can color gathered white wool by crafting it with a dye, or you can cut out the middleman and dye the actual sheep by right-clicking the dye on a sheep. Dyed wool is a colorful building block; just be aware that wool is fairly flammable, so use it wisely. You can craft a thin carpet block using two wool of the same color. You can also create dyed carpet by crafting white carpet with a dye.

Challenge: Wool Wizardry

Craft the sixteen dyes (see Table 8-1 on page 119) and use them to dye sheep so that you have one sheep in each color. Shear your colorful sheep and craft carpet from each one.

Functional Items

Items are objects you hold in your hand and perform some action with, like tools, weapons, and buckets. Here are a few items you may not come across in your average day, but can greatly enrich your experience.

BOOK AND QUILL

A *book and quill* is crafted from a book, an ink sac, and a feather. To craft a book, you first need to craft paper from three sugar cane. You then craft the book with one leather and three paper. To collect ink sacs, you'll need to kill squids; feathers are dropped from killing chickens and parrots.

Once you've crafted the book and quill, right-click it to open the book and write in it. Click **Done** to finish your entry and close the book. If you click **Sign**, you finalize the text so that the book can no longer be edited, and it becomes a written-in book.

BOTTLE O' ENCHANTING

The *bottle o' enchanting* is a bottle that contains experience, anywhere between three and eleven points. It can't be crafted; you can only find it in treasure chests or through trading with cleric villagers (see Chapter 12). Equip the bottle and right-click it to throw it on the ground, which smashes the bottle and releases the experience orbs.

CLOCK

A clock, crafted from four gold and one redstone, displays where you are in the day/night cycle. The central dial sports a sun on one side and a moon on the opposite side. As the dial moves, you can see the position of the sun or moon relative to the Overworld's surface.

COMPASS

A compass—crafted from four iron ingots and one redstone dust—points back to your world spawn and doesn't work in the Nether or End. However, you can connect a compass to a placed lodestone (crafted with eight chiseled stone bricks and a netherite ingot) by right-clicking to make the compass point to that lodestone.

DYES

You craft sixteen dyes from flowers, various natural resources, and even from combining existing dyes. You can use dyes to color wool, sheep, pet collars, glass, terracotta, concrete powder, beds, candles, sign text, firework stars, banners, and leather armor (including leather horse armor). To dye blocks, you typically combine one or more of that block with a single dye. A few crafted blocks and items, like firework stars and concrete powder, require a dye in their original crafting recipe.

To dye a pet collar (see Chapter 10 for taming dogs and cats), right-click that animal with a dye. If two dyed sheep have compatible colors and breed, they produce offspring with that combined color. For example, a green sheep and a blue sheep have a chance of breeding a cyan sheep. If the sheep's colors aren't compatible (say, black and purple) their offspring will have one of its parents' colors.

Sixteen Minecraft Dyes and Where to Get Them

Dye	Source
White	Lily of the valley; bone meal
Light gray	Azure bluet, oxeye daisy, or white tulip; gray dye and white dye; two black dye and white dye
Gray	Black dye and white dye
Black	Wither rose (a drop from the Wither boss mob discussed in Chapter 16); ink sac (a drop from squid)
Brown	Cocoa beans
Red	Poppy, rose bush, or red tulip; beetroot
Orange	Orange tulip; red dye and yellow dye
Yellow	Dandelion or sunflower
Lime	Sea pickle (smelting); green dye and white dye

Dye	Source
Green	Cactus (smelting)
Cyan	Green dye and blue dye
Light blue	Blue orchid; blue dye and white dye
Blue	Cornflower; lapis lazuli
Purple	Blue dye and red dye
Magenta	Lilac or allium; purple dye and pink dye; red dye and blue dye and pink dye; two red dye and blue dye and white dye
Pink	Peony or pink tulip; red dye and white dye

FIREWORKS

You can make a wide variety of impressive fireworks in Minecraft. Used alone, firework rockets don't create explosions but can be used to boost your Elytra flying speed and height with Elytra (see Chapter 16 for more on Elytras) and as ammunition in crossbows. Firework rockets are made with one to three gunpowder (each additional gunpowder increases flight duration) and one paper.

To make decorative fireworks that explode, you craft the firework rockets with a *firework star*. A basic firework star is made from one gunpowder and one dye and creates a small spherical burst. You can then include additional items in crafting the star to change color, shape, and any additional effects of the firework.

Create different fireworks shapes

Add one . . .	To get the shape . . .
Feather	Burst
Fire Charge (crafted from one blaze powder, one coal/charcoal, and one gunpowder)	Large sphere
Gold Nugget	Star
Mob Head (any)	Creeper
Diamond	Trail
Glowstone Dust (from the Nether)	Twinkle

Once you've crafted a firework star, craft the firework with one to three gunpowder, one paper, and the star. To set the firework off, place it on the ground and right-click it. You can also use a dispenser to set them off for you—see Chapter 13 for more on using redstone.

> **NOTE:** YOU CAN COMBINE THE DIAMOND AND GLOWSTONE DUST TO MAKE A TWINKLING TRAIL. NONE OF THE OTHER FEATURES CAN BE COMBINED.

FROM LEFT TO RIGHT, PAPER, GUNPOWDER, FIREWORK STAR, ROCKET.

MAPS

In Chapter 7, you learned how to use explorer maps to find specific structures and items. You can also create your own maps of any area you choose. First, craft a blank map using a compass with eight paper. To fill the map with your current location, simply right-click and hold the map. The map should then show the 128x128-block area you're in, with north at the top; one map pixel represents one block. If parts of the map are blank, travel to these areas with your map in hand to fill them in. Maps will only fill in when they're equipped in your hand.

You can duplicate a map by crafting it with an additional blank map. If something changes in an area you've already mapped (for example, you've since built a road and new home), you can revisit that area with your map in hand to update it. You can use also a cartography table, found at a cartographer villager's workstation (see Chapter 12) to increase the area that a single map covers and lock maps so they can no longer be updated.

Functional Blocks

The following blocks perform some action, often with your interaction, and are often used to make other tasks easier. For example, you can install a lightning rod block to protect an area from lightning strikes.

> NOTE:
> WE'LL LOOK AT MORE FUNCTIONAL BLOCKS RELATED TO VILLAGERS AND REDSTONE IN CHAPTERS 12 AND 13.

CANDLES

Candles are a light source crafted from one honeycomb and one string. You can light a candle with a flint and steel. Each candle emits a light level of 3, and you can place up to four candles in a block for a light level of 12. You can dye candles with any of the sixteen dyes and can place single candles on cakes. To extinguish candles, either right-click them or use a water bucket or water bottle on them.

CHISELED BOOKSHELF

You can craft a chiseled bookshelf with six wood planks and three wood plank slabs in a line in the middle of the crafting grid. You can place up to six books (any type, including books and quills and enchanted books) in one by right-clicking the book on the bookshelf. To remove a book, use (left-click) the occupied book slot. You'll need an axe enchanted with Silk Touch to retrieve the chiseled bookshelf, otherwise, breaking the shelf will drop just the contained books. You can't use this type of bookshelf to increase the power of an enchanting table.

CONDUIT

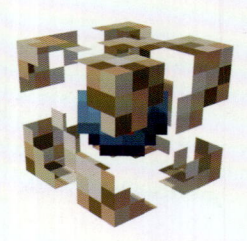

A *conduit* is a 5x5x5 multiblock object that you build underwater. It provides you and any other players within a certain radius an effect called *Conduit Power*, which combines the effects of Haste (ability to mine underwater), Night Vision (ability to see underwater), and Water Breathing. You can craft the conduit's heart from eight nautilus shells, dropped from the drowned or from fishing, and one *heart of the sea*: a unique spherical item you can only get from buried treasure.

The conduit needs to be placed underwater within a 5x5 square frame constructed from prismarine blocks, which can include prismarine, prismarine bricks, dark prismarine, or sea lanterns. The frame activates the conduit's power, indicated by the conduit opening and rotating. Once activated, the conduit power has a base radius of thirty-two blocks. You can increase the radius by adding up to two square frames, perpendicular to each other. With all three frames, the conduit is complete and extends its range to a ninety-six-block radius. A completed conduit will also inflict damage to nearby underwater hostile mobs.

BOTH THE CENTRAL EYELIKE BLOCK AND THE ENTIRE MULTI-BLOCK STRUCTURE ARE REFERRED TO AS CONDUITS.

JACK O' LANTERN

Jack o' Lanterns are carved pumpkin blocks that emit light levels of 15. To craft them, use shears on a pumpkin block to carve a face into the pumpkin, and then craft the carved pumpkin with a torch.

JUKEBOX

A jukebox, crafted from eight planks and a diamond, can play music discs found in treasure chests or dropped from a creeper if it is shot by a skeleton. As of Minecraft 1.21, there are nineteen different music discs to collect. To play a disc, equip the disk and right-click on a jukebox. You can find music discs in loot chests in ancient cities, bastion remnants, dungeons, strongholds, and woodland mansions.

LIGHTNING ROD

Lightning rods, crafted from three copper ingots, will attract lightning strikes within a 128-block radius, keeping nearby areas like your house (and you!) safe from being struck by lightning and igniting fires.

SCAFFOLDING

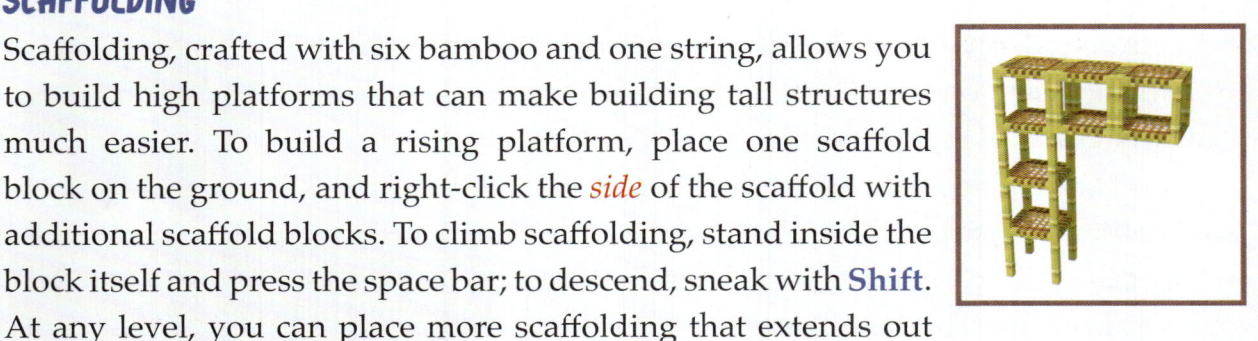

Scaffolding, crafted with six bamboo and one string, allows you to build high platforms that can make building tall structures much easier. To build a rising platform, place one scaffold block on the ground, and right-click the *side* of the scaffold with additional scaffold blocks. To climb scaffolding, stand inside the block itself and press the space bar; to descend, sneak with Shift. At any level, you can place more scaffolding that extends out horizontally. To do this, right-click on the top of the block you want to extend from, making sure to face the direction you want the scaffolding to go. You can remove scaffolding easily by breaking the lowest blocks of a platform, as this instantly breaks the connected blocks above.

Decorative Blocks

The following blocks are used primarily to spruce up your surroundings.

BANNERS

Banners are two-block-tall decorations you can craft with six wool of a single color and one stick. They can be placed on the tops or sides of block surfaces. Using a loom, you can choose up to six colored patterns on top of the base banner color, each overlaid on the previous. The *loom* is a shepherd villager's workstation. (See Chapter 13 for more on using this block.) If you craft a banner with a shield, it will transfer the banner's pattern to the shield. You can also find banner patterns, rarely, in loot chests, that you can use in the loom.

CHAINS

Chains are a decorative block that you can craft from an iron ingot and two iron nuggets. You can place them vertically or horizontally and you (or a chicken) can even walk on them.

FLOWER POTS

You can craft a flower pot with three bricks and fill it with any one-block-high flower or plant, including ferns, bamboo, cacti, mushrooms, saplings, and azalea bushes.

ITEM FRAMES

Item frames are small picture frames that you can craft from one leather and eight sticks. You can place these frames on block surfaces and right-click an item or block on the frame to place that item in the center of the frame. You can right-click the displayed item to rotate. To place item frames on chests, sneak with **Shift** while you right-click the chest. You can use item frames to display maps, even connecting maps. This allows you to make a wall of seamlessly connected maps.

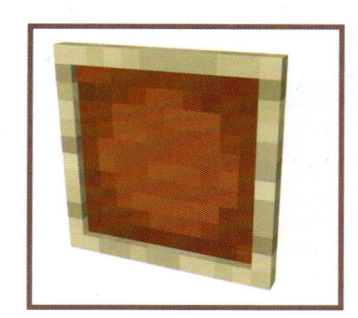

> **Challenge: Map Mastery**
>
> To make a 3x3 wall map depicting the area around your base, first craft nine empty maps (you'll need nine compasses and seventy-two paper). Starting at your base, equip one map to show the immediate 128x128 area. Travel north so that your player icon leaves the map's area and becomes a circle rather than an arrow. You're now in the map area just north of your base. Open a second empty map to record the 128x128 area north of your base, and travel as you need to fill it. Continue in a circle around your base in this way to the next seven areas, opening up a new empty map when you reach each one.
>
> Return to your base and choose a wall to display your map. Craft nine item frames from nine leather and seventy-two sticks. Place your item frames in a 3x3 square on the wall. Add each map to its correct item frame. If you're having difficulty keeping track of which map is which, arrange them in a memorable order in your inventory, or you can rename each map using an anvil for the cost of 1 XP.

MOB HEADS

Mob heads are the disembodied heads of hostile mobs, including creepers, zombies, or skeletons. They'll drop when killed by a charged creeper, a creeper that has been struck by lightning (see Chapter 11). Wither skeletons found in the Nether also have a chance of dropping their head when you kill them, and you can find dragon heads in the End dimension. You can place these heads decoratively or even wear one in place of a helmet; for Overworld mobs, wearing a mob head as a helmet decreases the distance at which that mob sees you by 50 percent.

PAINTINGS

You can craft a painting with one wool and eight sticks, and place them by right-clicking on a block or wall of blocks. Paintings range in size from 1x1 to 4x4. One of twenty-six paintings is randomly chosen, depending partly on the number of blocks on the wall adjacent to the target block. To create a painting of a certain size, limit the wall temporarily to the size you want. You can walk through paintings, so they're often used to disguise secret entrances.

SIGNS

You can make signs from six wood planks and one stick. A sign can be freestanding or placed against surfaces. The type of wood you use determines the color of the sign. Once you place the sign, you are prompted to enter the text, if any, you'd like the sign to display.

You can change the text's color by using a dye on the sign and can make the text glow with a glow ink sac, dropped by glow squid. You can change a sign's text or add text to its back by right-clicking the sign (or the back of the sign). You can craft a hanging sign (to place underneath blocks) using six stripped logs of the same wood and two iron chains. You can also use a honeycomb on a sign to prevent the sign from being edited again.

> ### Challenge: Sign Skills
> Collect three different types of wood and turn the wood into planks. Collect three sticks. Craft three signs, each made of a different type of wood; one for your farm, one for your home, and one for your livestock area.
>
> Place each sign in front of its designated location and enter some text on each sign. Make the text in front of your home glow with a glow ink sac. Change the text of the sign in front of your livestock area to be a different color with any of the sixteen dyes.

Up Next

The Minecraft world is rich with oddities and unusual features, and the developers add more every year. It's always great fun to keep up with their additions. Maybe you'll feel inspired enough to use these features as a focus in your game—creating in-game books of quests and lore or making map art by coloring in the area of a map with different blocks to show a scene or pattern.

In the next chapter, we'll turn our focus to the tools, weapons, and armor you need to advance in mining and combat.

9
WEAPONS, ARMOR, AND TOOLS

Tools and weapons are often necessary to craft or perform activities such as fighting, chopping trees, and mining. Likewise, armor is important in protecting yourself from hostile mobs, harsh environments, and more. In this chapter, we'll take an in-depth look at your equipment and how best to use them.

Materials

As discussed in Chapter 3, the material used to craft your tools, weapons, and armor makes a huge difference in their durability and strength.

The materials used for making tools and weapons are (in increasing order of quality): wood, gold, stone, iron, and diamond.[1] For armor, the materials are leather, gold, chainmail, iron, and diamond. Strive to have diamond armor, tools, and weapons, especially those you use most often, like your axe and sword. Unless you're going to the Nether, avoid using gold armor and tools, as they have low durability and will break quickly.

THE DURABILITY BAR BENEATH THE WEAPON OR TOOL SHORTENS AND CHANGES FROM GREEN TO RED THE CLOSER A TOOL OR WEAPON IS TO BREAKING.

---

[1] Using netherite, a material originating in the Nether, you can make diamond tools and armor into more durable netherite tools and armor. See Chapter 14 for more on the Nether and finding netherite.

Durability is the number of times you can use a tool, weapon, or armor before it breaks. Each use costs one durability point. Using the wrong tool for an action, like a pickaxe (instead of a shovel) to break sand, costs two durability points.

You can get a sense of how long your equipment will last by looking at its status bar in your inventory. The bar turns from green to red as the item wears down.

Weapons

Minecraft's main weapons are the sword or axe for melee (hand-to-hand) combat and the bow and arrow for ranged (distance) combat, but you can use other weapons and tools to strike an opponent. Even a shovel is better than nothing!

SWORD

The sword is your designated weapon for close-range, melee combat. You can use a sword by placing it in your hand and clicking when your cursor is over an enemy. After you strike, there's a short cooldown (.625 second) while your sword recharges; it won't strike at full strength until the recharge is complete. You can turn on an indicator to show a weapon's cooldown in your video settings.

Swords can give additional damage and Knockback to any mobs close to your target opponent; this is called a *sweeping attack*. It works only if your sword is at least 85 percent recharged and you're standing or walking. You can also perform a *sprint knockback* by running at your opponent while striking. The force of your speed will knock back your opponent.

The sword is also a legitimate tool for breaking cobwebs, which drop string.

BOW AND ARROW

For ranged attacks, you'll want a bow and arrow. Craft a bow with three sticks and three string; craft four arrows with one flint, stick, and feather. To use the bow, you must have at least one arrow in your inventory. Hold the bow in your hand and right-click it to charge. As the bow charges, it rises up in your screen and will shake slightly once it's fully charged. You can fire the bow before it's fully charged, but it will deal up to 6 points of damage. A fully charged, quivering bow has a chance of delivering a stronger, critical hit between 8 and 11 points. As you charge your bow, your walking speed is slowed to a sneak.

You can also craft specialty arrows that have various effects. *Spectral arrows*, crafted with an arrow and four glowstone dust from the Nether, will show the outline of the target for ten seconds—even through blocks! This makes it much easier to track foes. Lingering potions, which require resources from the End, can be combined with arrows to create *tipped arrows*, which give the target a special effect, like Weakness or Slowness. See Chapter 15 for more on crafting tipped arrows.

> **Challenge: Bow Mastery**
> Craft a few blocks to act as targets from colored wool. Set the blocks varying distances apart. Now, practice, practice, practice! You can retrieve any arrows you've shot.

CROSSBOW

Crossbows cost more to craft than bows (three sticks, one iron, one trip wire hook, and two strings), but they deliver more damage—between 6 and 11 points. Like bows, you'll need at least one arrow to use them. You have to fully charge your crossbow, which can take a while (they're slow), and then use it again to fire the shot. You don't need to fire a fully charged crossbow; you can carry it in your hotbar. A charged crossbow has an extended string to show that it is loaded.

> **NOTE:**
> YOU CAN USE A FIREWORK ROCKET WITH A CROSSBOW TO DEAL AN AMAZING 18 POINTS OF DAMAGE!

TRIDENT

Tridents can be acquired only by killing a drowned that's carrying a trident. Even then, there's a small chance that the drowned will drop it. You can throw a trident to deal 8 points of damage, or strike a foe with it to deal 9 damage. You'll need to pick a trident up once thrown, unless it's imbued with the Loyalty enchantment, which automatically returns it to your hotbar.

SHIELD

Although it's not a weapon, the shield is one of the most important fighting tools, especially against skeleton arrows and creeper explosions. However, shields are vulnerable to axes and guardian laser beams. To use a shield, place it in your off-hand slot. Right-clicking will raise and activate it, and will slow you to sneaking speed. It blocks incoming damage in a half-circle from where you're facing. You can decorate a shield with a custom banner using a villager's loom.

> **NOTE:** I RECOMMEND CRAFTING A SHIELD WITH YOUR FIRST IRON INGOT BEFORE MAKING IRON ARMOR.

Challenge: Get Good at Crits

Regardless of the weapon, you can add 50 percent more damage points to a melee attack if you perform a *critical hit*. To do this, you have to be falling while you strike—such as jumping and then striking as you start to fall. Achieving a critical hit will display sparkles on your foe. To practice, breed a bunch of farm animals in a pen. When you have a group of ten or so, critical hit the animals by jumping up and swinging your weapon on your descent. If you're having difficulty, place a block in the pen to stand on and jump from it as you strike.

Other Weapons

There's less conventional weaponry available to you as well, though most may only be useful in specific circumstances. An axe is also a suitable substitute for a sword—read more about this in the Tools section below.

MACE

You can craft a mace with a heavy core (which you can get as loot only from an ominous vault in the underground trial chambers) and a breeze rod, dropped by a breeze. The mace delivers a heavy wallop (called a smash attack), as long as you are falling when using it. The longer the drop in height you make before hitting an enemy with it, the greater the damage. You can also use it in regular combat, although, without a critical hit, it will only give 6 points of damage.

TNT

Crafted with four sand and five gunpowder, an ignited block of TNT will cause an explosion that can kill mobs and players. The blast radius depends on the blast resistance of the block. For example, the blast radius of a grass block is about three to four blocks. You can set off TNT with a flint and steel. TNT is gravity-affected once it's lit. Setting off TNT in water won't explode any blocks, but will still damage mobs.

FIRE CHARGES

You can craft fire charges from gunpowder, blaze powder (from the blaze, a Nether mob), and coal or charcoal. Right-click a fire charge to start a fire, light a Nether portal, or fire them from a redstone dispenser to deal up to 9 points of damage (see Chapter 13 for more on redstone).

WIND CHARGES

You can throw wind charges at enemies to knock them back and deal a small amount of damage. You craft them from breeze rods dropped by breezes. Wind charges can also interact with some blocks, like doors and levers, opening, closing, pressing, or flipping them.

> **NOTE:**
> FIRE CAN SPREAD TO NEARBY NATURAL BLOCKS LIKE TREES, LOGS, WOOL, MANY VEGETATION BLOCKS, AND WOOD-BASED CRAFTED BLOCKS. LAVA CAN ALSO IGNITE NEARBY FLAMMABLE BLOCKS. YOU CAN TURN FIRE SPREAD OFF WHEN YOU FIRST CREATE YOUR WORLD BY TURNING UPDATE FIRE OFF UNDER THE CREATE WORLD/GAME RULES OPTIONS.

SPLASH POTIONS

Throw harmful splash potions at your enemies to inflict debuffs, including Harm (damage), Poison, Slowness, and Weakness. (You can take beneficial potions yourself, to heal or get stronger.) See Chapter 15 for more information on brewing potions.

LAVA BUCKET

Lava damages players and mobs, except most Nether mobs; make sure not to step in it. To use a lava bucket, right-click it at your opponent's feet.

SNOWBALLS AND EGGS

Snowballs and eggs can't do damage when you throw them; however, they can knock an enemy back. In the Nether, these items will damage a blaze.

Of the weapons listed in this section, the most useful in combat are the lava bucket and splash potions.

Challenge: Blow Stuff Up!

TNT is one of the most fun blocks in Minecraft, but it can do a lot of damage. You might use it to blast a tunnel through a mountain or collect large amounts of materials.

Craft at least three TNT blocks and make your way to a desert. Place a line of TNT about four blocks apart in a level area. When your TNT is placed, set off one end of the line with a flint and steel, and run ten or so blocks away to protect yourself from blast damage. Reignite the chain if needed. Once your TNT chain has finished exploding, go pick up the dropped sand.

Armor

Armor is your first line of defense, especially against mobs that will attack you by surprise before you can hold up your sword or shield. You have four armor slots in your inventory that hold a helmet, chestplate, leggings, and boots. Each item provides a certain number of defense points; for example, a full set of diamond armor provides 20 defense points. You'll craft each of the four pieces with pieces of the same material: leather, iron ingots, gold ingots, diamonds. You'll need four pieces of material for boots, five for hats, seven for leggings, and eight for chestplates.

DEFENSE POINTS FROM THE ARMOR YOU ARE WEARING ADD UP TO DISPLAY IN YOUR ARMOR BAR IN THE HUD. ONE CHESTPLATE ICON REPRESENTS TWO POINTS. THE MORE ARMOR YOU WEAR, AND THE HIGHER THE QUALITY, THE MORE PROTECTED YOU ARE.

The material of the armor piece, alongside any enchantments, will change the armor's damage. In general, chestplates and leggings provide the most protection. Armor doesn't typically protect against noncombat damage, like suffocating, drowning, falling, starving, and some magic. However, you can enchant armor to provide additional protection, grant certain abilities, or protect against a specific type of damage, like fire or explosions.

DECORATED ARMOR

You can decorate your armor with a *trim* by combining any armor piece with a smithing template and a trim material in a smithing table. There are sixteen types of smithing templates you can find in loot chests in various structures and by brushing suspicious gravel in trail ruins and suspicious sand in ocean ruins and desert pyramids. Trim materials decide the color of the

SMITHING TEMPLATES ARE SMALL RECTANGULAR ITEMS WITH A DESIGNS ON FRONT.

Display Your Armor

You can show off your armor on an armor stand, as shown in this chapter's opening image. Craft the stand with six sticks and one smooth stone slab. After you've placed it, right-click it with a piece of armor in hand to transfer the armor onto the stand.

trim: these are amethyst shard, copper ingot, diamond, emerald, gold ingot, iron ingot, lapis lazuli, Nether quartz, netherite ingot, and redstone dust.

You can duplicate a smithing table by crafting it with six diamonds and a material specific to that template. To create netherite tools and armor, you use a smithing table to craft it from diamond tools and armor pieces with a netherite upgrade smithing template.

THIS IRON ARMOR SET IS TRIMMED WITH AMETHYST USING THE RIB SMITHING TEMPLATE.

SPECIALTY ARMOR

You may find chainmail armor pieces in treasure chests or as occasional drops from killing skeletons or zombies. Chainmail falls between gold and iron in terms of the amount of protection it offers.

The turtle shell helmet improves underwater breathing. You can craft it from five scutes, which are the shell fragments dropped by baby turtles when they mature into adults.

THE BENEFIT OF LEATHER

Although your goal is to level up to diamond, don't throw away your leather armor. Leather armor is a must for exploring mountains, as it prevents you from freezing and sinking into powder snow. Leather armor can be dyed using any combination of the sixteen dyes, providing over twelve million possible tints.

Challenge: Booty Beauty

First, craft yourself some leather boots with four leather. Place your boots in the crafting grid of a crafting table and add any combination of up to eight dyes (for a reference on how to make dye, see page 119). You can do this over and over to achieve different colors.

To start over and remove the dye, right-click the boots on a cauldron (crafted from seven iron ingots) filled with water.

ARMOR FOR HORSES

You can craft horse armor from seven leather, which can also be dyed with any combination of the sixteen dyes. Leather armor will protect horses in powder snow. You can also find iron, gold, and diamond horse armor in treasure chests. See Chapter 10 for more on taming, riding, and equipping horses.

WOLF ARMOR

You can craft armor for a tamed wolf (dog), with six armadillo scutes. Right-click your dog with the armor to place the armor. To remove the armor, use shears. The armor adds an armor value of 11 (similar to diamond horse armor) to help protect your dog. If your dog does die, it will drop its armor. Wolf armor has constant durability, so it will never break and need to be replaced.

Tools

The speed, durability, and attack damage of your four main tools—the pickaxe, axe, shovel, and hoe—depend on their material. Wood and gold are at the bottom of the list in all three attributes, followed by stone, iron, diamond, and netherite.

PICKAXE

As you've seen in previous chapters, you use your pickaxe for mining stone, ore, other hard blocks like metals and bricks, and crafted blocks made from stone and metals (like furnaces and lanterns). The pickaxe's material also determines what kinds of ore it can break.

Wood or gold pickaxe and better:
Coal ore, stone, bricks, and crafted and other blocks not mentioned below.

Stone pickaxe and better:
Iron ore, lapis lazuli ore, and blocks of iron and lapis lazuli.

Iron pickaxe and better:
Diamond, emerald, gold and redstone ore, and blocks of diamond, emerald, and gold.

Diamond and netherite pickaxe:
Obsidian and the Nether-origin blocks crying obsidian, respawn anchors, ancient debris, and blocks of netherite.

AXE

You use your axe to chop trees; break wooden objects, like fences; strip logs of their bark; remove wax or the greenish tinge from waxed or oxidized copper blocks; and harvest melons, pumpkins, bamboo, large mushrooms, and cocoa. The material of your axe doesn't determine what you can break with it, but the higher the level of material, the faster you'll break a block. You can also use your axe in battle; in fact, it can deliver as good or better than an unenchanted sword made of the same material. However, each strike with an axe will use up two durability points rather than one, as it isn't the primary weapon for battle. Other reasons to use swords for melee include cooldown times (a full second for an axe), attack speed (axes are slower), and enchantments (swords have more battle-related enchantments).

SHOVEL

Use a shovel to dig dirt and dirt variants like podzol and soul soil, as well as clay, sands, gravel, snow, and concrete powder. You can also create path blocks with a shovel by right-clicking a dirt or grass block.

HOE

You can use a hoe to create farmland from dirt or grass blocks, and to quickly break some plant-related blocks, including dried kelp, hay bales, leaves, moss, and sponges.

FISHING ROD

Check out page 47 in Chapter 4 for the basics of using a fishing rod.

> **Challenge: Ride a Pig!**
> For this challenge, you'll need a saddle, fishing rod, and carrot. Saddles can be found in loot chests, as a treasure item when fishing, when trading with a master-level leatherwork villager (see Chapter 12), or as a drop when killing ravagers (see Chapter 13).
>
> Craft a fishing rod with a carrot to create a *carrot on a stick*. Equip the saddle and place it on a pig, and then right-click the pig to ride it. You can steer the pig by holding your carrot on a stick, and make the pig run faster by right-clicking with your carrot on a stick in hand. Sadly, the only way to remove a saddle from a pig is by killing it.

SHEARS

Use shears to get wool from sheep and honeycomb from beehives, and to harvest fragile plant blocks like ferns, vines, and leaves. You can halt the growth of cave vines (and vines in the Nether) by right-clicking the end of the vine with shears.

OTHER TOOLS

Many other tools can be very handy in certain situations.

Brush

Use a brush on suspicious gravel, which you'll encounter in trail ruins and cold ocean ruins and suspicious sand. Suspicious sand generates in the hidden rooms below desert pyramids, the bottoms of desert wells, and warm ocean ruins.

Flint and Steel

A flint and steel—crafted from one iron ingot and one flint—is used to activate Nether portals, detonate TNT, and light candles and campfires. You can also set fire to flammable blocks and entities like leaves, wood, and even sheep. Be careful, as fire can spread to nearby flammable blocks.

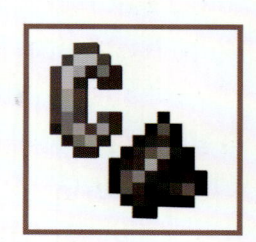

Spyglass

You can craft a spyglass from two copper ingots and one amethyst shard to take a closer look at distant scenes.

Lead

You can attach leads (crafted from four string and one slimeball) to most nonhostile mobs (never hostile mobs or villagers) and drag them around. Once attached, the other end of the lead should be in your hotbar. You can attach the other end to a fencepost to keep the mob in place.

Bucket of Water

To create a bucket of water, first craft a bucket from three iron ingots, then right-click the bucket on a water source. It's a good idea to always carry a bucket of water in your inventory, as it can save you from some perilous situations.

Right-clicking a bucket of water on the ground will create a flow of water. This can be helpful if you've managed to catch on fire. Right-click the bucket at your feet to put yourself out and right-click again with the bucket equipped to pick the water back up.

Water also stops fall damage, so if you've just fallen off a cliff and have your bucket of water in hand, repeatedly right-click it on the block you're going to land on before you crash. If you manage to place water even a split second before you land, you've saved yourself from possible death.

As stated in Chapter 4, a bucket of water can be used on standing lava to create obsidian, and flowing lava to create cobblestone.

Finally, if you're at the edge of a ravine and need a quick way to descend, use your bucket of water on the ground before you to create a stream down into the ravine. Jump into the stream and float down, making sure to lean your head out of the water to prevent drowning. You can even use water to climb; place a stream above your head on a sheer wall or cliff, swim up, then pick the water up and place it again, even farther above your head. The delay in water disappearing after you've picked it up allows you to swim several blocks up at a time.

Boat

Craft a boat with five planks of the same wood—you can also craft a flat raft if you use bamboo planks. You can also craft a chest with a boat to make a boat with a chest in it, which will help you transport extra resources. A boat can be invaluable beyond simply transportation. For example, if you place a boat on the ground directly in front of a mob, there's a very good chance it'll walk right into the boat. Once in the boat, the mob can't get out, making them easy to kill. Note that skeletons can still fire arrows, and creepers will still explode if you get too close.

Boats can be a good way to transport passive mobs, since they can acccomodate two passengers (including yourself). Boats can travel slowly over dry land as long as it's flat land or descending blocks. At your destination, you'll need to break the boat with an axe to get the mob out.

You're also safe from fall damage when you're riding in a boat, meaning you can ride a boat over a cliff to fall gently to the ground.

Of the tools listed in this section, the bucket of water is probably the most important to keep in your inventory, as it can be used in a variety of ways—from catching tropical fish and axolotls to converting lava into obsidian.

Repairing Armor, Tools, and Weapons

Before your sword with Sharpness V and Looting III wears out and disappears forever, repair it! There are several ways to repair tools, weapons, and armor.

IN A CRAFTING GRID

Combine two items of the same type in a crafting grid (or a weaponsmith villager's grindstone) to create a new item with their combined durability (and up to 5 percent more durability). Note that the created item loses any enchantments. If you're using the villager's grindstone, you'll get experience points.

WITH AN ANVIL

You can craft an anvil from three iron blocks and four iron ingots. An anvil allows you to combine your worn item with either an item of the same type or additional material. For example, you can combine iron ingots with an iron sword or chestplate. Using an anvil to repair equipment will keep and combine enchantments, but costs experience points (noted in the figure as Enchantment Cost). Anvils can last about twenty-five uses. You'll see it start to wear down with use, eventually breaking with a clang.

Additionally, the anvil is one of the few blocks in Minecraft that is affected by gravity; you can do serious damage to a foe by dropping an anvil on its head.

PLACE YOUR WORN TOOL IN THE LEFT BOX. IN THE MIDDLE BOX, YOU CAN PLACE REPAIR MATERIALS, OR ANOTHER WORN TOOL OF THE SAME TYPE. YOU CAN ALSO REPLACE THE TOOL'S NAME WITH A NEW NAME, COSTING EXPERIENCE POINTS.

Name Tags and Anvils

In addition to repairing items, you can also use an anvil with name tags to name mobs in the world. Naming a mob prevents it from despawning, which can be useful for advanced mob farms. (Most passive mobs don't despawn, but hostile mobs do.)

Name tags are tricky to find; you can get them through trading with librarian villagers, finding them in loot chests, or (rarely) from fishing. To use a name tag, place it in the left slot of the anvil interface and type a name in the top text box. Retrieve the named name tag from the right slot, then right-click a mob with the tag to name it.

Minecraft includes several Easter eggs in its naming mechanics. Name a mob *Dinnerbone* (a game developer), and the mob will display upside down. Name a sheep *jeb_* (another developer) and it will change colors in a rainbow cycle.

Up Next

Now that you're armed with the general details of how armor, tools, and weapons work, we're going to take a close look at the mobs you can use them on! In the next chapter, we'll look at passive mobs, like horses and turtles, and their habitats and uses. Then, in the following chapter, we'll examine hostile mobs, how difficult they are to battle, and where you'll find them.

10
MOO! OINK! THE PASSIVE MOBS

In Minecraft, the word *mobs* is short for *mobile entities* (or *mobiles*)—characters that move around by themselves. This includes cows, spiders, and even villagers. Mobs are sorted into three main categories: passive (they don't attack players), neutral (they are passive until provoked), and hostile (they always attack). In this chapter, we'll focus on passive mobs.

Passive mobs are primarily animals and villagers. Because villagers have complex behavior and are a huge part of the game, we'll look at them in more detail in Chapter 12.

Passive Mobs

Many passive mobs are based on real-life animals, and some can be bred, tamed, or healed with a favorite food. Each mob also has specific spawn locations; farm animals will spawn in any biome with grassy areas, but they won't spawn in the desert or snow. Some mobs have special behaviors, called *AI (artificial intelligence)*.[2] For example, a dolphin may play with items dropped in the sea, and a goat may ram you. Most passive mobs have 10 HP; smaller mobs will have 3–4. Many mobs also have drops that are related to their nature—a cow drops leather and raw beef, while a squid drops ink sacs. The number of drops is often random; a chicken will always drop raw meat, but feathers are less common. Remember, baby mobs don't drop anything—including experience points!

---

[2] In this context, AI doesn't refer to real-world artificial intelligence, but simply the use of complex algorithms for behavior.

MOO! OINK! THE PASSIVE MOBS

Passive Mobs: Spawns, Food, and Drops

MOB	SPAWN	FOOD	DROPS
Allay	In jail cell rooms in woodland mansions and in dark oak cages at pillager outposts	None	Any items they are holding
Armadillo	Badlands and savannas	Spider eyes	Armadillo scutes
Axolotl	Underwater in dark caves	Bucket of Tropical Fish	None
Bat	Dark caves below y=63	None	None
Camel	One spawns in a village center	Cactus	Only a saddle if it was equipped with one.
Cat	Villages; swamp huts (black cats)	Raw cod or salmon	String
Chicken	Grassy areas	Seeds (beetroot, melon, pumpkin, wheat)	Raw chicken, feathers
Cod	Lukewarm, normal, and cold oceans	None	Raw cod, bone meal
Cow	Grassy areas	Wheat	Raw beef, leather
Donkey/Horse/Mule	Plains; savannas; villages	Breeding: Golden carrots or golden apples Healing: Sugar, wheat, apples, golden carrots, golden apples, hay bales (tamed adults only)	Leather
Frog	Swamps and mangrove swamps	Slimeball	
Glow Squid	Underwater in dark caves	None	Glow ink sacs
Mooshroom	Mushroom Fields	Wheat	Raw beef, leather
Ocelot	Jungles	Raw cod; raw salmon	None
Parrot	Jungles	Seeds (beetroot, melon, pumpkin, wheat); cookies will kill them	Feathers
Pig	Grassy areas	Beetroot, carrot, potato	Raw porkchop
Pufferfish	Lukewarm and warm oceans	None	Pufferfish, bone meal

(Continued on next page)

MOB	SPAWN	FOOD	DROPS
Rabbit	Deserts, Flower Forests, Groves, Meadows, Taigas, Snowy biomes	Carrots, golden carrots, dandelions	Raw rabbit, rabbit hide, rabbit foot
Salmon	Rivers, Cold and frozen Oceans	None	Raw salmon, bone meal
Sheep	Grassy areas	Wheat	Raw mutton, wool
Sniffer	Spawns only from sniffer eggs used by a player	Torchflower seeds	None
Snow Golem	Player spawned	None	None
Squid	Oceans and rivers	None	Ink sacs
Strider	Nether biomes	Warped fungus	String
Tropical fish	Lukewarm and Warm Oceans	None	None
Turtle	Beaches	Seagrass	Seagrass
Wandering trader	Random	None	Leads, milk bucket, potion of Invisibility

ALLAY

The allay is a tiny, passive mob that has a chance to spawn in the jails in pillager outposts and woodland mansions. If you right-click it with an item, the allay will follow you (if you're within sixty-four blocks), pick up any dropped identical items (up to a stack) within thirty-two blocks of you, and deliver them back to you. Right-click the allay to remove any item it is holding and searching for. You can have the allay drop the items it collects at a note block if you place a note block within sixteen blocks of it while it is searching. The allay will dance near a jukebox playing a music disc, and you can duplicate the allay by giving it an amethyst shard while it's dancing.

ARMADILLO

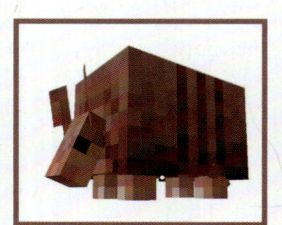

You can find armadillos in badlands and savanna biomes. It is a small creature and will roll up into a ball when undead mobs are near or if a player is sprinting or riding an animal nearby. Spiders and cave spiders will run away from armadillos. Armadillos will drop armadillo scutes (shell pieces) over time, or if you brush them.

AXOLOTL

Axolotls are cute creatures that swim in lush caves and come in pink, cyan, blue, gold, and brown. They attack other aquatic mobs, including the drowned, and excepting turtles and dolphins. (Apparently the axolotl is keen on protecting endangered species!)

After attacking an enemy, axolotls play dead for a few minutes to regenerate health. If you kill a mob that an axolotl is battling, the axolotl will also give you a few moments of regeneration and cure any Mining Fatigue effects.

> **NOTE:** AXOLOTLS ARE GREAT COMPANIONS TO BRING TO AN OCEAN MONUMENT RAID. YOU CAN PICK THEM UP WITH A BUCKET OF WATER TO EASILY TRANSPORT THEM.

The blue variant is the rarest—there's only a 1/1200 chance to get a blue axolotl by breeding two other types. However, once you have a single blue axolotl, you can breed it with a common variant for a 50 percent chance of getting a blue offspring.

BAT

Bats spawn in caves; when they're not hanging from the ceiling, they squeak and fly in your face. During Halloween (late October through early November), they'll spawn much more frequently.

CAMEL

Camels spawn singly, in village centers, and are already tamed and ready for a player (or two) to saddle and ride it. While you are riding a camel, you are high enough to be safe from zombies and other hostile mobs that can't jump or use a ranged weapon. Spiders can still jump up to you, and skeletons still strike you with an arrow. However, camels are pretty slow. They can sprint and, if they have a saddle, perform a dashing charge for up to twelve blocks. You can ride them in water up to three blocks deep; any deeper and they will dismount you.

CAT

There are eleven types of cat varying in color and markings. Cats spawn in villages or swamp huts (black cats). You can tame them with raw cod or salmon (you'll need to be *very* slow and cautious). Once tame, they'll follow you unless you right-click them to make them sit. If you move more than twelve blocks from your tamed cat, it should instantly transport to you, unless it's sitting or you're in water. A tamed cat will sport a collar (that you can dye) and can give you gifts, like strings or feathers, when you wake after sleeping. You can also heal your tamed cat with raw cod or salmon. All cats can scare away creepers and phantoms; untamed cats will attack baby turtles and rabbits and avoid players.

> **NOTE:**
> YOU MAY NEED TO FEED AN ANIMAL ITS RAW COD OR SALMON MORE THAN A FEW TIMES TO TAME IT. AN UNSUCCESSFUL TAMING CAUSES BLACK SMOKE PARTICLES TO COME OFF THE MOB RATHER THAN RED HEARTS.

CHICKEN

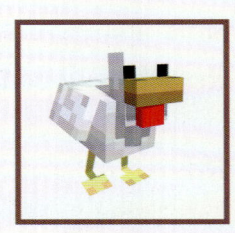

Chickens can be bred and killed for food and feathers to craft arrows. They're the choice of food for untamed cats, ocelots, and foxes, so be sure to protect them. Adult chickens will occasionally lay an egg that you can throw with a 1/8 chance of spawning a chick and a 1/256 chance of spawning a cluster of four chicks.

COW

Like other farmyard mobs, cows are found in bright, grassy areas and have a calm demeanor. Cows have some worthwhile drops, so it's a good idea to breed them consistently. You can cook raw beef to make steak, one of the highest-quality food items offered. Use an empty bucket on a cow to get a bucket of milk, which can cure any status effect. Their leather is crucial in making books for enchanting.

DONKEY

You'll find donkeys most often in grassy biomes. They behave identically to horses, except that, once tamed, you can permanently equip them with a chest to carry stuff around. If you breed a donkey with a horse, you'll get a mule!

FISH

You can find cod mostly in oceans, salmon in rivers, and tropical fish and pufferfish in warm oceans. Tropical fish come in many different colors and markings. Watch out for pufferfish—although they are categorized as passive, if you get too close they will poison you for several seconds. You can catch fish individually using a bucket of water, and you can carry them in your inventory and use (right-click) on a block or in water to place the fish. Fish will die if they're removed from water.

FROGS

Frogs spawn in swamps and mangrove swamps and can be generated by a tadpole growing up. There are three types of frogs: warm-biome frogs that are off-white, temperate-biome frogs that are orange, and cold-biome frogs that are green. The type of frog depends on which type of biome (warm, temperate, or cold) the tadpole matures in. Tadpoles themselves spawn from frogspawn, a horizontal, vine-like block that rests on water and is created by a frog when it is bred.

Frogs can jump up to eight blocks high, and they will attack small slimes (and small magma cubes). When they kill a small magma cube, the frog will drop a froglight block. Froglights come in three colors, ochre (from orange frogs), pearlescent (from white frogs), and verdant (from green frogs). Froglights emit a light level of 15.

TADPOLES WILL MATURE INTO ORANGE, WHITE, OR GREEN FROGS.

HORSE

Horses are a fast way to travel, and they can jump up several blocks to make climbing mountains easier. They come in different colors and markings and have varying health points, speeds, and jumping abilities.

You can tame an adult horse by right-clicking with an empty hand (it will be more receptive to taming if you first feed it an apple). This will put you on top of the horse, which will buck you off after a few moments. Continue to right-click and mount the horse until it stops bucking and hearts float above it. The hearts mean it's been tamed. Now that you've tamed the horse, press **E** while you're sitting on it to open its GUI. Here you can add a saddle (to ride it) and horse armor. (You can also right-click saddles and armor on a horse to add them.) Press **Shift** to get off a horse you're riding and use the WASD keys to control your movement. Horses will throw you off if you try to ride them in water deeper than two blocks, but you can bring them through water as you swim or boat by using a lead.

You can breed horses by feeding them golden apples or golden carrots and feed their foal to make it mature faster. If they are injured, you can help heal them by feeding them (from least effective to most) sugar, wheat, apples, golden carrots, golden apples, or hay bales.

> **NOTE:**
> UNFORTUNATELY, SADDLES ARE ONE OF THE FEW UNCRAFTABLE ITEMS IN MINECRAFT, MEANING YOU HAVE TO FIND ONE IN ORDER TO USE IT. YOU CAN FIND A SADDLE BY FISHING, TRADING WITH A MASTER LEATHERWORKER VILLAGER (SEE CHAPTER 12), LOOTING TREASURE CHESTS, OR KILLING RAVAGERS (SEE CHAPTERS 11 AND 12).

WHEN YOU MOUNT A HORSE, THE HUD SHOWS THE HORSE'S ARMOR LEVEL ABOVE YOUR HEALTH ON THE LEFT. ON THE RIGHT IT SHOWS THE HORSE'S HEARTS. BELOW THIS IS THE JUMPING METER, WHICH HELPS YOU PERFORM JUMPS.

To jump up more than one block with a horse, press the space bar as you approach the jump. A jump meter will appear in your HUD.

As you press the space bar, its jump meter fills up with a blue line that turns orange at the very end. For the highest jump, you want to release the space bar right before the jump meter turns orange. Many horses can jump over two blocks, and very few can jump up to five blocks. Horses with a high number of hearts aren't necessarily the fastest or the best jumpers.

Challenge: Champion Horse Breeder

There are seven colors of horses and five possible coat markings (including no special markings). Travel your lands and collect as many different types of horses as you can. Horse colorings are black, gray, dark brown, brown, chestnut, creamy, and white. The four horse markings are white stockings and blaze, white field, white spots, and black dots. Build a stable with stalls for your horses. You can use signs for each horse's stall if you don't have name tags to name your different horses. For each, take note of its health (hearts). Set up a speed and jumping test to note how fast each horse is and how many blocks each can jump. Once you know how your horses perform, try to breed even better horses. When you breed two horses, the abilities of the parents are combined so that their foal should be an equal or better runner or jumper. Can you breed a horse with high hearts, fast speed, and good jumping ability?

MOOSHROOM

The red mooshroom is a cow with mushrooms growing on its back that can be found only in the Mushroom Fields biome. They act identically to cows, except that you can right-click them while holding a wooden bowl to receive mushroom stew. If a red mooshroom is struck by lightning, it will turn into the even rarer brown mooshroom. Breeding two red mooshrooms gives you a very small chance (1/1024) of producing a brown mooshroom. Mooshrooms can produce suspicious stew by right-clicking one of the suspicious stew flowers on it before clicking it with a wooden bowl. (See Chapter 2 for more on suspicious stew.)

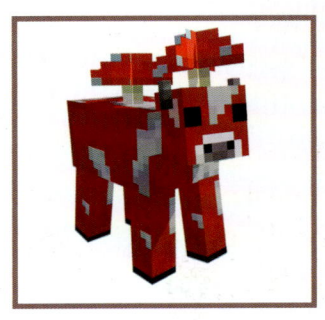

MULE

The mule behaves almost identically to a horse or donkey. Mules do not spawn naturally; you must breed a horse with a donkey to produce one. You can saddle them and give them chests, but you can't breed them.

OCELOT

You can find the rare ocelot in jungles. To breed ocelots, feed them raw salmon or cod; this will also gain their trust, which means they'll no longer run away from you. Like cats, they'll attack baby turtles and chickens and scare off creepers and phantoms.

PARROTS

Parrots can also be found in jungles. They can be blue, green, red, cyan, or gray. If you tame parrots by feeding them seeds, they'll follow you, sit on your shoulder, and even dance to music from a jukebox. Like tamed cats and wolves, parrots will sit when you right-click them, and teleport to you if you are far away. If you get a pet parrot, brace yourself: They'll imitate the sounds of any hostile mobs within about twenty blocks, and sometimes even mobs that aren't nearby. Don't feed them cocoa beans as these are poisonous to them.

PIG

Pigs drop raw porkchops, and you can ride them using a saddle and a carrot-on-a-stick. If struck by lightning, they'll turn into zombified piglins (see Chapter 11).

RABBIT

Rabbits are skittish and difficult to catch or kill. Their coloring and markings depend on which biome they spawned in. Desert rabbits are sandy; snowy biome rabbits are white or black and white; and other biomes spawn brown or black rabbits.

> **NOTE:**
> IF YOU USE FIRE TO KILL AN ANIMAL (LIKE A SWORD WITH THE FIRE ASPECT ENCHANTMENT), IT WILL DROP THE COOKED VERSION OF THAT MEAT.

One of their potential drops, the rabbit foot, is used to make Potions of Leaping. They can also drop rabbit hide—to be used for crafting bundles and leather—and raw rabbit. Wolves and foxes will attack rabbits.

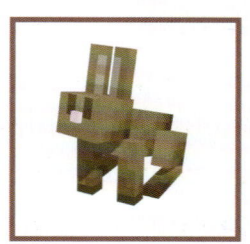

Challenge: Your Own Zoo

Create your own zoo by bringing two or more of each passive animal into an enclosed area. You can transport many mobs overland by lead, some can be picked up with a bucket of water, and others by pushing them into boats and sailing them across water. Remember to carry the mobs' favorite food on hand so they follow you!

Make sure to separate animals that will attack others, like wolves and foxes.

You can make ponds for fish, axolotls, and squids by digging out an area of ground and filling the space with buckets of water. Keep your axolotl separate, as they'll attack the other mobs. Put coarse dirt around the pond's edges for a muddy look, gravel and sand as the pond bed, and decorate with sugar cane, lily pads, and kelp.

Consider decorating each fenced area so it's specific to the mob(s) inside. For example, plant a couple of oak trees in your horse/donkey/mule enclosure; for your turtle enclosure, replace the ground with sand and add a pond and seagrass. You might even choose to add signs to signify different areas of your zoo!

SHEEP

Sheep spawn with natural colors—like gray, white, and brown—and very rarely, a pink sheep will spawn. Sheep eat grass blocks, which will turn into dirt blocks. Wolves will attack them.

SNIFFER

The sniffer is a one-of-a-kind "ancient" creature that you can only spawn yourself from hatching a sniffer egg. You can find sniffer eggs by using a brush on suspicious sand found around warm ocean sandstone ruins, much as you do when excavating in trail ruins (see Chapter 8 for more on trail ruins and excavating.) Each suspicious sand has just a chance to drop a sniffer egg. If you want to be able to breed more sniffers, you'll need to find two sniffer eggs. Place a sniffer egg on the ground to begin the hatching process, which will take two Minecraft days. (You can double this speed by placing the egg on a moss block, which you find in lush caves.) When the egg hatches, it turns into a baby sniffer, or snifflet. When the snifflet grows up into an adult sniffer, which takes about one Minecraft day, it will start sniffing for ancient seeds in nearby grass, dirt, mud, or moss blocks (as long as there is at least a 6x6 patch of this). By sniffing, it can find ancient pitcher pods and torchflower seeds, which you can plant in farmland and grow into pitcher plants and torchflowers.

SNOW GOLEM

The snow golem is a *utility mob*, which means it helps other mobs or players. The snow golem can only be created by a player. To do so, stack two snow blocks and place a carved pumpkin or Jack o' Lantern on top. Snow golems will throw snowballs at hostile mobs to knock them back (snowballs only hurt blazes, however.) Snow golems will melt in hotter biomes (savanna, desert, badlands) as well as in rain, though a roof will protect them from rain.

SQUID

Squid display a toothy red mouth, but they are passive. Upon death, they drop ink sacs, which are a source of black dye. They often produce a cloud of inky particles after being attacked as they try to flee. Squid are relentlessly attacked by guardians, elder guardians, and axolotl. A variant of the squid is the glow squid, which spawn in dark underwater areas, like flooded ravines and caves. The glow ink sacs they drop can be used to make Glow Item Frames; you can also apply them to signs to make the text glow.

STRIDER

The strider is a Nether mob that walks in lava. If they leave the lava, they'll start shivering and turn purple until they get back in. You can equip a strider with a saddle and ride it, controlling their direction with a *warped fungus on a stick* (crafted with a fishing rod and a warped fungus). To dismount and avoid lava, face a solid block before pressing **Shift**.

TURTLE

Turtles spawn on beaches and swim in oceans. If you breed them with seagrass, one of the pair will become pregnant and swim to its spawning or home beach, where it will lay a group of one to four eggs. The eggs will hatch in four to five days but are in danger of being attacked by untamed cats, foxes, ocelots, and wolves, zombies, and skeletons. When the baby turtles grow up, they drop a scute, or turtle shell part.

Wandering Trader

The wandering trader looks like a villager, but spawns randomly near players and villages, leading two llamas. Right-click the trader for a selection of items it will offer you in exchange for emeralds; these are usually nature-related items like saplings and dyes. Traders are at risk of zombie attacks and may take an invisibility potion at night to escape detection. If you kill a wandering trader while it's drinking a potion, there's a small chance it will drop a bucket of milk or a potion. It will also drop the leads to its llamas.

Up Next

As you've seen, passive mobs offer a lot of fun gameplay, from farming animals for their drops, to experimenting with breeding, and even building farms, zoos, and stables. In the next chapter, we'll take a look at the mobs that you should treat with a bit more caution—the ones that attack!

11
GRRR! MOBS THAT ATTACK

Both neutral and hostile mobs can attack you. While neutral mobs are typically passive until you attack them, hostile mobs are always out to get you. Some neutral mobs can be tamed and bred like passive mobs, while others—like spiders—are more similar to hostile mobs. Most mobs we'll discuss have unique drops, behaviors, and spawn locations. For example, many hostile mobs in the Overworld spawn only in complete darkness.

Hostile and neutral mobs have set *damage points*—the amount of health points they'll take away from a player or other mob. The amount of damage usually depends on your difficulty level; on Hard difficulty, mobs will cause more damage than on Easy and Normal. Damage can be from melee or ranged attacks, or from a special effect they can inflict on you, like Poison or Slowness. If you're playing on Easy or Hard difficulties, the attack will be weaker or stronger. In general, smaller mobs inflict less damage than bigger, fierce-looking mobs.

Neutral Mobs

If a mob doesn't always attack on sight, but will under specific circumstances, it's called a neutral mob.

Neutral Mobs: Spawn, Food, and Drops

NEUTRAL MOBS	SPAWN	FOOD	DROPS
Bee	Plains and forests, in bee nests	Flowers	None
Cave spider	Cave spider spawners in abandoned mineshafts	None	String
Dolphin	Oceans, lukewarm Oceans, warm oceans	Raw cod and salmon	Raw cod

(Continued on next page)

NEUTRAL MOBS	SPAWN	FOOD	DROPS
Enderman	Overworld, Nether, and End	None	Ender pearls
Fox	Giant tree taiga, snowy taiga, taiga	Glow berries; sweet berries	Items they're holding or spawned with
Goat	Snowy slopes, jagged peaks, frozen peaks	Wheat	None
Iron golem	Villages; player crafting	None	Iron ingots, poppies
Llama	Windswept hill, gravelly hills, and forests and savanna biomes	Wheat (healing and growth) Hay bales (healing, growth, and breeding—tamed llamas only)	Leather
Panda	Bamboo jungles and jungles	Bamboo	Bamboo
Piglin	Nether, in crimson forests and nether wastes; bastion remnants	None	Armor or weapons they've picked up or are wearing (occasionally)
Polar bear	Snowy plains, ice spikes, and frozen oceans	None	Raw cod, raw salmon
Spider	Overworld at low light levels; spider spawner dungeons; woodlands mansions	None	String, spider eyes
Wolf	Forest, sparse jungle, grove, savanna plateaus, wooded badlands, and and taiga biomes	Most meat foods including rotten flesh; bones are used only for taming	None
Zombified piglin	Nether: crimson forests and nether wastes	None	Rotten flesh, gold nuggets, rarely gold ingots, and occasionally weapons and armor.

BEE

Minecraft's bees are relatively enormous—roughly equivalent to the size of your head. They spawn in trios with a nest on an oak or birch tree in plains and forests. During the day, they'll collect pollen from flowers and bushes, and then pollinate nearby berry bushes and crops (causing the plants to grow to the next stage). After pollination, bees fly back to their nest to make honey.

Bees will ignore you so long as you do not attack them, steal their honey or honeycomb, or break their nest or hive. Doing any of these will anger all nearby bees, which will try to attack you. If you get stung by a bee, you'll be poisoned, and the bee will die within a minute or so. If you want to collect their honey (use a glass bottle) and honeycomb (use shears), you must place a campfire below their hive and wait until enough honey has been made (five bee visits). You can use a pickaxe enchanted with Silk Touch to collect a natural nest with its bees intact; you can also craft a beehive to house new bees.

CAVE SPIDER

Theoretically, the cave spider is neutral at higher light levels, but in practice, it's always out to poison you. They spawn from metallic cave spider spawner blocks hidden behind walls of cobwebs in abandoned mineshafts. Be warned: Cave spiders are smaller than a block, so they can fit through one-block holes.

DOLPHIN

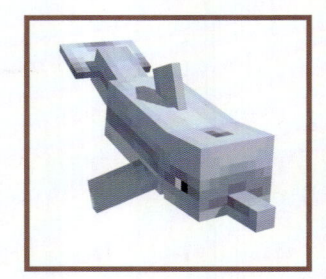

Dolphins spawn in small pods in any of the warmer ocean biomes. They'll play with you by nosing or tossing items you've dropped into the water and will chase you if you're in a boat. If you attack a dolphin, it and other nearby dolphins will attack back. You can't breed or tame dolphins, but you can build trust by feeding them raw cod or salmon; a fed dolphin might lead you to a treasure chest! If you swim near a dolphin, it will give you the Dolphin's Grace status effect (fast swimming) for five seconds repeatedly, so long as you are next to it. You can cover an amazing amount of ocean swimming with the dolphins but be sure to have a boat handy for when the dolphin loses interest.

ENDERMAN

Endermen spawn in the Overworld, Nether, and the End. They won't bother you unless you look at (or your cursor crosses) their body or head. If you do this, they'll shriek and run or teleport to you and attack. They're three blocks tall, so you can run into a two-block-high space to safely attack them or try to trap them in a boat. Endermen hate water and will teleport away from it. They can also randomly pick up and put down natural blocks like clay, dirt, grass, or melons.

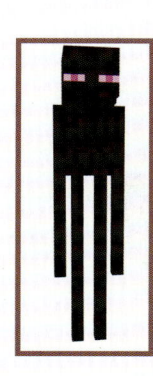

FOX

Foxes are immensely cute, though they'll attack rabbits, chicken, baby turtles, and fish—even pouncing over fences to get them. They're attracted to villages and will wander them at night looking for chickens. Foxes are one of the few mobs that sleep; they're nocturnal, so they typically sleep during the day. Foxes run pretty fast and will flee from you unless you sneak up to them. They're considered neutral because they will attack mobs that attack you.

While you can breed wild foxes, you can't tame them. However, a baby that you've bred will *trust* you, meaning it won't flee from you (unless it's following a parent) and it will attack your attackers. A fox has a chance of spawning with an item in its mouth (like leather, an egg, and very rarely an emerald), and can pick up dropped items in its mouth. If they find an edible item, they'll eat it when hungry. Foxes born in a snowy biome have white fur.

NOTE:
IF A FOX PICKS UP AN ITEM YOU WANT, THROW FOOD AT IT, LIKE SWEET BERRIES. IT WILL PICK THE FOOD UP AND DROP THE ITEM.

GOAT

You'll find goats in the mountainous jagged peaks, frozen peaks, and snowy slopes biomes. They can jump up to ten blocks high and can be milked like cows—their milk can also cure any status effects. If you stand still for at least thirty seconds, a nearby goat may ram you and catapult you off the mountain. Some goats spawn as screaming goats. You'll know it when you hear them. Goats can drop one or both of their horns when they ram into a solid block. If you use a goat horn, it will emit one of eight goat horn sounds.

IRON GOLEM

The iron golem spawns in villages and will protect villagers by attacking incoming hostile mobs. They sometimes offer poppies to villagers. As they battle hostile mobs and lose health, their iron exterior becomes more and more fractured. You can heal them by right-clicking an iron ingot on them. If you harm a villager or the golem itself, it will turn its wrath on you. If for any reason you need to kill an iron golem, punch them, quickly run away a short distance, pillar up three blocks, and use your sword to defeat them.

> **Challenge: Build an Iron Golem to Protect Your Base**
>
> If you create your own iron golem, they won't attack you but will attack any hostile mobs that enter your base. To craft an iron golem, stack four iron blocks in a T-shape and place a carved pumpkin or Jack o' Lantern on top. Note that this happens in your world, not through a crafting table or grid. When you're building your golem, make sure there aren't any blocks or grass beneath its arms. Remember to repair your golem with iron ingots if you notice cracks in its exterior. You can use a lead on an iron golem to keep it from wandering, although leads do occasionally break.

LLAMA

Llamas spawn in windswept hills and savannas and will attack (by spitting) any mob or player that attacks them, as well as wolves and pillagers. Llamas can't be ridden, though you can tame them by jumping on their backs, as you do with horses. While you can't put a saddle on them, you can give tamed llamas a chest to store items and a dyed rug (carpet) for their backs. To equip a chest, right-click a chest on the llama. To give it a rug, mount it and press E to open its interface, then add a carpet to the left slot. Chest storage slots are on the right (between three and fifteen) and show up after you've added the chest on the right. Note that you can't take a chest from a llama without killing it. You can also attach a lead to a llama to have it follow you. Leading one llama will cause other nearby llamas to follow, so you can create a caravan transporting several chests of goodies via llamas.

> **Challenge: Ten Llamas Moving Company**
> Llamas spawn with three, six, nine, twelve, or fifteen inventory slots. When you breed them, their baby has a chance of having more slots than the strongest parent. Breed a company of llamas with fifteen slots each to help carry your loot when you move. Try to start with llamas with larger inventories, as this will make the breeding process much easier. (You'll have to tame them and then equip them with a chest to evaluate them.) You can also use multiple hay bales (fourteen or so) on offspring to quickly mature them into adults ready to breed.

PANDA

Pandas will only attack you if you hurt them; otherwise, they're content to eat bamboo and amble about. Pandas are the only mob whose traits vary: they can be normal, aggressive (they'll attack a predator more than once), lazy (they're slower), playful (they somersault and jump), weak (they sneeze more), and worried (they avoid players and mobs and shiver in thunderstorms). Some pandas are brown rather than black and white. Pandas can only breed if there are eight or more bamboo blocks nearby.

PIGLIN

The piglin is a Nether humanoid mob with piglike features. They often spawn with a crossbow or sword and will attack you unless you're wearing a piece of gold armor. They'll also attack you if they see you breaking any type of gold-related block, like Nether gold ore, or opening any type of chest.

Piglins are serious about their gold. So much so that you can barter with them by throwing them gold ingots. They'll inspect the ingot and throw you back an item or two in return, primarily Nether or Nether-mob related items and blocks, like obsidian, Ender pearls, and potions of Fire Resistance. A variant of the piglin is the zombified piglins—piglins that turned into zombies at some point in the past. Like zombies and skeletons, they can pick up dropped armor and weapons. They spawn in the Nether holding a gold sword, but unlike piglins, they're not obsessed with gold and will only attack you if you attack them. If you do, they'll join forces with other nearby zombified piglins to attack you together. If a regular piglin enters the Overworld or the End dimensions, it transforms into the zombie version.

POLAR BEAR

You'll find polar bears in the snowy biomes and frozen oceans. They often have a passive cub with them. If you get close to their cub or attack them, they'll attack you. Both adults and cubs will attack nearby foxes.

SPIDER

Although spiders are one of the most common enemies, they're actually passive during the day (at light levels of 12 or more). Be wary of them, though, as they can see through blocks, climb walls, and make a jumping attack. When battling, back away from them or get in a higher position to prevent them from jumping on you. If you play on Hard difficulty, spiders can spawn with status effects (see Chapter 15) like Speed, Strength, or Invisibility (you'll see only their red eyes). You'll occasionally find spider spawners in underground dungeons.

WOLF

Wolves live in forests—especially taiga—and will attack nearby sheep, foxes, rabbits, skeletons, and baby turtles. They'll attack you only if you attack them and will bring other nearby wolves into the melee. You can tame wolves by feeding them bones; a tamed wolf will follow you forever, much like a cat. Once tamed, the wolf will wear a collar you can dye. They'll continue attacking skeletons on sight, but not other prey, and they'll attack anyone that harms you. Right-click your tamed wolf to make it sit or stand. You can judge the health of your wolf by the angle of its tail; if upright, it's at full health. To heal your tamed wolf, feed it raw or cooked meats as well as rotten flesh. You can also equip it with wolf armor crafted from six armadillo scutes. There are 9 color variants of wolves: ashen, black, chestnut, pale, rusty, snowy, spotted, striped, and woods, that you can find in different biomes.

Hostile Mobs

Hostile mobs are always ready to attack; if you're within sixteen blocks of them and they see you, they'll come after you. Most will stop attacking you if you get out of their line of sight. These mobs almost always spawn in low-light areas, like dark forests, caves, unlit mineshafts, and at night.

> **NOTE:**
> NAMING HOSTILE MOBS WITH A NAME TAG WILL STOP THEM FROM DESPAWNING. YOU MIGHT WANT TO DO THIS IF YOU'RE CREATING A FARM OR CONTRAPTION THAT NEEDS A HOSTILE MOB TO WORK, OR IF YOU WANTED TO MAKE A HOSTILE MOB ZOO. OR MAYBE YOU JUST FEEL ATTACHED TO LIL BILL THE BABY ZOMBIE AND WANT TO KEEP HIM IN A CAGE IN YOUR KITCHEN. YOU DO YOU!

Hostile Mobs: Spawn and Drops

HOSTILE MOB	SPAWN	DROPS
Blaze	Nether fortresses; blaze spawner platforms	Blaze rods
Creeper	Overworld in low light	Gunpowder
Drowned	Oceans and rivers in low light	Rotten flesh, copper ingots, tridents, nautilus shells
Elder guardian	Ocean Monument top room and wings.	Prismarine shards, wet sponges, raw cod, or other fish.
Endermite	With thrown Ender pearl	None
Ender dragon	The End	Dragon Egg
Evoker	At thrown Ender pearls	None
Ghast	The Nether: in basalt deltas, soul sand valley, and Nether wastes	Ghast tears, gunpowder
Guardian	Ocean monuments	Prismarine shards, prismarine crystals, raw cod, or other fish
Hoglin	Nether, in crimson forests and some bastions	Leather, porkchops

(Continued on next page)

HOSTILE MOB	SPAWN	DROPS
Husk	Desert biomes in low light	Rotten flesh, iron ingots, carrots, potatoes; held weapons and worn armor
Magma cube	Nether: basalt deltas, nether wastes, Nether fortresses; magma cube spawners in bastions	magma cream
Phantom	Overworld, aboveground, at night when a player hasn't slept in three days or more.	Phantom membranes
Piglin Brute	Bastion remnants	Golden axe, occasionally
Pillager	Overworld as patrols, Pillager raids, and at Pillager outposts	Crossbows, arrows, banner (when captain is killed)
Ravager	In Pillager raids on villages	Saddle
Shulker	The End, in End cities	Shulker shells
Silverfish	Infested stone and stone variant blocks in mountain biomes, igloo cellars, and woodland mansions; silverfish spawner in stronghold end portal rooms.	None
Skeleton	Overworld at low light; skeleton spawner dungeons; in the Nether in soul sand valleys and Nether fortresses	Bones, arrows, bows; worn armor
Slime	Overworld in low light aboveground in swamps; below level 40 in swamp chunks	Slimeballs
Stray	Snowy plains, ice spikes, frozen oceans and rivers	Bones, arrows, arrows of Slowness
Vex	Spawned by evokers	None
Vindicator	Woodlands mansions; Pillager patrol and raids	Emeralds, iron axe, banner (when captain is killed).
Warden	Spawned one at a time by sculk shriekers in deep dark biomes.	None
Witch	Overworld at low light levels, swamp huts	Sticks, sugar, spider eyes, redstone, gunpowder, glowstone dust, glass bottles; when killed while drinking, a chance of dropping a potion of Healing, Fire Resistance, Swiftness, or Water Breathing
The Wither	Spawned by player	One Nether star
Wither Skeleton	Nether fortresses	Bones, coal, wither skeleton skulls, stone swords

HOSTILE MOB	SPAWN	DROPS
Zoglin	When a hoglin enters the Overworld or End dimension	Rotten flesh
Zombie	Overworld in low light; zombie spawner dungeons	Rotten flesh, iron ingots, potatoes, carrots; worn armor and held equipment
Zombie Villager	As part or regular zombie spawns, when a zombie kills a villager	Rotten flesh, iron ingots, potatoes, carrots; worn armor and held equipment.

BLAZE

Blazes are floating Nether mobs that shoot fireballs at you from up to forty-eight blocks away. If you attack it, other nearby blazes will attack you. While they'll spawn randomly in and around Nether fortresses, most fortresses also include platforms holding blaze spawners. Blazes drop the blaze rod, which you need for crafting brewing stands, potions, Eyes of Ender, fire charges, and magma cream.

BREEZE

Breezes are similar to blazes in terms of their size and shape. They're found only in underground trial chambers and spawn when you approach a breeze trial spawner. The breeze fires wind charges at you, knocking you back. A wind-like creature, it will repel any ranged attacks (sending back arrows and other projectiles) and can leap quickly around the chamber. It will drop breeze rods when killed, which you can use to create the mace weapon and wind charges.

CREEPER

The iconic creeper spawns in the Overworld and will sneak up behind a nearby player. Once it's within a few blocks of you, it will hiss, inflate, and explode, leaving a small crater of destruction. Their explosion can kill you if you're unprotected, so if you hear their hiss, hold a shield up as you face them. Creepers will stop their explosion process if you step out of their line of sight. They're afraid of cats and ocelots and will rush away from them. If a lightning bolt strikes a creeper, it transforms into a charged creeper with a doubly deadly explosion. To fight a creeper up close, sprint to it, strike with your sword, and back away quickly until it stops sizzling. Repeat until it's dead. You can also strike and then hide behind a wall or solid barrier to break its line of sight to you, then step out again to strike once it is calm.

> ### Challenge: Record Collector
> To get most of the game's music discs, you're going to have to get a skeleton to kill quite a few creepers. Set up a record farm to make this a bit easier—a space where you can lure a skeleton and a creeper into cells that are positioned so that you can aggravate the skeleton, but its arrows will hit the creeper in between you. You'll need three pits or cells in a row, separated by wall blocks or fences. The skeleton goes in the first cell, the creeper in the second, and you in the third (to taunt the skeleton into shooting your way). Make sure you can stay at least 3 blocks away from the creeper in the middle cell to keep it from exploding. To get the mobs in place, you can use trapdoors along the wall of the cell. Mobs will see these as walkable blocks, even when they are vertical. They will walk into the trapdoor space as they follow you and drop into their cell. Use a name tag to name the skeleton so you can reuse it; and you will want a block above the skeleton's pit to make sure it doesn't burn in the sun. Once the creeper dies, you'll want a way to stay safe from the skeleton, retrieve the disc, and get out of the pit.

ELDER GUARDIAN

The elder guardian is a larger, deadlier relative of the guardian mob that scans the area around the ocean monument to find players within a fifty-block radius. Only three elders spawn in the upper levels of each ocean monument. Like guardians, elders attack by shooting lasers out from their eye or jabbing you with their spikes. They can also inflict you with Mining Fatigue for five minutes, which makes it near impossible to use a pickaxe; when this happens, you'll see its ghostlike apparition overtake your screen in one of Minecraft's few jump scares.

ENDERMITE

Endermites spawn randomly when a player throws an Ender pearl to teleport. This tiny mob may appear at the end destination and will attack any nearby players. Endermen will attack endermites on sight.

ENDER DRAGON

The Ender dragon is a boss mob that lives in the End realm. There is only one of its kind. See Chapter 16 for more on the End and the Ender dragon.

GHAST

The ghast is one of the largest mobs. It can only be found in the Nether and has the ability to shoot fireballs at a distance; you're in danger if you're within sixty-four blocks and in their line of sight. You can use your empty hand or a weapon or tool to return volley; if you hit the ghast back, you'll earn the coveted accomplishment *Return to Sender*. If you're being attacked by a ghast, move perpendicular (sideways) to its fireball trajectory and hide. They'll lose interest if they can't see you.

GUARDIAN

Guardians are aquatic mobs that spawn in and around ocean monuments. They have lasers that shoot from their eyes, and spikes that emerge to attack you.

HOGLIN

Hoglins are large, boar-like creatures that spawn in the Nether, attacking and ramming players within a thirty-two-block radius. Even baby hoglins are hostile, though they deal less damage than adults. If you attack one hoglin, all nearby hoglins will join in the attack against you. Hoglins will avoid warped fungi, respawn anchors, and Nether portals. If one is chasing you, pillar up four blocks and attack them from above. Unlike most hostile mobs, hoglins can be bred with crimson fungi, although you'll have to be very careful luring them into a pen. A variant of the hoglin is the zoglin, which is created when a hoglin enters the Overworld or the End dimension. This undead hog will attack and ram players, armor stands, and any mobs except for creepers, ghasts, and other zoglins. They can't be bred, and baby zoglins won't mature into adults.

ILLAGERS

Illagers are gray-faced hostile mobs that look similar to villagers. There's the cross-bow-armed pillager that attacks players, villagers, iron golems, and wandering traders. You'll find them walking in small patrols, guarding their outpost buildings, and attacking villages in raids if the village has been visited by a player with Bad Omen status. For more information on pillagers, see Chapter 12. Vindicators are illagers that often wield iron axes. You'll find them in woodland mansions, as well as pillager patrols and raids. They're hostile to players, villagers, wandering traders, and iron golems. They can move fairly fast and open doors. If you use a name tag to name a vindicator *Johnny*, it will become hostile to every mob except its own illager ilk and will aggravate most hostile and neutral mobs. The evoker is an illager also found in woodland mansions and pillager raids. They raise their arms to cast a fang attack—a zipper-like string of fangs that rise from the ground and snap at you. They can also call upon the vex mob to attack you. Evokers may cast a spell on any nearby sheep with blue wool that changes their wool to red.

MAGMA CUBE

A slime-like Nether mob, the magma cube comes in big, medium, and small sizes and will bounce around you relentlessly. Killing a large magma cube will spawn several medium magma cubes; killing a medium will spawn several of the smallest magma cubes.

PHANTOM

The phantom is an undead Overworld mob that spawns only when you haven't slept for three days. Typically, a group of phantoms will appear at night or in a thunderstorm about twenty blocks overhead. You'll likely notice their breathy screeches first as they swoop toward you. When daylight hits, they'll burn alongside their zombie and skeleton compatriots.

PIGLIN BRUTE

The piglin brute is a deadlier variant of the piglin; it only spawns in Nether bastion remnants. They won't barter with you, don't care about gold, and will always attack. Their high health and attack points make them especially tough to kill. Brutes will also attack Wither and wither skeletons and any mob attacking their fellow piglins.

RAVAGER

The Ravager is a humongous, tusked, boar-like creature that spawns only in pillager raids. They'll ram and attack players, villagers, wandering traders, and iron golems. They can also trample and destroy vegetation like leaves, melons, and bamboo. They're sometimes ridden into battle by a pillager or evoker. You can kill them pretty easily by digging a four-block hole in the ground and attacking them as they stand over you.

SHULKER

Shulkers are purple box-shelled creatures that spawn on End City structures in the End dimension. When you approach them, their shells open to reveal a haggard-looking face, and they'll begin shooting bullets at you. When a bullet hits you, you'll be inflicted with Levitation effect; this causes you to slowly float upward until the effect stops, at which point you'll plummet back down. Shulkers can teleport a short distance away when you attack them; when killed, they may drop a shulker shell, which can be crafted into a portable chest called a shulker box.

SILVERFISH

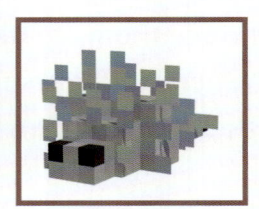

Silverfish are a tiny mob that dwell, like an infestation, inside stone blocks in mountain biomes, Woodlands Mansions, igloo cellars, and strongholds. In the End portal room, each stronghold holds a single silverfish spawner. When you break the infested block, they'll emerge to attack you. Infested blocks break quicker than regular blocks. If you use a pickaxe enchanted with Silk Touch, the infested stone block will simply drop a regular stone block and will not spawn a silverfish.

Silverfish can infest stone, stone brick blocks and variants, cobblestone, and deepslate. If you attack one, it will call other silverfish in nearby blocks to attack you en masse. Killing them in one shot with a strong sword or indirectly (with lava, for example) will prevent a recurring surge of silverfish.

SKELETON

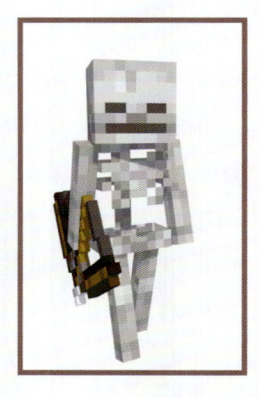

Skeletons are fierce, accurate bowmen; they're difficult to defeat unless you protect yourself with a shield. With your shield raised, you should wait until the skeleton hits the shield with an arrow, and then strike at it. Like zombies, skeletons will burn in direct sunlight; you'll see them rushing to shaded areas during sunrise. A skeleton can spawn riding a spider; this unnerving combo is called a spider jockey. During thunderstorms, there's a rare chance that a skeleton horse, called a skeleton trap horse, will spawn. If you approach the skeleton horse, a lightning strike will transform it into four armed skeletons riding skeleton horses. Run! Skeleton variants include the bogged, which shoot poison arrows and spawn in swamps and trial chambers, and the stray, which shoots slowness arrows and spawns in snowy biomes.

SLIME

Slimes, like magma cubes, will bounce on you to inflict damage; when you kill them, they split into smaller slimes. They spawn in very specific circumstances: Aboveground in swamps at night, or below level y=40 in predetermined areas called slime chunks.

SLIME CHUNKS

In addition to being divided into blocks of space, the Minecraft world is also divided into chunks. Each chunk is a 16x16-block portion that stretches from the top to the bottom of the world. It's the basis for a lot of beneath-the-hood programming and memory management of the infinite landscape. One particular attribute of chunks is whether a chunk will spawn slimes or not. The slime mob can only spawn underground in predetermined (according to the world's programmed generation) chunks called slime chunks. You can see the chunk borders in your world by pressing **F3**+**G**.

Challenge: Spawn Slimes!

The slimeballs dropped by slimes are used in crafting, enchanting, and redstone contraptions. It's a good idea to begin collecting slimeballs sooner rather than later, especially if you want to use leads on animals and other mobs.

You can find your world's slime chunks using online slime chunk finders, such as http://chunkbase.com, where you can type in your world seed to get a map of your slime chunks. To find your world seed, press **T** to open chat and type **/seed**. The seed will be shown in chat, and you can click it to copy it to your clipboard.

Once you have your map, locate the coordinates of a 16x16 chunk near you. If you can find two chunks side by side, that's even better—there will be double the space for slimes to spawn! You can use the debug screen (F3) to track coordinates. To see where chunks start and end in your world, press **F3**+**G**.

Slimes only spawn below y = 40 (at any light level) in slime chunks, so you'll need to dig down and excavate a spawning chamber the width and length of the chunk(s) and at least three blocks high. Light up the chamber to stop other mobs from spawning with Jack o' Lanterns or other light-emitting blocks. *Don't* use torches, as these take up spawning spaces.

For slimes to spawn, you'll need to be at least twenty-four blocks away. You can dig a simple corridor twenty-four blocks long where you can retreat to or excavate a larger waiting area. Be patient: you'll have to wait a while, as slimes don't spawn as frequently as zombies and skeletons.

VEX

Vexes are tiny flying mobs who can fly through solid blocks and carry swords that inflict major damage. They can only be summoned by evokers. Vexes attack players, villagers, wandering traders, and iron golems.

WARDEN

Wardens are the terrifying, blind denizens of the deep dark, spawned nearby a sculk shrieker only when the sculk shrieker is activated four times. A shrieker is activated by a player walking over it or by a player walking within eight blocks of a sculk sensor. The warden will inflict the darkness effect on players within twenty blocks, and hunt players by sensing their vibrations (movements and other actions like eating). Each time a warden senses a player or mob, it will grow ever angrier. After three or four times sensing the intruder, they are angry enough to attack. They can also sense a player just by sniffing if the player is within six blocks horizontally or twenty vertically, even if the player isn't moving. They have massive health and can kill you with one or two attacks.

    The angered warden will roar and chase after the player, trying to swipe at the player with its arms. If it can't reach a player to attack it but the player is still within fifteen blocks horizontally and twenty blocks vertically, the warden will perform a sonic boom attack, a deadly sound that passes through blocks to the player and is unable to be dodged. Once a warden is spawned, the best response is to flee or fly to an exit that you have hopefully clearly marked with lights or special blocks. Watch out though, the warden can fit in spaces just one block wide and three blocks tall and they aren't affected by lava, fire, or Knockback. Wardens don't drop anything special, they aren't affected by shields, and their health is astonishingly high (500 points), so it really is best to just escape them. After sixty seconds of not sensing a player or mob, the warden will cool down and despawn. The only time to attack a warden is when you are twenty blocks higher than it and can use a powerful bow and arrow multiple times against it.

WITCH

Witches spawn singly in a hut in the swamp biome, as well as in darkness and pillager raids. A villager struck by lightning will transform into a witch. Of the common Overworld mobs, the witch is probably the deadliest; it has high health and consumes health potions while battling. Witches will throw debuff potions at you, like Slowness, Poison, Weakness, and Harming. Either have a great sword and attack quickly or run and shoot arrows from a distance.

THE WITHER

The Wither is a very tough endgame boss you spawn with wither skeleton heads. Details about creating and fighting the Wither are covered in Chapter 16.

WITHER SKELETON

The wither skeleton is a Nether mob that spawns exclusively in Nether fortresses. It holds a stone sword and will inflict you with the Withering effect, which temporarily turns your health bar black and lowers your health about half a heart every two seconds. Like other skeletons, some can pick up dropped armor and weapons.

ZOMBIE

Another iconic Minecraft mob, the zombie spawns in the Overworld in darkness and attacks nearby players and turtle eggs. Some may spawn with weapons or armor; if they wear a helmet, they'll be protected from direct sunlight. Zombies sometimes spawn near villages at midnight in large groups (up to sixty, depending on the number of beds and villagers) in a deadly siege.

Some zombies spawn as babies, which can run through one-block spaces to get at you. Because they're so fast, babies can cause a lot of damage quickly. Baby zombies (and baby zombie villagers and baby zombified piglins) have a chance of spawning on chickens—a deadly duo referred to as a chicken jockey. You can slow a baby zombie down by luring it into a body of water, which will give you a little more time to attack it. Zombie variants include the husk, which spawns in deserts and can inflict you with a Hunger effect, and the drowned, which spawn in rivers and oceans and occasionally have a trident to attack you with. There is also the zombie villager, which can be created when a zombie kills a villager. They behave the same as regular zombies, except they can be cured by feeding them a potion of Weakness and then a golden apple. Some zombie villagers spawn as babies, which behave like baby zombies.

Up Next

You've pretty much seen the worst of the Minecraft denizens and what makes them tick: how they can scare you, attack you, and how you can defeat them. In the next chapter, we'll look at the most complex mob of all—villagers—and the unique villages they live in.

12
VILLAGES AND VILLAGERS

Villages are active locations, with occupants bustling to and from work, stopping to gossip, and trading food or goods. Villages and villagers are one of the game's most complex features, with multiple working parts that create a novel environment. Each village is home to a unique, random selection of building types set on varying landscapes, from coasts to mountaintops. In this chapter, we'll look at the various aspects of village life.

Village Features

You can find villages only in specific biomes—desert, meadow, plains, savanna, snowy plains, and taiga—although villages can extend into a nearby biome. The procedural way they are generated can make them look quite different, but ultimately, they all share some similar features, from the types of buildings and occupants to their daily activities.

STRUCTURES

Villages consist of houses with one or more beds and structures associated with the different professions a villager can take, like butcher shops, armorer's huts, and farms. These professional structures can be identified by a *job site block*—a functional block a villager can claim to take on that profession. For example, if a villager claims the barrel in a fisher's hut, they'll become a fisherman and offer fisherman-related trades, such as cooked fish or fishing rods in exchange for emeralds.

THIS PLAINS COASTAL VILLAGE EXTENDS OVER A WIDE RIVER.

Villages also include a central gathering place with a golden bell, paths, lampposts, and miscellaneous structures like animal pens and pumpkin patches. Each village's architecture uses materials found in the biome it's located in.[1] For example, desert village buildings are made from sandstone, savannah villages rely on logs from acacia trees, and taiga villages use spruce logs to build.

A SMALL PLAINS VILLAGE'S GATHERING PLACE.

SIZE

A village must have at least one bed and one villager claiming it. The maximum population depends on the number of beds. If there are three villagers in a village with seven beds, the villagers will breed (so long as other conditions are met) to bring the population to seven.

If you're creating a village, know that it will take a while for villagers to recognize any beds or job site blocks you have placed. The village radius is either thirty-two blocks from the village center or the distance from the center to the furthest bed. Villagers can wander farther than this radius to find new beds and blocks; if they do, the size of the village will be increased. If not, the villager will ultimately return to be inside the village area.

---
1   There's one exception: the meadow village uses the plains village style.

Challenge: Make a New Village

To create a new village, you'll need buildings with beds, a gold bell for the central gathering place, and job site blocks for professions. The hardest part will be getting at least two villagers there so they can mate and grow your population. The easiest way to do this is to move a villager from the nearest coastal village using a boat. You'll need to plan a path to the ocean that goes downslope only (boats can only travel on ground horizontally or down blocks). Then, find a plain, brown-coated (jobless) villager. You can also break a villager's job site block so that they turn into a brown-coated villager. Get the villager into the boat by placing the boat near them and pushing them into it (easier said than done, but this does work). Then get into the boat yourself and travel down your path to the ocean, and then to the coast near to the new village. Get out and break the boat carefully so that you don't harm the villager, and it should hop up to land. Then, you can move the villager across land by placing any job site block to attract the villager, then breaking that block and placing it farther along in the direction you're headed. (Villagers will see job site blocks within forty-eight blocks.) You can also transport villagers using a minecart and rails—see Chapter 13 for more on rails technology.

RESIDENTS

You'll find the same types of residents in each village: villagers, farm animals, and cats. Villages are the only places cats spawn, except for black cats that spawn singly in witch huts. Villagers naturally spawn an iron golem when a village is generated. If a hostile mob enters the village and villagers don't see an iron golem within about thirty seconds, new iron golems will be spawned.

There are four main types of villagers. Professional villagers, who claim a profession like butcher or weaponsmith, wear the robes of their profession and are often seen at their job site. Unemployed villagers wear simpler robes and cannot trade. However, if they find an unclaimed job site block, they will take that profession and change into their new robes. The green-robed villagers, *nitwits*, are unable to get jobs or trade. Finally, baby villagers wear unemployed robes until they mature and take a job.

A random number of unemployed villagers, baby villagers, and nitwits are generated with each village. Unemployed adults immediately look for nearby job site blocks (within forty-eight blocks) and claim the first profession they find. All villagers also look for beds they can claim, which they'll return to every night to sleep.

ROUTINES

Villagers keep similar daily schedules. Upon waking up, they wander the village before the professionals go to work. Baby, unemployed, and nitwit villagers wander instead of working. In the afternoon, villagers gather at the village's gathering place to exchange information (such as good trades) or food, and even breed. After this, villagers explore the town to see if there are new buildings, job site blocks, and beds. At sundown, they go to their beds and sleep, although nitwits stay up a little later. If a villager doesn't have a bed, they'll usually stand inside a house.

MATING

Villagers will mate with each other under specific circumstances. There must be a free, unclaimed bed in the village, and they must be *willing*. To become willing, a villager must have an adequate supply of food in their inventory—this can be twelve beetroot, carrots, or potatoes, or three bread. This food supply is used up when breeding. When breeding, two willing villagers will stand close to each other, hearts will float around them, and a child will appear shortly after. To speed up the population growth of your village, add beds and throw bread at your villagers.

YOUR POPULARITY RANKING

You're assigned a popularity ranking in each village you visit that ranges from −30 to 30. You start at 0, with points added or subtracted as you perform positive or negative actions. Positive actions include trading with villagers, curing a zombie villager, and successfully defending a village from a pillager raid. Negative actions include attacking or killing villagers and iron golems.

A naturally spawned iron golem (as opposed to player-created) will attack you if your rating reaches −15 or if it sees you hitting a villager. As your reputation increases, you'll typically receive better trading prices.

TRADING WITH VILLAGERS

There are five levels of trade that unlock as you continue to trade with a professional villager; these villagers wear a badge that shows their level. Professional villagers begin at the novice level, and graduate to apprentice, then journeyman, expert, and master. At each stage, new trades are unlocked, and the badge they wear upgrades from black (novice) to diamond (master). At first, only the first level of trades is available. Villagers don't commit to their profession until you've traded with them. You can change a villager's profession by breaking their job site block and placing a new one. If you aren't happy with their initial trades, you can replace their job site block to generate new trades. You can do this as many times as you like, but once you trade, the villager's profession is set.

To trade with a villager, right-click that villager to open the trading menu. The left column of the trading menu shows a list of available trades; the items you can trade are on the left and the item the villager will give you in return is on the right. Each villager's trades are related to their profession. For example, the armorer will trade armor and the farmer will buy crops.

To trade, select the deal you want in the left column, and then place the item(s) you are selling for that trade in the left slot(s) of the right column. You can make the same deal multiple times until the villager refuses to trade—when this happens, a red X appears over the trade in the trading menu. The villager can open the trade again twice a day.

> **NOTE:**
> IF YOU HOLD AN EMERALD IN YOUR HAND AND APPROACH A VILLAGER, IT WILL HOLD THE ITEMS IT WILL TRADE IN ITS HANDS, ONE AT A TIME. IF YOU'RE HOLDING SOMETHING THE VILLAGER WOULD BUY FROM YOU, IT'LL HOLD UP EMERALDS. THIS VILLAGER ANIMATION DOESN'T CHANGE ANYTHING ABOUT THEIR TRADES.

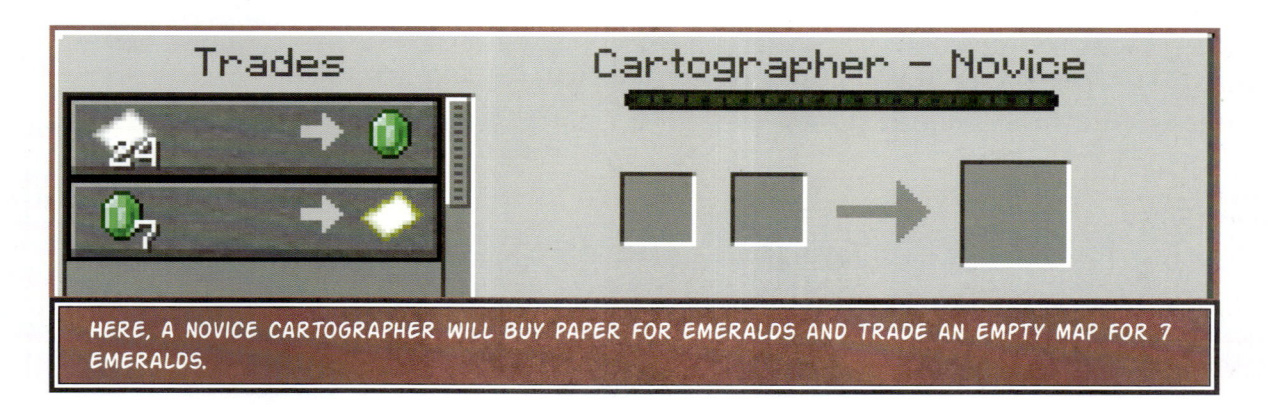

HERE, A NOVICE CARTOGRAPHER WILL BUY PAPER FOR EMERALDS AND TRADE AN EMPTY MAP FOR 7 EMERALDS.

The prices a villager charges depend on demand, the player's reputation, and whether a player has the Hero of the Village status effect. The most significant way to improve your reputation, outside of Hero of the Village, is to cure a local villager that has been zombified. To cure a villager, first capture a zombie, and let it attack a villager in a controlled setting. Then, feed the villager a golden apple and splash it with a splash potion of Weakness, making sure the zombie villager is safe from the sun and from attacking other villagers.

Villager Professions

While villagers wear different robes depending on profession and village style, each profession has some key markers. For example, all librarians wear a hat made of a book. The badge worn by each professional villager shows what level of profession they've reached, from a brown novice badge, to black (apprentice), to gold (journeyman), emerald (expert), and diamond (master). Rarer and higher quality trades are opened at higher villager professional levels.

Let's take a look at each profession, its job site block, and the types of trades you can expect.

ARMORER

The armorer wears a welding mask and uses a blast furnace in the armorer's house. Possible buys (from you, in exchange for emeralds) are coal, iron ingots, lava buckets, and diamonds. Possible sells (to you, in exchange for emeralds) are iron armor, chainmail, enchanted diamond armor, and gold village bells.[2]

The armorer's blast furnace smelts metals twice as fast as a regular furnace. You can craft one from a furnace, five iron ingots, and three smooth stone.

BUTCHER

The butcher wears a red headband and white apron and uses the smoker in the butcher shop. Possible buys are raw meats,

---

[2] Not every professional sells or buys the same items for the same price.

coal, dried kelp blocks, and sweet berries. Possible sells are rabbit stew, cooked chicken, and cooked porkchops.

You can craft the butcher's smoker—which cooks food at twice the speed of a furnace—from a furnace and four logs of any type.

CARTOGRAPHER

The cartographer wears a golden monocle and uses the cartography table in the cartographer's house. Possible buys are paper, glass panes, and compasses. Possible sells are empty maps, ocean explorer, trial chambers, and woodland explorer maps, item frames, banners, and the globe banner pattern.

You can use a cartography table—crafted from four planks and two paper—to clone maps, lock maps, or zoom maps.

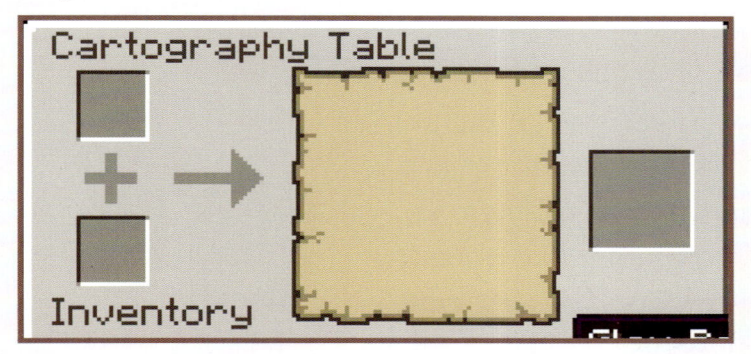

PLACE YOUR MAP IN THE TOP LEFT SLOT. TO CLONE IT, ADD AN EMPTY MAP TO THE BOTTOM SLOT. TO LOCK A MAP (PREVENT IT FROM UPDATING), PLACE A GLASS PANE IN THE BOTTOM SLOT. TO ZOOM A MAP OUT (ENLARGE THE AREA THEY COVER), PLACE A SINGLE PAPER IN THE BOTTOM SLOT. THE RESULTING MAP(S) WILL APPEAR IN THE RIGHTMOST SLOT.

CLERIC

The cleric wears a purple and gold tunic and uses the brewing stand in a temple. Possible buys include rotten flesh, gold ingots, rabbit's foots, scutes, glass bottles, and Nether wart. Sells include redstone dust, lapis lazuli, glowstone, Ender pearls, and bottles o' enchanting.

You can craft a brewing stand from three cobblestone and one blaze rod (from killing a blaze in the Nether). It is used to brew potions (see Chapter 15).

FARMER

The farmer wears a straw hat and uses a composter, located near a farm. Possible buys are beetroot, carrots, potatoes, wheat, pumpkins, and melons. Possible sells are bread, pumpkin pies, apples, cookies, cakes, suspicious stew, golden carrots, and glistering melon slices (a potion ingredient).

The farmer is one of the few villagers that has specific activities to perform. They plant seeds, harvest nearby crops, and put seeds in the composter. The composter—which you can craft with six wood slabs—can take many types of plant and food material, as well as meat and fish. With each item you add to the composter, it slowly fills up. Once the composter is full, it pops out a piece of bone meal and the composter is emptied. The farmer will pick up the bone meal.

FISHERMAN

The fisherman wears a hat and a belt with fish and netting and uses a barrel in the fisher cottage. Possible buys include string, coal, raw fish, and boats. Possible sells are cooked fish, buckets of cod, campfires, and enchanted fishing rods.

The barrel functions as a storage container like a chest, with the same number of inventory slots. You can craft your own from six planks and two wood slabs.

FLETCHER

The fletcher wears a cap and feather and uses a fletching table found in a fletcher house. Possible buys are sticks, gravel, flint, string, feathers, and trip wire hooks. Possible sells include arrows, flint, bows, crossbows, enchanted bows or crossbows, and tipped arrows. Early on, fletchers will typically trade sticks for emeralds.

The fletching table—which you can craft from four planks and two flint—currently has no functionality in the game (other than to turn an unemployed villager into a fletcher), although it is suspected it will in the future.

LEATHERWORKER

The leatherworker wears a leather apron and gloves and works at the cauldron in a tannery. Possible buys are leather, flint, rabbit hide, and scutes. Possible sells are dyed leather armor, dyed leather horse armor, and saddles.

You can craft a cauldron from seven iron ingots. Cauldrons hold water, lava, and powder snow—all of which can be gathered with a bucket. A cauldron can also be filled slowly by rain or snow or dripstone dripping with lava or water. You can use a water-filled cauldron to remove dyes from leather armor or to save yourself if you're on fire.

LIBRARIAN

The librarian wears glasses, a red and gold book hat, and a cream tunic. They use a lectern found in a library. Possible buys include paper, ink sacs, and books and quill. Possible sells are enchanted books, bookshelves, lanterns, glass, clocks, compasses, and name tags.

You can craft a lectern from a bookshelf and three wood slabs. It's used to hold and display a single book and quill, from which multiple players can read at the same time (see Chapter 8 for more on the book and quill).

MASON

The mason wears black coveralls and gloves and uses the stonecutter found in the mason's house. Possible buys are clay balls, stone, granite, andesite, diorite, and Nether quartz. Possible sells are bricks, chiseled stone bricks, polished granite, andesite or diorite, dripstone blocks, colored and glazed terracotta, and quartz blocks.

A stonecutter is used to craft blocks of stone, stone variants, and copper into shape variants—like slabs, stairs, and chiseled versions—generally at a lower cost than regular crafting. For example, while six stone blocks in the stonecutter create six stairs, this will produce only four stairs on a crafting table. You can craft your own stonecutter using one iron ingot and three stone.

To use a stonecutter, place your stone block in the left slot. The craftable variants appear in the middle section. Select one and retrieve it from the rightmost slot.

SHEPHERD

The shepherd wears a short-brimmed hat and woolly tunic and uses a loom found in the shepherd's house. Possible buys are wool (white, brown, black, or gray) and dyes. Possible sells are any color of wool, carpet, beds, and banners, and paintings.

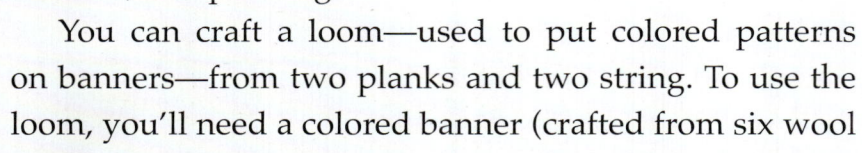

You can craft a loom—used to put colored patterns on banners—from two planks and two string. To use the loom, you'll need a colored banner (crafted from six wool and a stick) and one or more dye. The color of the banner will be the base color that the patterns are imposed on. The loom interface includes a number of standard patterns, but you can find or craft six other unique banner patterns, as listed in the table below.

Unique banner patterns

To create . . .	You'll need . . .
Creeper face	One paper and one creeper's head
Flower	One paper and an oxeye daisy
Skull and crossbones	One paper and a wither skeleton skull
"Thing" (the old Mojang logo)	One paper and an enchanted golden apple
Snout	To find in chests in bastion remnants in the Nether
Globe	To purchase from a cartographer

In the loom interface, place your banner and dye in the top left slots. In the central area, choose a pattern, scrolling down for more selections. If you want to use one of the unique banners, place it in the bottom slot on the left.

VILLAGES AND VILLAGERS

Once you've chosen a pattern, a preview displays on the right. You can retrieve your patterned banner from the bottom right slot. You can add multiple patterns to the same banner; each new pattern will appear on top of the older ones.

YOU CAN PLACE UNIQUE PATTERNS IN THE BOTTOM LEFT SLOT OR CHOOSE ONE OF OVER THIRTY BUILT-IN PATTERNS.

TOOLSMITH

The toolsmith wears a dark brown leather apron and uses a smithing table in the toolsmith's shop. Possible buys include coal, iron ingots, flint, and diamonds. Possible sells are stone tools, bells, enchanted iron tools, and enchanted diamond tools.

You can craft your own smithing table from four planks and two iron ingots. The smithing table is used to upgrade diamond gear to netherite gear.

To upgrade your gear, place your diamond item in the left slot and a netherite ingot in the next slot. Retrieve your upgraded item from the right slot. Any enchantments and durability levels will be kept.

THE SMITHING TABLE INTERFACE. THE SMITHING TABLE IS THE ONLY WAY TO CREATE NETHERITE GEAR, BY UPGRADING DIAMOND EQUIPMENT WITH NETHERITE INGOTS.

WEAPONSMITH

The weaponsmith wears an eyepatch, black gloves, and a dark brown apron. They use the grindstone in the weaponsmith shop. Possible buys are coal, iron ingots, flint, and diamonds. Possible sells are iron axes, enchanted iron axes, golden bells, and enchanted diamond axes and swords.

You can use a grindstone—crafted from two sticks, a stone slab, and two planks—to repair two tools or disenchant a tool.

To repair, place two tools in the left slots and retrieve an unenchanted tool with their combined durability plus 5 percent from the right slot. To disenchant, place a single enchanted tool in a left slot. When you retrieve the unenchanted tool from the right slot, some experience orbs will drop. The grindstone can't remove any curse enchantments. Disenchanting is helpful if you've found or traded for an enchanted item in a loot chest, but you're not happy with its enchantments. You can disenchant the item, enchant it with the enchantments you want, and gain a little XP as you go.

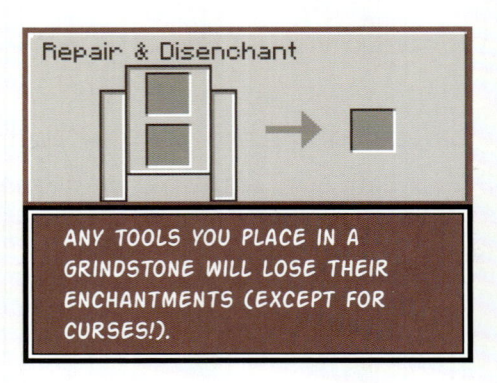

ANY TOOLS YOU PLACE IN A GRINDSTONE WILL LOSE THEIR ENCHANTMENTS (EXCEPT FOR CURSES!).

Challenge: Village Security

Even with an iron golem or two standing guard, villagers are very vulnerable to hostile mobs as well as their own surroundings! And once a village has lost its villagers, you've lost a valuable source of trading. To protect a village, first lock up the villagers so that zombies can't attack them. You can do this by digging a three-block-deep hole, adding a torch to keep the hole lit, pushing a villager into it, and then covering the hole with blocks. Use a distinctive block to cover the hole so you can remember where your villagers are. You can also block the doors of the buildings villagers are in. This is easiest in the evening when the villagers enter their house, though you can bang a gold bell to encourage villagers to go indoors.

Once the villagers are safely in their homes, you should inspect the landscape to remove anything that might hurt villagers. Block entrances to caves and ravines that villagers could fall into (and mobs might come out of) and fence off or fill lava pools. Villagers can accidentally walk into cacti or prickly sweet berry bushes, so remove any you find. Look for water features they could fall into and place a block at water level so they can jump onto land.

After you've villager-proofed the landscape, build a wall or fence around the village—preferably with a stronger material, like stone. Villagers can't open fence gates, so you can place these for your own entrances through the walls. Finally, light up the village so that there are no dark spots.

These security measures will stop zombies, pillagers, and other mobs from infiltrating the village, but *not* zombie sieges.

Villages Under Attack

Villages are almost always under attack while you're visiting or nearby. Any dark cave or overhang is prime territory for spawning the villager's nemesis: the zombie. At nighttime, zombies will approach from all sides. The village golem will dispatch most of these, but a golem is slow and may not catch an attacking zombie in time. If you don't protect your favored villages, it's all too easy for them to fall victim to zombies. Then who are you going to trade with? Because you need two villagers to breed and increase the population of a village, it's a good idea to protect at least two villagers in the towns you pass through.

On top of these already dangerous circumstances, a village is also vulnerable to zombie sieges and to pillager raids. You have little control over zombie sieges, but pillager raids can only be caused by you.

Zombie Sieges

If you're in a village with at least ten beds and twenty villagers, there's a 10 percent chance for a zombie siege to spawn at midnight.[3] In a zombie siege, a large group of zombies—including baby zombies and chicken jockeys—spawns at the edge of a village, regardless of light level. Your best bet here is to first make sure at least two villagers are fully protected behind blocked doors so you can repopulate if needed. You can build other iron golems to help defend the village and use a ranged weapon like a bow and arrow.

Pillager Raids

A pillager raid starts when a player drinks an ominous bottle (from killing one or more pillager captains), which gives them the Bad Omen Effect, and enters a village. If you change your mind about enjoying a pillager raid, drink a bucket of milk before the raid starts, which will be within thirty seconds of entering the village, or wait an hour for the effect to wear off. Pillager raids entail several increasingly hard waves of attackers; you must kill all attackers before the next wave begins. A raid ends successfully when you kill all attackers in each wave or unsuccessfully if the raid kills all villagers.

---

[3] Zombie sieges are exclusive to Java edition.

The attackers and total number of waves depends on the difficulty level and the level of Bad Omen you have. The more pillager captains killed, the higher the Bad Omen level. A raid will have three waves in Easy difficulty, five in Normal, and seven in Hard. At Bad Omen level 2, an additional wave is added, and at higher Bad Omen levels, mobs have increasing chances of having enchanted gear.

When a raid starts, a red bar appears at the top of your screen that represents the overall health of incoming attackers. With each wave, a villager will ring the village's bell, causing the villagers to run inside, and a horn will blow from the direction that the attackers are coming from. The villagers rarely stay put, instead often panicking and running around the village.

In each wave, between four and nineteen attackers will spawn outside or near the village. In early waves, the attackers are pillagers and vindicators; in later waves, witches, ravagers, and evokers join in the fray. At higher difficulties, later waves will include ravagers ridden by evokers and vindicators.

SURVIVING A RAID

If you're experienced at fighting, you can win a raid by shooting arrows from a high, protected position, like a roof, with somewhere you can retreat to regain health. Building a wall can help keep the marauders from getting close, and making extra iron golems can help out a lot. Iron golems are great at offense, but poor at defense—they'll take a lot of damage from arrows. You can heal golems by using iron ingots on them.

> **NOTE:** YOU'LL USUALLY GET DROPS FROM HOSTILE MOBS ONLY WHEN YOU KILL THEM YOURSELF WITH A WEAPON.

If you're less confident with a bow and arrow, you can set traps. For example, you can set out clusters of boats to trap pillagers, which gives you time to attack pillagers individually. You can also create a trench to trap them. Dig a trench that is at least three blocks wide, three blocks deep, and as many blocks long as you can manage. Along each side of the trench, place trapdoors (crafted from six wood planks) and right-click them so they're flush with the wall. Mobs see the opened trapdoors as being solid blocks they can walk on, meaning you can lead attackers toward the pit, where they'll fall in. You can kill them once they are trapped, or you can also put something at the bottom of your trench to kill them, like lava.

Evokers release flying vexes that can fly through solid blocks, so try to kill these first along with any witches, who heal pillagers. Most important, before you initiate a raid, ensure your villagers are protected in their houses with blocked doors. Set your spawn somewhere nearby and protected, with access to weapons and armor, so you can jump back into battle if you're killed.

It's not unusual for attacking pillagers to become trapped somewhere in the landscape, like a cave or pond, or for the last few pillagers to be difficult to find. To find them, ring a gold bell in the village, which will show the outlines of nearby pillagers.

If you successfully finish a raid, villagers will emerge from their houses (once you unblock their doors) and celebrate with fireworks. You'll be given a Hero of the Village status effect, which will make village professionals (once they've exchanged gossip) throw gifts at you. A raid that goes on for more than forty minutes will end automatically. If all villagers are killed, the pillagers win, and they will have a little celebration.

Why start a raid? In addition to free goodies, you'll also get valuable loot from dying pillagers, including saddles from ravagers, plenty of emeralds and crossbows, and totems of undying from evokers. Totems of undying will prevent you from dying *once*, as long as you hold them in your hand or off hand. This is especially helpful if you are playing in hardcore mode, when dying will delete your world, or when you want to avoid the dying/respawning process (which is immensely helpful when you're fighting an Ender Dragon or Wither).

Up Next

Now we've looked at the inner workings of villages, it's time to delve into the engineering side of Minecraft with redstone. You can use this technology to simplify chores or dive in deep to make amazing contraptions.

13
TECHNOLOGY: REDSTONE AND RAILS

While you can play Minecraft without delving into its engineering feature, *redstone*, it can really enhance your gameplay. It's true that redstone contraptions and tinkering can be incredibly complex—one very clever player even built a functioning computer within Minecraft! That said, there are many simple contraptions that can make your daily (in-game) life more efficient and enjoyable.

We'll begin by discussing some basics of redstone and how it works. Then, we'll look at the various redstone-related devices and blocks, building helpful contraptions along the way. Finally, we'll learn how to use redstone-powered rails and minecarts. We'll combine everything we've learned to build an automatic sugar cane farm.

Redstone Basics

At the core of redstone engineering is the redstone ore found underground. When you mine it (below level y=16 and with an iron pick or better), the ore drops redstone dust, which is used both by itself and in crafting other redstone components. Redstone refers not just to the ore and dust, but to the use of redstone components and circuits to create contraptions as well.

Redstone is similar to electricity in that its power runs along a line to power up devices, like doors and note blocks. The devices then react to that power by performing an action, like opening or emitting a musical note. Redstone's signal strength, or power, varies from 0 to 15, with most power sources emitting a level 15 power and most devices activating at any level (1–15)

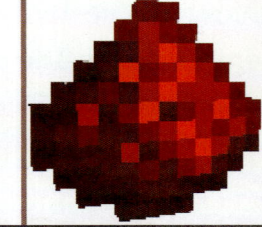

REDSTONE ORE MUST BE MINED WITH AN IRON PICK OR BETTER; IT WILL DROP FOUR TO FIVE REDSTONE DUST. WHEN YOU RIGHT-CLICK A BLOCK OF REDSTONE ORE, IT WILL LIGHT UP AND SPARKLE FOR A FEW MOMENTS.

of power. The most common way to transmit that power is through redstone dust (see "Transmission Components").

Times and delays (such as the length of time a button is pressed, or how quickly a hopper transfers items) often become important in making complicated contraptions. Redstone times are measured in *redstone ticks*, where one redstone tick is 1/10 of a second. These redstone ticks are different from game ticks (used to describe game mechanics) which are 1/20 of a second. However, the contraptions in this chapter don't need that level of focus on timing; where possible, times will be mentioned in regular seconds.

Each redstone contraption has three parts: a source of power, a path that transmits the power, and a device or mechanism that receives that power and reacts to it in some way. To get an idea of how this works, let's walk through an example.

One of the simplest power sources is a lever (see next section for more on levers). If you switch the lever on, the lever begins emitting a redstone signal with full power. To connect this signal to a device it can power, you can place a line of fifteen redstone dust starting at any side of a lever and traveling away from it. With each redstone dust placed, the signal strength decreases by 1. This means the signal decays completely after fifteen blocks. (There are ways to reset the signal power back to full, which we'll look at later in the chapter.) You can place a redstone device at the end of the line of redstone dust to receive that power. For example, you could place a redstone lamp, which only lights up when it is receiving redstone power.

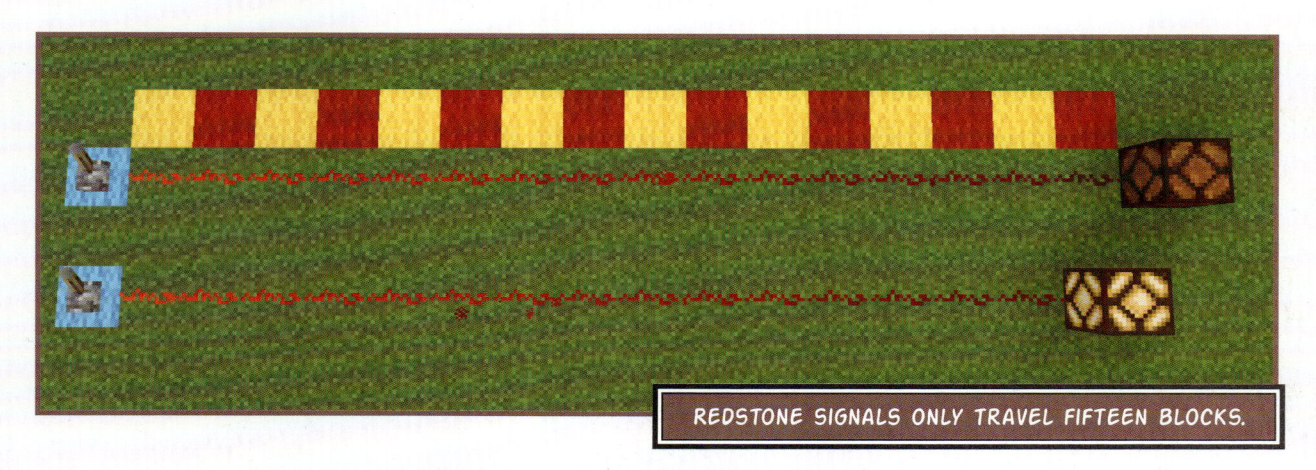

REDSTONE SIGNALS ONLY TRAVEL FIFTEEN BLOCKS.

Redstone power signals only last for fifteen blocks. In the image above, both lines, a lever on the left is switched on, which powers the lines of redstone dust. The redstone dust beneath the first yellow block is level 15, dropping to 14 in the next block (below the first red block). The top redstone line is sixteen blocks long; at the sixteenth block, there is no more power in the redstone to light up the redstone lamp. In the bottom line, the redstone line is fifteen blocks long. At the final block, its power is only 1, but that is enough to power the redstone lamp on.

Power Components

Some redstone power components send a constant redstone signal, while others send only a brief signal. This signal is sent to any adjacent redstone devices or redstone dust, and typically the blocks the power component is attached to. A few components also send power to any solid block *adjacent* to the block they're attached to; these include buttons, levers, and pressure plates. Most power sources produce the highest signal strength, 15.

REDSTONE TORCH

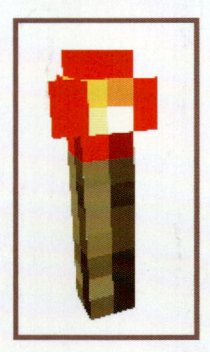

A redstone torch, crafted from one stick and one redstone dust, provides constant power to the block above it and to adjacent redstone dust and devices. It does not power the block it's on; if that block receives power from another source, the torch will turn *off*. Redstone torches are often used in complicated contraptions to *invert* a signal (turn it off if it's on, and vice versa) or to move a signal vertically. For example, when you place torches on every block in a tower, each torch alternately toggles the torch above it on or off. The top torch in the tower can then carry the signal horizontally. This enables a tower of torches to transmit a redstone signal vertically without taking up much horizontal space.

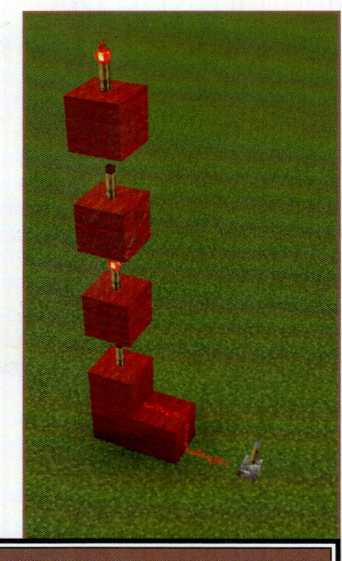

A REDSTONE TORCH TOWER FOR MOVING A SIGNAL VERTICALLY.

In this torch tower, a redstone signal is emitted by the lever at bottom right. (The lever here represents a signal coming from part of a contraption.) The power turns the first, bottom torch off. With the bottom torch off, the second torch remains lit, as it's not receiving any signal. However, the power of the second torch turns the third torch off, and the top torch remains on. Turning the lever at the bottom reverses all of this. Using towers of redstone torches is a common way to move a signal vertically in the least amount of space.

REDSTONE BLOCK

A redstone block is crafted from nine redstone dust. It provides constant power to adjacent devices. These are sometimes used with sticky pistons that push the blocks to turn contraption circuits (like a clock) on and off.

LEVER

A lever, crafted from one stick and one cobblestone, needs to be switched on to provide constant power to the block it is on and any adjacent devices. To switch a lever on, right-click its handle, and right-click it again to turn it off.

BUTTON

Buttons provide only a short burst of power—one second for a stone button and 1.5 seconds for a wood button. Buttons send power to the block they're on as well as adjacent devices. You can craft a stone button from one stone block and a wood button from one wood plank.

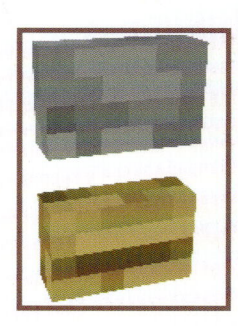

PRESSURE PLATES

Pressure plates provide a short burst of power lasting for the length of time an entity is on the plate. If a plate is just pressed once quickly, its power lasts for one second. Stone pressure plates (crafted from two stone blocks) are activated by entities: mobs, players, or even minecarts with mobs in them. Wood pressure plates (crafted from two wood planks) also activate when items are thrown on them, as well as by arrows and any minecarts.

WEIGHTED PRESSURE PLATES

Weighted pressure plates operate like regular pressure plates but give out a signal strength dependent on the number of mobs or items on them. The light weighted pressure plate (crafted from two gold ingots) sends full signal strength when fifteen mobs (or items) are on it. The heavy weighted pressure plate (crafted from two iron ingots) increases its signal strength by 1 for every ten mobs on it, up to a maximum of 15 for over 140 mobs.

TRIP WIRE HOOK

A trip wire hook device is made from two trip wire hooks placed up to forty blocks apart and connected with string. When someone stands on or walks through the string, both hooks provide full signal strength.

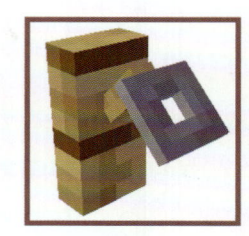

TRAPPED CHEST

A trapped chest is crafted with a trip wire hook and a chest. They provide power level 1 when they're opened, increasing the signal strength by 1 for each player opening the chest at the same time, up to a maximum of 15. You can identify a trapped chest by the red border around its latch. These are typically used for pranks or in PvP (player-versus-player) combat, as a lure. Target players open the chest, which sets off an explosion or other series of events.

DAYLIGHT SENSOR

A daylight sensor provides a signal strength relative to the amount of sunlight it's directly receiving, with a maximum of 15 at full light, that decreases at sunset. You can invert a daylight sensor by right-clicking it to cause its signal to increase the less sunlight there is. You would use a daylight sensor to set off a contraption when it turns day or night; for example, to turn on outside lights at night.

CONTAINERS

Containers are blocks that store items and have inventories. Chests and furnaces are containers, as are hoppers, droppers, dispensers, and brewing stands. Containers provide power only to a comparator device (see the next section), and their signal strength depends on how full they are. A full container will provide 15 power. The fullness of a container takes into account the number of slots and the size of the stacks (most items stack to sixty-four, but some stack only to sixteen, and unique items like swords stack to only one). A chest with twenty-seven swords will read as full, while a chest with twenty-seven wood blocks will be seen as near empty.

SCULK SENSORS

Sculk sensors will emit a redstone signal for two seconds when it senses a vibration within eight blocks of it. The strength of the redstone signal depends on how far away the vibration comes from: the closer the vibration, the stronger the signal. Wool blocks will block the vibrations from reaching the sculk sensor. After hearing a vibration, the sculk will cool down for ten seconds before it can be activated again. Vibrations are caused typically by actions you associate with sounds, like dropping an item, eating, moving, etc.

You can craft a *calibrated sculk sensor* using a sculk sensor and three amethyst shards. The calibrated sculk sensor can detect vibrations within sixteen blocks and respond more quickly with a shorter cooldown.

LIGHTNING ROD

A lightning rod, crafted from three copper ingots, sends a full-strength signal when it is hit by lightning. The rods divert lightning bolts to it during thunderstorms within a 128-spherical-block radius, or when hit by a trident enchanted with Channeling. You'll find that it's pretty common for a lightning rod to be struck during a storm.

The most common power sources used in contraptions are redstone torches, redstone blocks, buttons, and levers.

Challenge: Automatic Iron Door

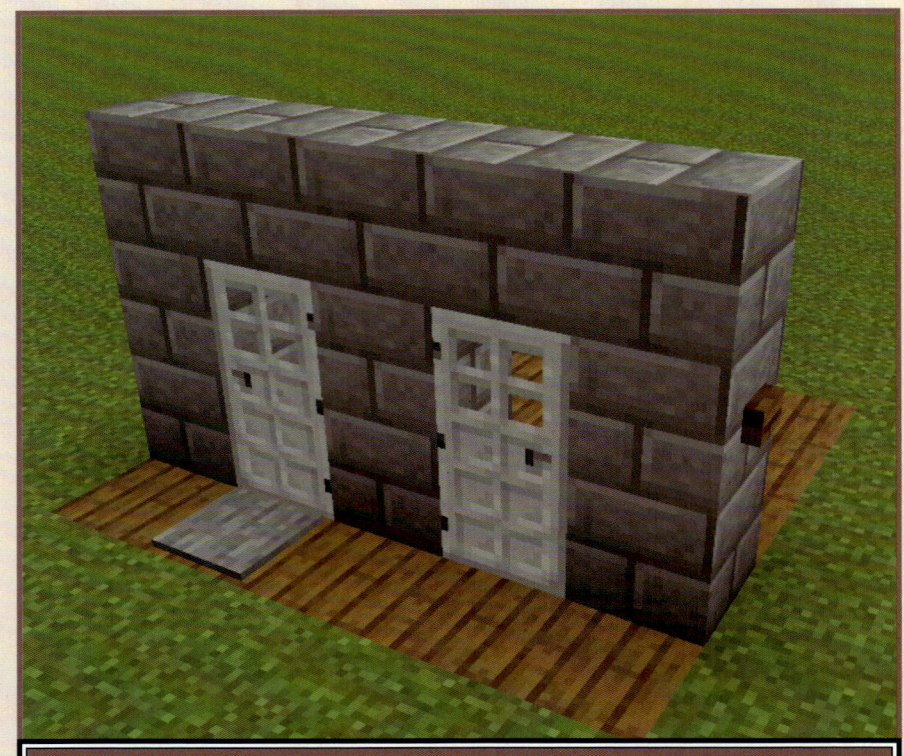

THE IRON DOOR CAN BE ACTIVATED (OR OPENED) BY REDSTONE POWER COMING FROM AN ADJACENT SOURCE (THE PRESSURE PLATE) OR IN THE CASE OF A BUTTON, FROM AN ADJACENT BLOCK THAT IS POWERED BY THE BUTTON.

In this challenge, we'll take a look at how door-opening contraptions work. Iron doors can only be opened with a redstone signal, so we'll practice with two of these. First, craft two iron doors from six iron ingots each, a stone or wood pressure plate, and a stone or wood button. Build a 3x5 wall with spaces to fit the two doors as shown below. Place the doors in these gaps.

In front of one door, place a pressure plate. Note that we don't need to add a line of redstone dust with the pressure plate because it's right in front of the door. Place the button on the side of the block *next to* the second door, as shown. Buttons, and other redstone power components, can power opaque blocks—like the stone bricks used in my example—strongly enough that they will carry a signal through the block.

Now, test out these door-opening contraptions!

Transmission Components

In complicated contraptions, redstone devices often can't be placed right next to a power source, so the power signal needs to be transmitted one or more blocks from the power source to the device. This can be done using transmission components: blocks that affect the redstone power signal that travels between a power source and a redstone device.

REDSTONE DUST

Redstone dust is the mainstay for transmitting redstone signals, though it comes with a couple of quirks. For one, it can't be placed on most transparent or non-solid blocks, like glass or stairs. The line of redstone also must point *directly* at a device in order to power it. You can place lines of redstone dust to have corners and go down blocks. You can gather redstone dust by mining redstone ore with an iron pickaxe. Lines of redstone dust, extended with repeaters, are a typical solution for transmitting a signal over a distance.

REPEATER

Repeaters take a signal heading into their back, reset, and send it out their front at full strength. The signal is delayed one redstone tick (1/10 of a second). You can further delay the output of the signal up to four redstone ticks by right-clicking the sliding button.

Repeaters are used to extend a redstone dust signal. They can also be helpful when you want to make sure a signal is traveling only in one direction or doesn't connect to any nearby redstone dust. A faint arrow etched into the base of the device points to the front, or output side. You can craft a repeater from three stone blocks, two redstone torches, and one redstone dust.

COMPARATOR

A comparator takes a signal coming into their back and compares it to any signal coming from the side. In the default comparison mode, it outputs a signal the strength of the back signal unless the side signal is stronger, in which case it will produce no output signal. The comparator also has a subtract mode, in which it subtracts the greatest side signal from the back signal and outputs the result. To switch modes, right-click the comparator; when the subtract mode is selected, the torch on the front of it will light up. A faint arrow etched into this device points to the front. You can craft a comparator from three stone blocks, three redstone torches, and one Nether quartz crystal.

Simple Comparator Clock

When you're making contraptions, you'll often want to repeat certain actions, like firing a dispenser every second. You can do this with a *comparator clock*, a circuit that produces pulses continually. (There are many designs for clock circuits in Minecraft; this is one of the simplest.)

For this project, you'll need:

- One comparator
- One repeater
- Five redstone dust
- One lever

1. Place a comparator facing away from you and right-click it to activate subtract mode. The redstone torch at its front should light up.

TECHNOLOGY: REDSTONE AND RAILS

2. Place a repeater facing into the side of the comparator.

3. Place four redstone dust to connect the output side of the comparator to the input (back) of the repeater.

4. Place a lever one block away from the back of the comparator. Connect the lever to the back of the comparator with one redstone dust.

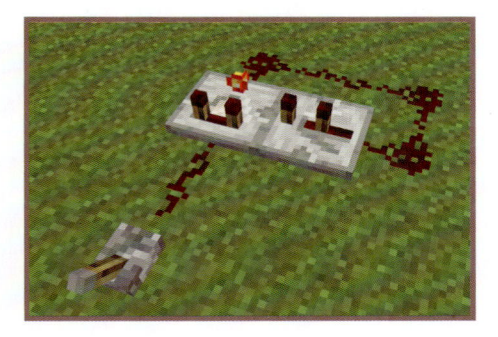

5. To turn on the clock, flip the switch on the lever. Once you turn on the lever, you'll see the line of dust from the comparator to the repeater turning on and off. This pulsing happens because the comparator is in subtract mode. First, the comparator receives the signal from the lever. At this point, there's no signal coming from the side, so the comparator outputs a full signal.

The signal then travels around to the side of the comparator, so now there *is* a signal coming from the side. Subtracting its strength from the lever's signal strength results in *no* signal being output from the comparator and no signal arriving again at the side of the comparator.

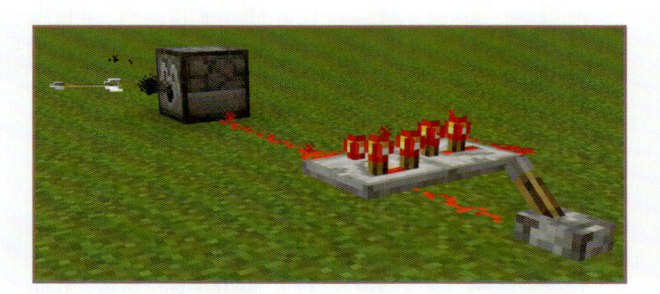

6. From here, you can add a redstone line to whatever device you want activated. This might be a dispenser holding arrows, as shown here (for more on dispensers, see the next section). To make this addition, you'll want five redstone dust, one dispenser, and at least a half-stack of arrows. Place a line of four redstone dust leading away from the clock's line of redstone dust. At the end of this line, add a dispenser and place arrows inside, in any slot. Now, the dispenser holding arrows will fire every two or three redstone ticks, along with the clock's timing.

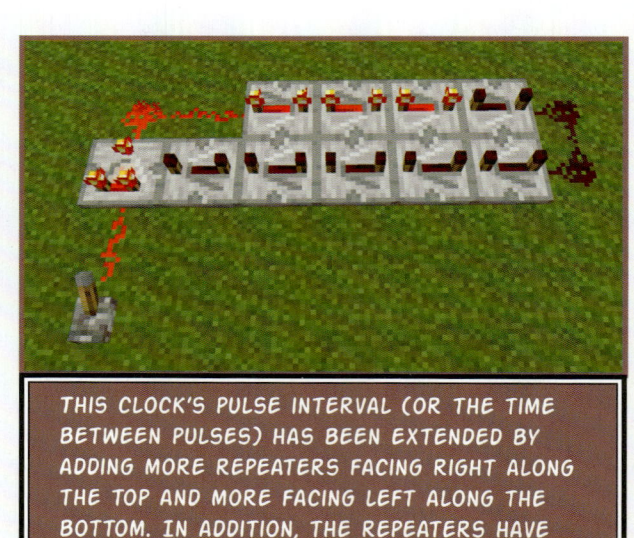

7. If you want to slow down the pulsing of your clock, right-click the repeater up to three times to increase the delay to four ticks. You can also increase the entire redstone dust transmission line from the comparator to the repeater by placing additional redstone dust, repeaters, and repeater delays. To shut off the clock, right-click the lever to turn it off.

THIS CLOCK'S PULSE INTERVAL (OR THE TIME BETWEEN PULSES) HAS BEEN EXTENDED BY ADDING MORE REPEATERS FACING RIGHT ALONG THE TOP AND MORE FACING LEFT ALONG THE BOTTOM. IN ADDITION, THE REPEATERS HAVE BEEN SET TO THEIR MAXIMUM FOUR-TICK DELAY.

You've officially built your very first redstone contraption!

Next, we'll look at the devices that actually do something when given redstone power. These are the blocks that contraptions are made out of; we can use them to strike a musical note, move blocks back and forth, drop and pick up items, and more.

Redstone Devices

Redstone devices are functional blocks that use redstone power to accomplish a task—from opening a door to moving your goods into a chest.

DISPENSER

A dispenser ejects one item at a time when it receives a redstone signal. It can also place some blocks on the block in front of it or activate specific items.

The actions a dispenser can perform, depending on what is in its inventory, include the following:

- Equip armor, shields, and mob heads on a player within one block.
- Place boats in water and minecarts on rails.
- Fire projectiles like arrows.
- Place (and pick up, on a second signal) lava and water.
- Use bone meal on plants, flint and steel to set blocks alight, and shears on sheep.
- Place and activate TNT and fireworks.
- Place shulker boxes.

A dispenser has an inventory with nine slots to place objects in. You can craft a dispenser from an arrow, one redstone dust, and seven cobblestone. To place objects in the dispenser, right-click it to open its inventory and drag in items from your inventory. You can also use a hopper to add things to a dispenser or to a dropper (see the following).

DROPPER

A dropper is similar to a dispenser in that it has a nine-slot inventory and ejects one item at a time when it's powered. However, it doesn't use, place, or activate objects. Instead, it can place items in containers directly in front of it. You can craft a dropper from seven cobblestone and one redstone dust.

HOPPER

Hoppers are used to transfer one item at a time, from one container to another. They have five slots of inventory space to hold items in and can be crafted from a chest and five iron ingots.

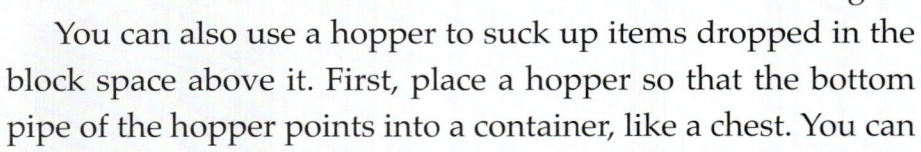

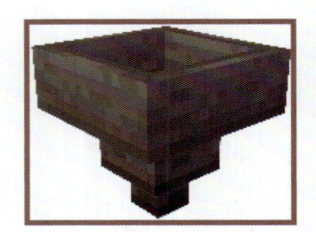

You can also use a hopper to suck up items dropped in the block space above it. First, place a hopper so that the bottom pipe of the hopper points into a container, like a chest. You can place a hopper next to a chest (rather than above it) by shift-right-clicking the chest with the hopper. The output pipe will then point into that chest and deliver items to it. If you send a redstone signal to a hopper, it *stops* transferring items.

PISTONS AND STICKY PISTONS

A piston is a block that can extend its front side (its *head*) out one block with redstone power. This pushes any block in front of its head out one block as well. It can move up to twelve blocks, so long as one block is directly in front of its head. When the piston's head retracts, however, it does not pull any blocks back with it. For that you need a sticky piston, which will pull back the block that its head touched.[4]

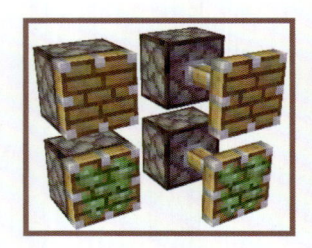

You can craft a piston with three wood planks, four cobblestone, one iron ingot, and one redstone dust. You craft a sticky piston with a piston and one slimeball (see Chapter 11 for more on slimes).

Some blocks—including obsidian, anvils, and functional blocks like droppers, chests, and dispensers—can't be moved by pistons. Blocks like melons, sugar cane, and cacti will drop into their item form when pushed by a piston.

---

[4] The only exception is slime blocks, which connect to each other when placed. The sticky piston can pull back up to twelve slime blocks, rather than just one.

Challenge: Furnace Upgrade

Why wait around to keep filling up and emptying your furnaces when you have a ton of materials to smelt? You can use chests and hoppers to make smelting loads of stuff much easier.

To create a single furnace upgrade, you'll want three hoppers and four chests. Place two chests on the ground to create a double chest. Then, place a hopper on top of the double chest, pointing into it. Place a furnace above this hopper, which will take all the smelted goodies and place them into your double chest.

Add two more hoppers pointing to the furnace, one on top, and one on the side (with shift-right-click). Finally, add a chest above both of these hoppers. The side hopper will bring fuel to the furnace, so fill its chest with coal or charcoal. The top topper will transfer items to be smelted, so in the top chest put all your raw ores or raw meats.

This furnace upgrade will keep your goods cooking so you can do other things!

OBSERVER

An observer is crafted from six cobblestone, two redstone dust, and one Nether quartz crystal. Observers output a pulse when they detect a change in the state of the block directly in front of them. (The front is the side with the face.) On the back of the observer is a small circular outlet, which flashes red when it emits a pulse.

A change in the state of the block might be a melon stem growing from stage 1 to stage 2 or the activation of a dispenser. The observer sees almost all block state changes, such as the activation of a dropper, hopper, or dispenser; the spread of grass; the placing of a block; and the growth of sugar cane and saplings. Exceptions include opening and closing chests (excluding shulker boxes and barrels), inventory changes in containers, activating beacons, and placing item frames.

Challenge: Create Tunes

In this challenge, you'll make a short tune with note blocks. Place three note blocks in a line with three blocks space between them. In these two spaces, place three repeaters each. Right-click the repeaters three times each to give them their full four-tick delay.

Before the first note block, place one redstone dust and one button. The button will be the power source. Next, right-click the first note block seven times (C#) and the second note block three times (A). Leave the final block as is (F#). Now click the button to set off a three-note creepy *duh-duh-duh* sound. If you don't like the notes, right-click the note blocks for new ones, or change the blocks that the note blocks are resting on.

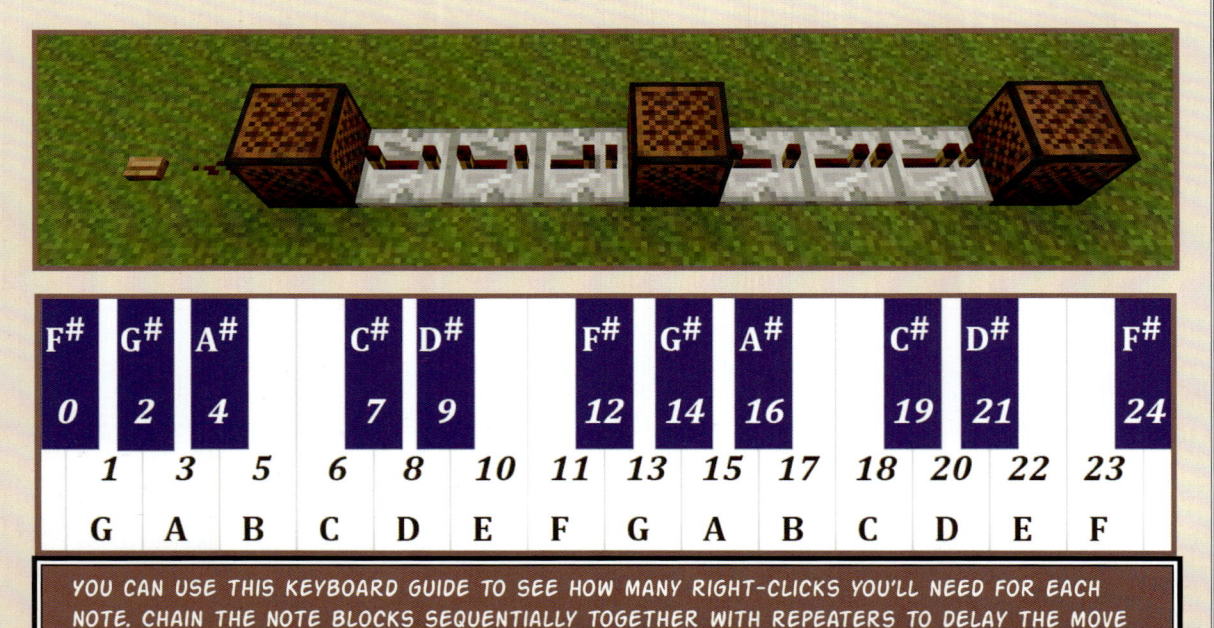

F#	G#	A#		C#	D#		F#	G#	A#		C#	D#		F#
0	2	4		7	9		12	14	16		19	21		24
1	3	5	6	8	10	11	13	15	17	18	20	22	23	
G	A	B	C	D	E	F	G	A	B	C	D	E	F	

YOU CAN USE THIS KEYBOARD GUIDE TO SEE HOW MANY RIGHT-CLICKS YOU'LL NEED FOR EACH NOTE. CHAIN THE NOTE BLOCKS SEQUENTIALLY TOGETHER WITH REPEATERS TO DELAY THE MOVE FROM ONE NOTE TO THE NEXT.

NOTE BLOCK

Note blocks are crafted with one redstone dust and eight planks; once they have a redstone power signal, they play a musical note when you click them.

The note block's initial tone is an F sharp, and right-clicking it will raise its pitch, up to two octaves higher, before returning to

TECHNOLOGY: REDSTONE AND RAILS

the lowest note. The default instrument sound for a note block is the harp (which also sounds like a piano), but you can place blocks beneath it to change the instrument, as shown in Table 14-1. Blocks that will change the sound of the note block include the hay bale (banjo), wool (guitar), wood (string bass), iron block (iron xylophone), pumpkin (didgeridoo), clay (flute), gold block (bells), packed ice (chimes), and the bass drum (most stone variants).

Other Devices

A number of devices can be incorporated into a creative contraption. For example, you can make doors, fence gates, and trapdoors open and close with a redstone signal.

When it's equipped with a book and quill, the librarian villager's lectern can be used as a power component, as it gives a .5 redstone tick signal when a player turns a page. A comparator also can measure approximately how far along in the book the current page is; for example, if the book is opened to page 7 of 15, the signal strength is 7. You might use this feature to set off a contraption only when a player reads a book on the lectern.

A target block is another power source that emits a signal for four redstone ticks when it's hit by a projectile; if that projectile is an arrow or trident, the signal will last for ten redstone ticks. The closer to the bull's-eye, the stronger the signal.

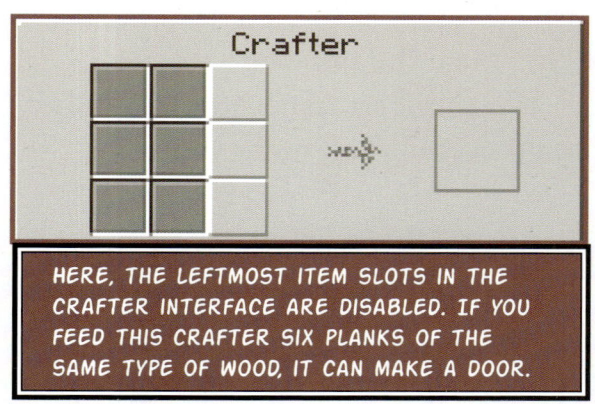

HERE, THE LEFTMOST ITEM SLOTS IN THE CRAFTER INTERFACE ARE DISABLED. IF YOU FEED THIS CRAFTER SIX PLANKS OF THE SAME TYPE OF WOOD, IT CAN MAKE A DOOR.

A copper bulb is a light source that lights up when you give it a redstone signal. You can craft it from three blocks of copper, one blaze rod, and one redstone dust.

A crafter is a type of crafting table you can use for automated crafting. You can feed it nine items through a hopper, dropper, or another crafter, on any side, and this fills its container slots from top left to bottom right, in order. If the items form a recipe, and the crafter is given a redstone signal, the crafted item will be ejected from the front of the crafter, and can be picked up by an adjacent container, even another crafter. For shaped recipes, the items must be in the recipe shape. You can disable slots by clicking them in the crafter UI.

Rails and Minecarts

Rails and minecarts are a subset of redstone; their primary use is to transport players and mobs. Boats—while an easy way to move mobs around—can't travel upward, and are tight quarters for a player and a hostile mob. With minecarts, you can place a mob by themselves in the cart, and then set the rails they travel on to go up and down terrain, as well as underwater.

MINECARTS

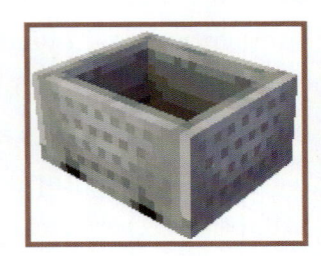

Minecarts, crafted from six iron ingots, can be placed only on a rail and can hold one player or mob. You can force mobs into minecarts by pushing a minecart up against a mob. To get into a minecart yourself, right-click it; to get out, press **Shift**. When you're in a minecart, press **W** to move ahead. We'll learn about rails soon but know that you can add momentum by placing the track on a downward slope so that gravity helps push the minecart.

You can craft minecarts with other functional blocks, which provide numerous functions but can't move mobs.

Hopper Minecart

Crafted from a hopper and a minecart, the hopper minecart will draw in any items that are in the block space above it or from a container in the space above it. Hopper minecarts have the same inventory space as a hopper. To retrieve the stored items, place a hopper below the minecart. You can also right-click the hopper minecart to add items from its inventory and remove them.

Chest Minecart

The chest minecart (crafted from a chest and a minecart) is used to transport items. They interact with hoppers in the same way as regular chests. A hopper placed below the chest minecart (rails can be placed on hoppers) will remove items from a chest, and a hopper pointing down at the chest minecart can add items to it.

TNT Minecart

You can craft the one-use TNT minecart from one TNT and a minecart. It will explode if it passes over a powered activator rail (see next section); if you break it while it's moving; if it's destroyed by lava, fire, explosions, or flaming arrows; or if it falls three blocks or more.

Furnace Minecart

Crafted from a furnace and minecart, furnace minecarts move on their own when fed coal or charcoal. They can pull up to four other minecarts; however, powered rails are more commonly used to move minecarts along a track (see next section).

> **NOTE:**
> THESE HYBRID MINECARTS DROP THEIR TWO SEPARATE PARTS WHEN YOU BREAK THEM. FOR EXAMPLE, IF YOU BREAK A FURNACE MINECART, YOU'LL GET A FURNACE AND A MINECART.

RAILS

You use rails to create the tracks that minecarts travel along. You can craft sixteen rails from six iron ingots and one stick. When you place a rail, it orients forward relative to where you're facing. To change a track's direction, just change the direction you are facing. As you continue to place rails, they'll connect to an adjacent rail.

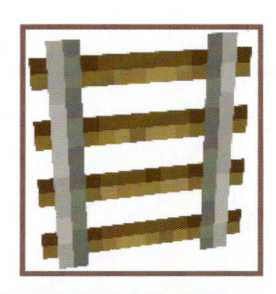

To create a curve to the left or right, place a rail at a 90-degree angle. When you do this, the rail at the intersection changes to a curved rail. Only standard rails can be curved; other rail types, which we'll discuss momentarily, can't curve. You can place rails up 1:1 block slopes, but you can't create curves on a sloping track.

> ANY RAIL TYPE CAN TRAVEL ON A 1:1 SLOPE, BUT ONLY STANDARD RAILS CAN BE USED TO TURN A CORNER.

Challenge: Four-Way Intersection

Rails behave in specific ways at intersections, so let's build a four-way intersection to see how these work.

Place a single track that will be the center of the intersection, and then build four tracks six rails long out from here in each direction. Note that the center track will be curved. (If it isn't, break it and replace it.) Now, we'll add stopping and starting rails at the end of each track. Place a powered rail, add a button next to it, and then place a single block at the end of the track (as shown in the image below).

The central curving rail appears to connect two sections of track. Add a minecart above the powered rail on one of the two "connected" tracks, get in it, and click the button next to you. Your course will follow the curved rail at the center. You can do this again from the other "connected" track.

But what happens if you approach the intersection via one of the "disconnected" tracks? Try this next, from both of the disconnected tracks. Your minecart will wobble a bit in the center but should go straight through, rather than following a curve.

If you design a railroad and have a T-intersection (with three tracks instead of four) that takes minecarts down a track you don't want, you can fix this with a lever. Break one of the four tracks coming to your intersection to make a T-intersection. Next, craft a lever and place it next to the central, curved rail. When you switch the lever on, the curve's direction should change.

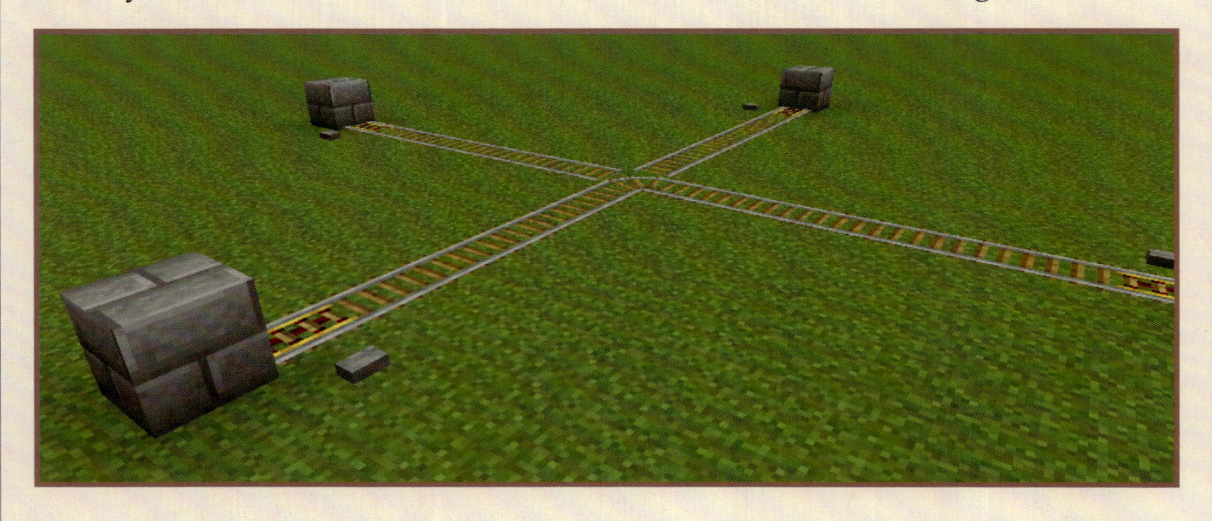

In addition to the standard rail, there are three other variations that provide unique functions.

Powered Rail

A powered rail can be used to increase or decrease the speed of minecarts moving along a track. You can craft six of them with six gold ingots, one stick, and one redstone dust.

> **NOTE:**
> YOU CAN PLACE RAILS PERPENDICULAR TO EACH OTHER IN A FOUR-WAY INTERSECTION SO THAT THE CENTRAL RAIL DOESN'T APPEAR CURVED, BUT CARTS WILL STILL BEHAVE AS IF IT IS CURVED. YOU CAN BREAK AND REPLACE THE CENTRAL RAIL TO DISPLAY THE CURVE.

Powered rails, contrary to their name, are powered only once you've connected a power source to it. You might, for example, place a redstone torch or lever next to the rail to power it. A single power source powers the rail it is next to as well as up to eight powered rails on either side. An unpowered power rail will act as a brake to minecarts and cause them to stop.

Once you've connected a redstone source to a powered rail, it will provide some acceleration to the minecart passing over it. The number of powered rails needed for a track depends on whether a minecart needs more power to travel up a slope or less power to go down a slope, and whether the minecart has a mob or player in it. For example, if your minecart needs to go up a slope while a player or mob is traveling in it, you'll need at least one powered rail every four blocks. An empty minecart traveling up a slope requires powered rails every second or third block.

On flat terrain, empty minecarts require a minimum of one powered rail every eighth block to continue moving. You can reach and maintain maximum speed with three powered rails shortly after the cart's starting point. For minecarts carrying mobs or players, you should place an additional powered rail every thirty or so blocks. Chest and hopper minecarts move faster and require fewer powered rails.

Challenge: Build Your Own Roller Coaster

Build your own roller coaster that travels up slopes, around corners, and finally screeches to a halt. For this challenge, you'll need a good number of rails and powered rails, a variety of blocks to build your track, and a minecart or two.

You might decide to keep it simple or use a theme, such as a haunted house, abandoned mines, or jungle tops. You can even make a short section underwater (you'll have to use redstone blocks to power the powered rails underwater).

You can use any solid blocks as the support frames and track base. For an old-school look, you might use wooden fences as support and wood planks to hold the tracks. For a modern look, you could use floating blocks to support the tracks.

To stop your minecarts, place two unpowered powered rails at the end of your track.

Detector Rail

A detector rail emits a full power signal when a minecart is on it. When a chest minecart or hopper minecart passes over it, the detector rail sends a signal relative to how full that container is, which is detectable by a comparator. You might use a detector rail to open a tunnel door whenever it detects a minecart, for example. You can craft six detector rails from one redstone, one stone pressure plate, and six iron ingots.

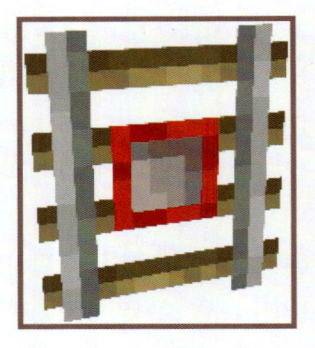

Activator Rail

When powered, an activator rail will eject any mobs and players inside the minecart running over it. This can be a fun way to exit your minecart! Activator rails will also activate a TNT minecart and disable hopper minecarts from picking up any items until the hopper minecart passes over an unpowered activator rail. Hopper minecarts are often used in automatic farms to pick up crops, and an activator rail can turn this ability on and off. You can craft six activator rails from six iron ingots, two sticks, and one redstone torch.

Build a Sugar Cane Farm

This automated sugar cane farm will grow tons of sugar cane to make paper, which you'll need for enchanting books or trading with villagers (see Chapter 15 for more on enchanting). It uses observers to track when the sugar cane grows and pistons to break the sugar cane. The dropped sugar cane is then picked up by a hopper minecart and deposited into a chest.

For this project, you'll need:

- Two hoppers
- One hopper minecart
- Two chests
- Eight standard rails
- Two powered rails
- Two redstone blocks
- Ten grass or dirt blocks (to plant sugar cane on)
- Six buckets of water
- Ten pistons
- Ten observers
- Ten redstone dust
- Fifty glass blocks, plus additional decorative blocks for enclosing the farm.
- Thirty-six spruce planks (or other building blocks of your choice)

Now, follow the directions below:

1. Dig out a 2x2-block hole in the ground. I recommend setting this up near your home base!

2. Place two chests on one side to create a double chest. Place two hoppers that point into the chest on the other side.

3. Place a track of eight rails centered across the hoppers, as shown. You'll need to shift-right-click to place rails on top of the hoppers.

4. Dig a one block hole at either end of the track.

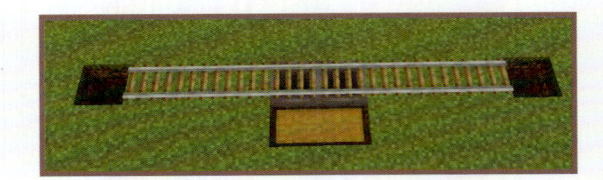

5. Place a redstone block in each of the holes and a powered rail above it.

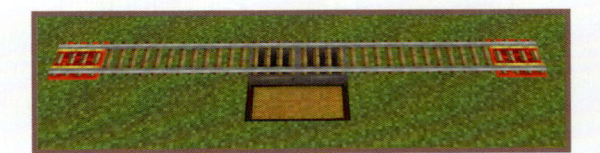

6. Add two spruce planks (or any solid block of your choice) at the ends of the track. These will stop the minecart and the powered rails will return it to the other side.

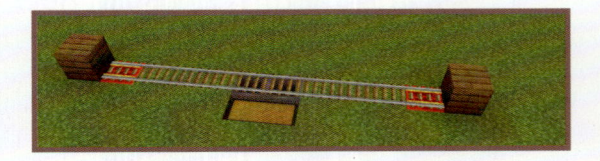

7. One block above the track, place a row of ten grass (or dirt) blocks. You can use a temporary block, like the yellow wool block shown, to help place the first grass block. Once you've placed all dirt blocks, remove the temporary block.

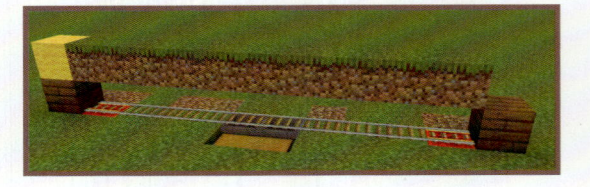

8. On the other side of the grass blocks, place twelve spruce planks on the ground to act as the bottom of the channel.

   Now we're going to make the water channel that allows the sugar cane to be planted on the raised grass.

TECHNOLOGY: REDSTONE AND RAILS 211

9. The water channel will be on top of the ten spruce blocks that you placed in Step 8, and behind the grass blocks, so we need to create walls around this. Add a row of twelve spruce planks (and two side walls of one spruce plank each) to enclose the water channel, as shown.

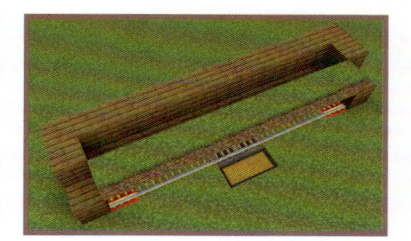

10. Fill in your water channel by placing a bucket of water at one end, then every other block, and then a last bucket at the other end.

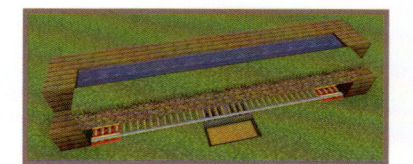

11. Plant ten sugar cane on the grass.

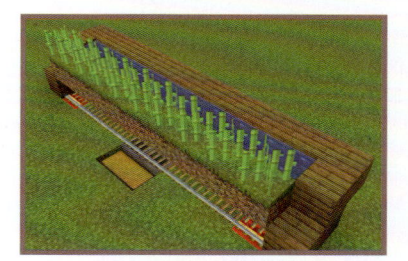

12. Cover the water channel with ten blocks of spruce planks.

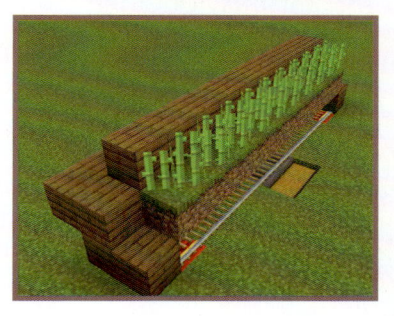

13. On top of the row of blocks you just added to cover the water channel, place a row of ten pistons facing toward the sugar cane. To position the pistons correctly, aim your cursor at the back of the block you want to place them on. In this case, face toward the back of the contraption, with the chests being at the front.

14. Place a row of ten spruce planks directly behind the pistons.

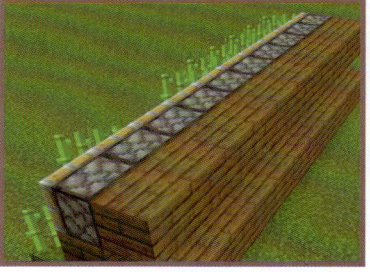

15. On top of the pistons, place a row of ten observers looking toward the sugar cane. To place these, stand behind the pistons and face toward the contraption's front.

16. On the blocks directly behind the observers, place ten redstone powder. These will transmit power from the observer to the pistons below.

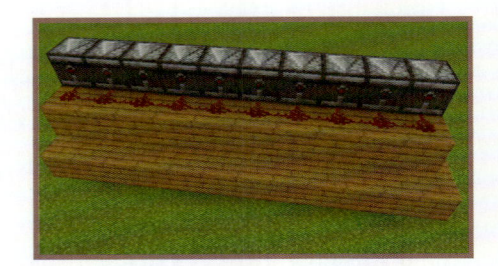

17. Place the hopper minecart on top of one of the powered rails, and it will start moving back and forth.

18. Finally, enclose the front of the farm with any blocks of your choice, in order to keep the harvested sugar cane falling on the grass blocks. Using glass, as I have, allows you to see your contraption at work. Make sure to leave an opening to access the chest and your sugar cane!

You've done it! Bask in your glory and prepare to reap the rewards of your efforts.

Up Next

The best way to learn about redstone is to experiment on your own and try to build other players' working contraptions to get ideas. You can find countless redstone tutorials on YouTube; some of my favorite redstone tutorial creators are Avomance and LogicalGeekBoy.

Now that you've delved into redstone, it's time to return to the adventurous side of Minecraft. In the next chapter, we'll explore the hellish landscapes of the Nether and their inhabitants. Buckle up!

14
SURVIVING THE NETHER

The Overworld is Disneyland compared to the Nether—a fiery, craggy, unforgiving landscape flooded with oceans of lava and populated by some of the most treacherous and bizarre denizens of Minecraft. It holds valuable materials you'll need for brewing potions and making redstone components, along with stunning decorative blocks you won't find anywhere else.

In this chapter, you'll learn how to enter and navigate the Nether, where you'll find its most precious goodies, and what mobs you should be on the lookout for.

The Lands of the Nether

The Nether is located theoretically "beneath" the Overworld; it's 128 blocks high with an uneven layer of bedrock at the top and bottom. A hellish underworld, most of the Nether's landscapes are dominated by netherrack, a reddish block that easily catches fire, and lava. Layers of netherrack cover the bedrock ceiling and floor, and present as massive outcroppings, mountains, cliffs, floating islands, and overhangs throughout. Lava is found dripping from the ceiling, and in oceans, pits, and springs around the netherrack landmasses. You can't mine down to the Nether. You can only get there through a Nether portal, discussed later in this chapter.

- The Nether has some unique characteristics:
- There is no weather, daylight, or day/night cycle.
- Water disappears with a sizzle if you try to pour it.
- Lava flows farther and faster than in the Overworld.
- Nether mobs, except for piglins and hoglins, are immune to lava damage.

- Clocks, regular compasses, and maps don't work.
- Beds are useless; right-clicking a bed will cause a bigger explosion than TNT!

The lands of the Nether are one-eighth the size of the Overworld (horizontally). This means that for each block you travel in the Nether, you are traveling the equivalent of eight blocks in the Overworld. For example, a portal at the (X, Z) coordinates of (8, 8) in the Nether will connect to a portal at (64, 64) in the Overworld. We'll learn how to build matching portals like this later on.

There are five biomes in the Nether, some more hospitable than others.

THE NETHER WASTES

The Nether wastes biome is the most common, with its rugged landscape of cliffs, mountains, islands, and plateaus of netherrack separated by ponds and seas of lava. You'll find soul sand, gravel, and clumps of magma blocks along its coastlines. Clusters of luminescent glowstone hang from cliffs and ceilings. Embedded in the landscape are veins of Nether gold ore and Nether quartz. Rare ancient debris ore blocks are found deeper within the masses of netherrack.

Zombified piglins and ghasts frequent the Nether wastes, with magma cubes, piglins, and Endermen appearing less regularly. You'll also find striders here and along the coastlines of every Nether biome.

THE BASALT DELTAS

The basalt deltas are arguably the most inhospitable biome, with uneven, towering columns of basalt and blackstone studded with lava pools and treacherous drops. Ghasts and magma cubes are prevalent here, both of whom can easily knock you back into a precipitous fall. The pale lavender air is riddled with ashy volcanic particles.

SOUL SAND VALLEY

The terrain of soul sand valleys consists of stretches and hillocks of soul sand and soul soil punctuated by columns of basalt and giant fossils made of bone block. The skies are a striking teal. Skeletons and ghasts make their home here, as well as the occasional Enderman. You should avoid walking on the soul sand, as it will slow down your speed by 50 percent. In soul sand valley, fire is blue. This *soul fire* inflicts more damage on a player than regular fire.

CRIMSON FOREST

The Nether is a fungal habitat, with brown and red mushrooms growing throughout. The two forests—crimson and warped—aren't populated with trees, but giant fungi that grow on *nylium*, a grasslike block. The fungi's stems can be used similarly to wood logs to create planks and other wood products.

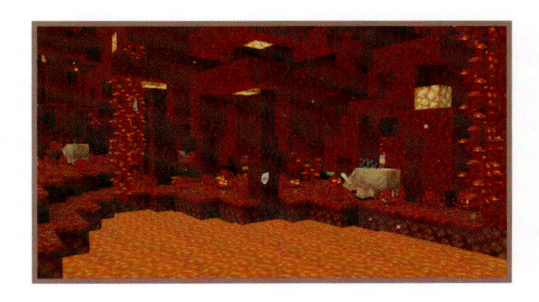

The Crimson Forest's fungi grow on crimson nylium. The giant crimson fungi's caps are made from Nether wart blocks studded with light-emitting *shroomlights*. The smaller fungi can be grown into their giant equivalents with bone meal. Weeping vines, a red vinelike fungus, grow from the ceilings or the caps of giant fungi.

The crimson forest is a dangerous biome, as it is home to hoglins, piglins, and the occasional zombified piglin. Piglins will attack you on sight unless you're wearing gold armor, and hoglins will attack you regardless. If you must fight, try to pillar up three blocks so you can strike these enemies without being hit yourself.

WARPED FOREST

The warped forest is similar to the crimson forest, except in color: its vegetation is teal and the skies are purple. Its warped fungi and roots grow on teal warped nylium, and twisting vines grow up from the ground. The huge fungi are capped by warped wart blocks.

This is one of the most hospitable biomes in the Nether, as only Endermen and striders spawn here.

The Nether isn't as intimidating as it looks, so long as you come prepared. Your main goal should be to find a Nether fortress and gather the supplies necessary for making potions: blaze rods and Nether wart. While you're in the Nether, you should also grab some glowstone for potion enhancement and Nether quartz for crafting redstone components, but your very first goal is to enter the Nether. To accomplish this, you'll need a portal.

Nether Portals

In Minecraft, a portal is a kind of door that transports you to another dimension. You'll need obsidian to construct a Nether portal, which can only be broken by a diamond pick.

You can build a Nether portal from either ten or fourteen blocks of obsidian in a 4x3 rectangular frame. You can choose to omit the blocks at the corners of the frame or replace them with other blocks. You can also create larger portals, up to 23x23-block frames.

BOTH OF THESE ARE VALID PORTALS; ON THE LEFT, A FULL FRAME WITH FOURTEEN OBSIDIAN BLOCKS AND ON THE LEFT, AN ABBREVIATED FRAME MADE OF TEN BLOCKS.

You might also choose to repair a ruined portal, which can appear randomly in the landscape and have obsidian blocks missing or replaced with other blocks, like crying obsidian. To repair them, you need to fill in the frame so that it is fully made of regular obsidian.

Once you've created a portal, activate it by using a flint-and-steel on the interior of one of the blocks. The swirly, purple portal will light up, ready for you to enter.

HOW NETHER PORTALS WORK

When you create a portal in the Overworld, a connecting portal is created in the Nether. It's placed as close as possible to the coordinates that correspond to your

Overworld portal, given that the Nether is eight times smaller than the Overworld. To find out an equivalent position in the Nether, divide the Overworld X and Z coordinates by 8. The Y coordinates are essentially the same in both dimensions.

Once you start building multiple portals, try your best to create them at matching coordinates in order to avoid portals connecting to the wrong place. For example, two portals close to each other in the Nether might link to the same portal in the Overworld, instead of to two separate portals.

Before You Step Through

Before you leap into the Nether, you'll want to take some specific supplies. As getting around in rugged Nether terrain can be difficult, you'll want at least one stack of blocks to use to climb up and down cliffs or make bridges over crevices. Cobblestone is a good choice, and several stacks are better than one. Extra blocks are also handy if you need to block yourself off from a hostile mob or pillar up away from one.

You may need to tunnel through a cliff, so bring a pickaxe and materials (cobblestone, wood, iron, and a furnace) to make new tools. Bring plenty of torches, as you'll want to place torches as you travel so you can find your way back to your portal. Have a copious supply of food, and wear quality armor. It is essential to wear at least one gold armor piece, or piglins will attack you on sight. Bring at least twenty gold ingots for trading with piglins.

In later trips, once you have potions brewing, bring a fire-resistance potion or two to help avoid damage from lava, blazes, and fire burning on top of netherrack (see Chapter 15 for more on potions).

IT'S A GOOD IDEA TO PLACE A BLOCK LIKE COBBLESTONE AT REGULAR INTERVALS AND USE A TORCH TO SHOW THE DIRECTION BACK TO THE PORTAL HOME.

Arriving in the Nether

Resist the urge to stride out boldly from your portal—take just one step. It's not uncommon for a portal to be generated high above a lava ocean or in another inconvenient position near fire or

NOTE:
THE NETHER HAS TWO FOOD SOURCES: MUSHROOM STEW, MADE FROM RED AND BROWN MUSHROOMS AND WOOD BOWLS, AND PORKCHOPS, WHICH YOU CAN GET BY KILLING HOGLINS.

hostile mobs. Once you're in the Nether, you should assess your portal's location and secure it if needed. If you're in a wide, exposed area, consider building cobblestone walls and a ceiling around your portal to protect it from ghast fireballs. If your portal is in a precarious position, it's a good idea to build a bridge to more traversable land.

You want to keep track of where your portal is because it's (almost) your only way out. There are ways to find the resources in the Nether for building a new portal (see "No Way Home" below). If you don't plan on using torches to guide the way, press **F3** to see your coordinates and take a screenshot with **F2**.

YOUR PORTAL CAN END UP ALMOST ANYWHERE IN THE NETHER, BESIDES IN LAVA. EXIT CAREFULLY!

NO WAY HOME

Having a ghast strike your portal with a fireball and break it (it breaks the swirly portal blocks) or losing your way back to your portal is a Nether nightmare. Thankfully, there are ways to fix the situation.

If your portal is no longer lit (say, because of ghasts hurling fireballs at it) and you don't have a flint and steel with you, you can find gravel to break for flint along coastlines in the Nether Wastes. To get the steel, you can trade with piglins for iron nuggets and use a furnace to smelt the iron into an ingot.

It's best to bring supplies for making or repairing a portal with you, as it might be difficult to find the right materials. With this in mind, you can sometimes find obsidian in Nether fortresses, through trading with piglins, or in the chests of ruined portals (which are rare).

SURVIVING THE NETHER

Challenge: Find a Fortress and Bastion

The Nether contains fortresses and bastion remnants, huge structures we'll learn about in the following sections. It's often hard to find these, as both structures can be wholly or partly embedded in netherrack.

The Nether is composed of grids of 432x432 blocks, starting from (0,0). Inside and toward the center of each grid square, there's a chance of either a fortress or a bastion being generated. Find (X, Z) coordinates that would place you somewhere around a grid center, for example, (200,200), and travel either north/south or east/west from there. The main bodies of Nether fortresses are around y=60 to y=70, so try to keep to that height. Once you find one of each, note their coordinates. Unless you're prepared to fight hoglins and piglin brutes, *keep clear of the bastion*.

Nether Fortresses

Nether fortresses are enormous structures made of wide pillars, walkways, bridges, platforms, halls, and corridors constructed from dark red Nether brick. Fortresses can generate in any Nether biome and can be difficult to reach. When you find one, you might have to pillar up or build a bridge to it using blocks.

In and around the fortress, you can find magma blocks, skeletons, zombified piglins, blazes, and wither skeletons. While you need to keep an eye out for all the hostiles, it's a good idea to proactively create wither skeleton barriers. To do this, place a row of blocks along the ceiling of interior corridors. This creates a two-block-high space that wither skeletons can't pass through; use this barrier to attack them.

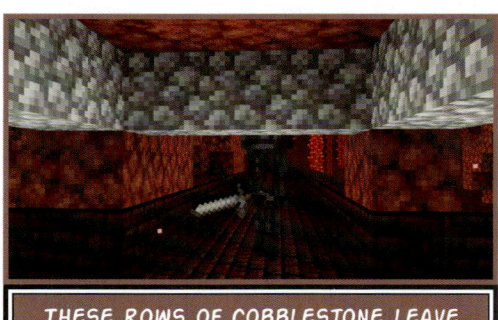

THESE ROWS OF COBBLESTONE LEAVE A TWO-BLOCK-HIGH GAP THAT WITHER SKELETONS CAN'T GET THROUGH.

The corridors inside a Nether fortress are meandering labyrinths, with staircases to different levels and platforms, so it's a good idea to mark where you've been with torches or something similar. If you encounter blazes in the fortress corridors, use your shield to fend off their fireballs and strike them with a sword immediately after they finish their three-fireball attack.

While you explore, look out for loot chests that might hold valuable items, as well as blaze spawning platforms, which should be destroyed on sight. You'll find Nether wart, a fungus-like plant, growing on soul sand at the bottom of some stairs. Nether wart can grow in the Overworld on soul sand and doesn't need water.

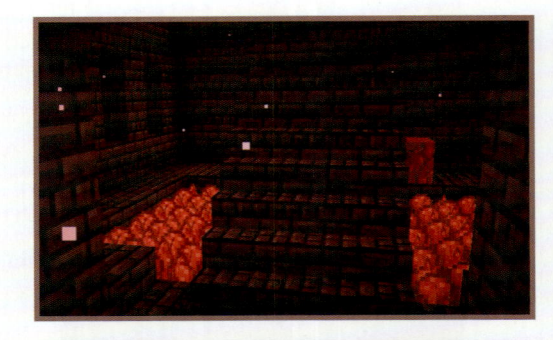

GLOSSY RED BULBS OF NETHER WART GROW BENEATH SOME OF THE FORTRESS STAIRCASES.

Bastion Remnant

Bastion remnants are large, partly ruined edifices made primarily from polished blackstone brick and basalt. You can find them in any biome, except basalt deltas. Bastion remnants are excellent looting spots, with ramparts that often hold multiple chests and secret locations that contain gold blocks. Piglins and piglin brutes spawn in these bastions, and hoglins spawn in the bridge and stable bastions.

Keep aware of your footing you as you explore a bastion, as the staircases, corridors, and walkways are ragged and ruined. It's easy to miss a hole and fall down to the next level, into a pool of lava, or even on top of a hoglin!

TYPES OF BASTION REMNANTS

There are four types of bastion you might come across in your travels:

- The *bridge* has a narrow bridge topped with a pile of gold blocks. The bridge leads to a rampart carved to look like a giant piglin face. Hoglins spawn in this bastion.
- The *hoglin stables* contain three ramparts and stables. These are occupied by many hoglins and are best to be avoided for now.
- The *housing unit* features multiple ramparts and an interior, central patch of Nether wart.

Challenge: Gather Blaze Rods

You'll want to kill blazes in order to get the blaze rods they drop, as these are used to make brewing stations and fuel the brewing stations.

Once you've entered the fortress, locate a blaze spawner platform. The blaze platforms should have a short set of stairs rising to them and will hold a blaze spawner at the top. As with spawners in the Overworld, if you move within sixteen blocks of the blaze spawner, you'll activate it; this will spawn several blazes every so often.

Look for a platform that is blocked off by netherrack overhead and on both sides. An enclosed platform is the best for fighting blazes, as the ceiling prevents blazes from rising up in the air. You're also able to block yourself off from the spawning blazes, which makes killing them much more efficient!

Block off the entrance to the spawner platform, as in the image below. You should leave a one-block-high gap right in front of the bottom step. This allows you to step partially into the staircase to look up at the blazes and lure them toward you, but it prevents the blazes from going any farther than the bottom step. Also be sure to block off areas behind you where wither skeletons or other mobs could approach you.

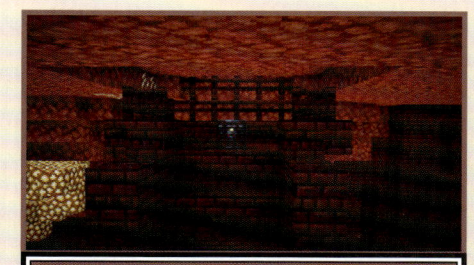

THIS BLAZE SPAWNER PLATFORM IS ENCLOSED OVERHEAD BY NETHERRACK, SO BLOCKING IT OFF FROM YOU WON'T BE TOO DIFFICULT.

THE GAP HERE ALLOWS THE BLAZES TO COME FORWARD JUST TO THE BOTTOM STEP, WHERE YOU CAN ATTACK THEM WITH YOUR SWORD. YOU CAN USE YOUR SHIELD TO DEFEND AGAINST THEIR FIREBALLS, TOO. THIS IS ONE OF THE BEST WAYS TO ATTACK BLAZES WHEN YOU WANT THEIR BLAZE RODS, AND ONCE YOU HAVE POTIONS AND CAN ENCHANT YOUR GEAR, YOU CAN IMPROVE THIS TECHNIQUE BY USING A FIRE RESIST POTION AND A LOOTING III SWORD.

- The *treasure room* has two main buildings connected by a bridge. The larger building has a central lava pool with a pier that holds numerous gold blocks and a top-tier treasure chest. Adjacent to this pier is a magma cube spawner that you should break as soon as possible.

Of all the bastion types, the treasure room bastion holds the best treasure, but they all are worthy of exploring and looting.

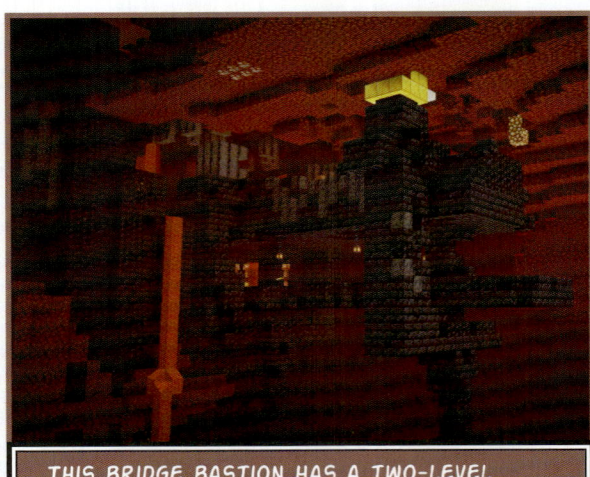

THIS BRIDGE BASTION HAS A TWO-LEVEL NARROW BRIDGE, WITH A HEAP OF GOLD BLOCKS AT THE TOP.

LOOTING BASTIONS

There's treasure to be found in all four bastion types, from gold blocks (oftentimes hidden behind the chiseled polished blackstone blocks that look like snouts) to the loot chests tucked away in corridors, at the bottom of stairs, and on roofs.

You can find rare loot in bastions, including enchanted crossbows, blocks of gold, diamond tools, diamond armor, ancient debris, and netherite scraps. Bastion remnants are the only places you can find the snout banner pattern and the Pigstep music disc.

Keep an eye out for piglins before opening chests or breaking gold-related blocks—they will be aggravated and attack, even if you're wearing gold. You may want to block yourself off from piglins with blocks or place a hopper beneath a chest to suck out the loot. The piglins won't be aggravated by you getting goods from a hopper.

PIGLIN BRUTES

Each bastion generates with several piglin brutes. They wear a black tunic with a gold belt and carry a gold axe. Unlike other piglins, piglin brutes will attack you on sight and can't be bartered with. It's best to attack them by shooting a ranged

SURVIVING THE NETHER | 223

weapon from afar in a safe position, or by pillaring up and pouring a lava bucket on them. Once a bastion's piglin brutes are killed, they won't respawn.

Challenge: Bartering with Piglins

To trade with piglins, just throw gold ingots at them. After inspecting the gold, they'll throw some Nether-related items or resources back at you. You might receive Ender pearls or potions, or you may end up with string or gravel. They may throw you enchanted boots or an enchanted book—both will be enchanted with Soul Speed, which allows you to move quickly over soul sand or soul soil. See Chapter 15 for details on using enchanted books.

The safest place to barter is in the Nether Wastes, as the other piglin spawning areas (bastions and Crimson Forests) are much more dangerous. Don't forget to wear a gold armor to appease them.

Nether Resources and Blocks

The Nether has building blocks you can't get anywhere else, as well as resources for crafting unique items.

ANCIENT DEBRIS

Ancient debris is a rare ore used to create netherite that can only be mined with a diamond or netherite pickaxe. Its highest level of distribution is around y=15. Ancient debris has a high blast resistance and won't break in explosions. To find some, you can explode areas of netherite with TNT.

NETHERITE

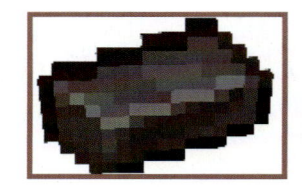

To make netherite, first smelt ancient debris. This produces one netherite scrap; you'll need to craft four netherite scraps with four gold ingots to create one netherite ingot. Netherite ingots are used to upgrade diamond gear into netherite gear, which is the highest-quality material. Netherite gear is resistant to fire, explosion, and lava damage.

> **NOTE:**
> WHEN YOU'RE MINING THROUGH ANY PART OF THE LANDSCAPE, IT'S VERY LIKELY YOU'LL OPEN UP A HIDDEN BLOCK OF LAVA THAT WILL FLOW VERY RAPIDLY TOWARD YOU. KEEP BLOCKS IN YOUR HOTBAR SO YOU CAN BLOCK THE FLOW AND REPLACE THE LAVA SOURCE.

BASALT

Basalt is a decorative stone block found in bastion remnants, the basalt delta, and soul sand valleys. You can craft four basalt to create polished basalt and smelt one basalt to create smooth basalt. Smooth basalt is also found in the Overworld in amethyst geodes.

BLACKSTONE

Blackstone is the Nether's version of cobblestone and can be used in many crafting recipes requiring cobblestone. You can find it in bastion remnants and basalt deltas, and occasionally as smaller veins in other biomes. You can craft four blackstone to make polished blackstone, and four polished blackstone to make polished blackstone bricks. You can craft slabs, stairs, and walls from blackstone, polished blackstone, and polished blackstone bricks. Polished blackstone slabs can craft chiseled polished blackstone, which have a piglin snout carved in them.

CRYING OBSIDIAN

Crying obsidian is a light-emitting version of obsidian. While it also has high blast resistance (and must be mined with a diamond or better pick), crying obsidian can't be used as part of a Nether portal. You can find it in ruined Nether portals and as loot in bastions. It's used for creating respawn anchors (see "Respawn Anchors" at the end of this list).

GILDED BLACKSTONE

Gilded blackstone is a type of blackstone found in bastions that sometimes drops two to five gold nuggets instead of itself when mined. Beware of nearby piglins if this happens!

GLOWSTONE

Glowstone is a light-emitting block (light level 15) that generates in clumps hanging from ceilings, cliffs, and overhangs. If you break it without a Silk Touch–enchanted pickaxe, it drops two to four glowstone dust; you can craft a glowstone block with four glowstone dust. Glowstone blocks are used to make redstone lamps and respawn anchors. The dust is used in firework stars, as a potion brewing ingredient, and in crafting spectral arrows.

LODESTONE

A lodestone is a block that you can make a compass point to. You can craft a lodestone from eight chiseled stone bricks and one netherite ingot. To use a lodestone, place it in the location you want your compass to point to. Then right-click with your compass on the lodestone to set the compass's origin.

You can use a lodestone in the Overworld, Nether, and the End but not between dimensions. You might use them to mark and find your way back to a portal, base, mob farm, village, or any other important location without having to open F3 and take screenshots of your coordinates.

NETHER GOLD ORE

Nether gold ore is found as veins in netherrack. You can break it with any level of pickaxe, and it will drop two to six gold nuggets. If you use a Silk Touch pickaxe to break it, smelting the Nether gold ore block will give you one gold ingot. Piglins will become aggravated if they see you mining it, even if you're wearing a piece of gold armor.

NETHER QUARTZ ORE

Nether quartz ore, found embedded in netherrack, drops one Nether quartz. You can craft four Nether quartz into a block of quartz, a decorative building block.

QUARTZ

Quartz is a decorative block made from four Nether quartz. You can craft the following variants from quartz: slabs (three quartz blocks); quartz pillars (two quartz blocks); chiseled quartz blocks (two quartz slabs); and quartz bricks (four quartz blocks). Quartz is also used to make comparators, observers, and daylight sensors (see Chapter 13 for more on redstone technologies).

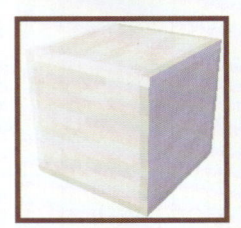

NETHERRACK

Netherrack is a soft stonelike block that is easily flammable and will burn indefinitely. (To put a fire out, click the block that is on fire.) You can smelt netherrack into Nether bricks, and craft four Nether bricks into a Nether brick block. You can craft Nether brick fences from four Nether brick blocks and two Nether bricks (there are no Nether brick fence gates).

RED NETHER BRICKS

Red Nether bricks are a decorative block that you craft with two Nether wart and two Nether bricks.

NETHER WART BLOCK

Nether wart block is a decorative block that you can craft from nine Nether wart. You can also find them naturally in crimson forests and should harvest them with a hoe.

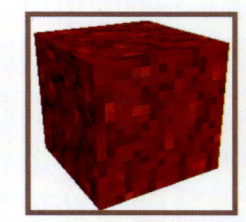

NYLIUM

Nylium, both crimson and warped, is a type of fungal netherrack. You'll need a pickaxe enchanted with Silk Touch to break it; otherwise, it drops netherrack. You can right-click bone meal on a fungi or mushroom that is on nylium to grow a huge fungi or mushroom. Using bone meal on netherrack placed next to nylium will change the netherrack into that type of nylium.

RESPAWN ANCHOR

You can set your spawn point in the Nether with a respawn anchor. This means if you die in the Nether, you'll return to wherever your respawn anchor is. You can craft it with six crying obsidian and three glowstone blocks.

To use your respawn anchor, place it where you want your spawn to be, and then charge it by right-clicking it with a block of glowstone up to four times. Charging the anchor once will give the anchor one respawn for you to use. Once it's charged, right-click the anchor to set your spawn. A notice in chat will confirm that your respawn point has been set. This respawn point overrides any respawn point you have in the Overworld, so if you die in the Overworld, you'll respawn in the Nether.

You can respawn at this anchor as many times as you've charged it (each respawn uses one glowstone charge), and you can continue to use glowstone blocks to recharge the anchor. If the anchor is broken or doesn't have any more charges, when you die, your respawn will be reset back to your original world respawn point. Don't try to use this in the Overworld or the End, as the respawn anchor will explode. Hoglins are scared of respawn anchors and will run from them.

SOUL SAND

Soul sand is a block found in the soul sand valleys biome. Soul sand has quite a few unique features: it slows you down considerably when you walk on it; if set alight, it creates a blue soul fire; and when submerged in water, it forms a bubble column above it that will push a player, mob, or item up to the top of the column.

SOUL SOIL

Soul soil is a dirt variant that generates in soul sand valleys. Unlike soul sand, it doesn't hamper a player's speed, but it will generate soul fire if it is lit.

You can craft a blue-fire version of a campfire by replacing the coal in the recipe with soul sand or soul soil. You can also create blue-fired torches by adding a block of soul sand or soil to the torch recipe. You can craft a soul lantern with a soul torch and eight iron nuggets.

Up Next

Now that you can confidently visit the Nether with the knowledge gained throughout this chapter, see if you can find all four types of bastion remnants and the five Nether biomes. Don't forget to keep a path of torches to find your way back to your portal! In the next chapter, we'll begin weaving some magic with enchantments and potions to amuse, alarm, and augment! Bring along your blaze rods, some glowstone, and the Nether wart.

15
MAGIC: ENCHANTING AND POTIONS

Magic—specifically enchantments and potions—is the means to taking your gameplay to the next level. And you'll need it, if you want to take on the most powerful bosses, like the Ender Dragon.

In this chapter, you'll learn to enchant your tools, weapons, and armor, and brew potions that will give you superhuman abilities, like invisibility and night vision! You'll also make your very own hostile mob spawner farm to gain all the experience points (XP) you'll need to perform enchantments.

Enchanting

Enchanting equipment is the process of using enchantments (or *enchants*) to give them more abilities than they ordinarily have. For example, you can give a sword heightened Knockback power, grant a bow infinite arrows, or even enable boots with the ability to walk on water. Enchanted items have a light purplish glow.

> **NOTE:**
> YOU CAN GAIN EXPERIENCE QUICKLY FROM KILLING MOBS (BESIDES VILLAGERS, GOLEMS, BATS, AND BABY ANIMALS). OTHER WAYS TO GAIN XP INCLUDE BREEDING, DISENCHANTING WITH A GRINDSTONE, FISHING, SMELTING WITH A FURNACE, AND TRADING.

You can enchant gear in two ways: by using an enchanting table, or by combining it with an enchanted book in an anvil. Both methods of enchantment will cost XP levels, depending on the level of enchantment and the number of enchantments an item already has. Enchanting with a table also requires lapis lazuli (see Chapter 5 for how to obtain lapis lazuli).

USING AN ENCHANTING TABLE

You can craft an enchanting table with four obsidian, two diamonds, and a book. To use your enchanting table, place it and right-click to open its interface. Put the item to be enchanted in the leftmost slot. A list of three enchants should appear on the right.

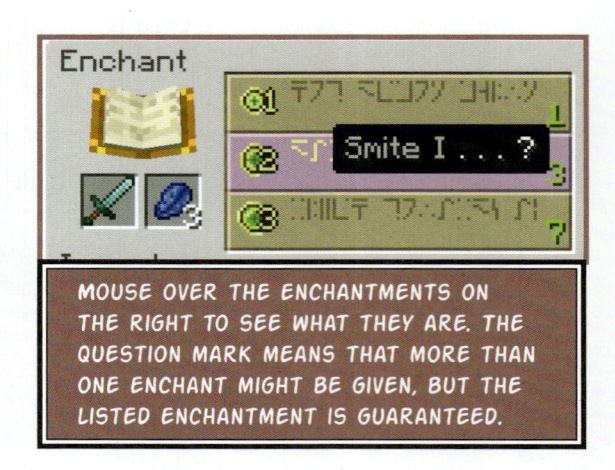

The enchants are listed in magical text in order from least to most lapis needed and XP levels that the enchant costs (1–3 on both counts). Mouse over the list to see a pop-up with the enchant's name in your language.

On the bottom right of each listed enchantment is the number of XP levels you must have overall in order to make the enchantments. Place the required amount of lapis lazuli for your desired enchant into the second slot on the left. The enchants you can apply should be highlighted. Select your enchantment. The lapis will disappear, the XP levels will be removed from your hotbar, and you can take your newly enchanted item.

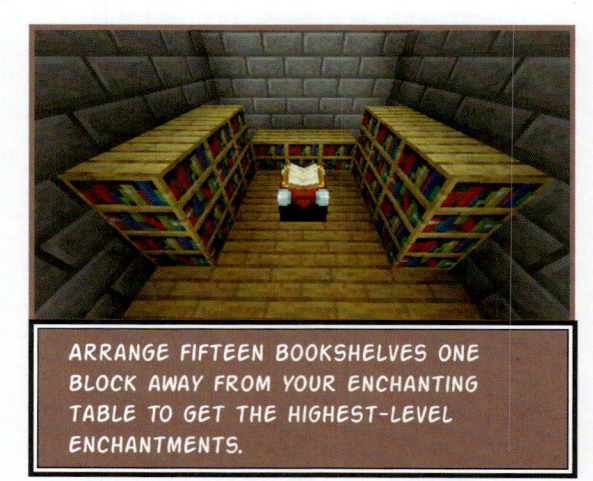

MOUSE OVER THE ENCHANTMENTS ON THE RIGHT TO SEE WHAT THEY ARE. THE QUESTION MARK MEANS THAT MORE THAN ONE ENCHANT MIGHT BE GIVEN, BUT THE LISTED ENCHANTMENT IS GUARANTEED.

ARRANGE FIFTEEN BOOKSHELVES ONE BLOCK AWAY FROM YOUR ENCHANTING TABLE TO GET THE HIGHEST-LEVEL ENCHANTMENTS.

To get access to stronger, higher-level enchants, you must surround your enchantment table with bookshelves. You can craft these from three books and six wood planks. These must be two blocks away at the same block height or one above, leaving one block of space in between the bookshelves and enchantment table.

Once a bookshelf is placed, you'll see magical text icons flowing in the air from the bookshelf to the enchantment table. For the maximum enchant levels, you will need fifteen bookshelves. These higher enchant levels enabled by the bookshelves will require you to have higher experience levels to make an enchant. With these bookshelves, you'll be offered fewer low-level enchants. If you want to return to lower-level enchants, you can disable a bookshelf by placing a torch on its front.

USING AN ANVIL

You might receive several enchants on an item through using an enchantment table, and you may not want them all. Let's learn how we can use an anvil and enchanted books to get the exact enchantments we want.

First, craft a book from three paper and one leather hide. To make three paper, craft three sugar cane. Leather is dropped from cows, horses, llamas, donkeys, mules, and mooshrooms.

Then, open up your enchanting table's UI and place your book. Select an enchant (books may have any enchants given to other gear), and add the necessary lapis. Your book is officially enchanted! (You can also find enchanted books through trading with a village librarian, fishing, or finding them in treasure chests.)

THE ENCHANTMENT COST REFERS TO HOW MANY XP LEVELS IT WILL TAKE TO PERFORM THIS ENCHANTMENT; IN THIS EXAMPLE, IT WILL COST SIX XP LEVELS. YOU CAN ALSO USE THE TOP TEXT BOX TO NAME YOUR GEAR.

NOTE:
YOU CAN ALSO TRADE FOR ALREADY ENCHANTED GEAR FROM VILLAGE ARMORERS, FISHERMEN, TOOLSMITHS, AND WEAPONSMITHS.

Next, craft an anvil using three blocks of iron and four iron ingots. Place your anvil and right-click it to open its menu. Place your equipment in the first slot and the enchanted book in the second.

You can also place two enchanted books to combine the enchants into a single book, and combine two enchanted items (of the same type) to combine their enchants as well. If you want to remove all the enchantments from a piece of gear (or a book), use a grindstone (see Chapter 13). You'll get XP back when you do this.

All enchantment combinations will cost experience levels. The item in the second slot in the anvil UI is the one "used up," so test each item in both slots to see if the enchantment cost lowers.

ENCHANTMENTS

There's a wide variety of enchantments for different types of tools and gear. Many have different levels, from I up to III, IV, or V. Higher-level enchantments produce their effects more quickly or strongly. While you can get higher levels through the enchantment table or books, you can also combine pieces of equipment that are at the same level to produce a tool or book at the next level. For example, combining two swords with Sharpness II in an anvil will result in a sword that is Sharpness III. To get to level IV, you'd need to combine two Sharpness III swords, or a Sharpness III sword and a Sharpness III enchanted book.

I've categorized enchantments by the gear they enchant below, but there are a few general enchantments you can apply to almost all gear that we'll go over first.

GENERAL ENCHANTMENTS

These enchantments can be given to most armor and equipment.

Mending:
Mending (from enchanted books only) will automatically repair an item, when held or in an armor slot, with XP orbs that are collected. A good source for Mending books is your local village librarian.

Unbreaking:
This enchant lowers the chance of an item losing durability when used, and can be used with armor, tools, and weapons. A book enchanted with Unbreaking can be used on an anvil with shields, fishing rods, shears, Elytra, and flint and steel.

Curse of Vanishing:
This enchantment will destroy its item when you die. You can only find this curse through obtaining enchanted books from fishing, looting chests, or trading with village librarians. Both Mending and Unbreaking are key enchants for keeping your tools from breaking.

Challenge: Mending Trades

In this challenge, you'll trade with a librarian villager to get Mending books.

First, you'll want to make some simple trades with a few villagers to acquire emeralds, like trading sticks with a fletcher. You'll also need non-enchanted books for each trade with the librarian, so make sure you have enough sugar cane and craft a bunch! Trade with the librarian to gather enough Mending books for all of your equipment. Then, add the enchantments with an anvil to your diamond tools, weapons, and armor.

ARMOR ENCHANTMENTS

Armor enchants are immensely helpful in traversing difficult terrain—such as underwater or the Nether—and in protecting yourself against hostile mobs. Many armor enchants are only for helmets and boots; these will be listed as such.

Aqua Affinity:
Helmets only. Allows you to mine underwater.

Blast Protection:
Reduces damage from explosions and reduces Knockback.

Curse of Binding:
An armor item enchanted with the Curse of Binding can't be removed until it breaks or the player dies. The enchantment can only be obtained through books from looting chests, fishing, or trading.

Depth Strider:
Boots only. Allows you to move more quickly underwater. Incompatible with Frost Walker. Only available from fishing, looting chests, trading, or pillager raid drops.

Feather Falling:
Boots only. Significantly reduces fall damage.

Fire Protection:
Reduces damage from fire.

Frost Walker:
Boots only. Allows you to walk on water by creating a circle of frosted ice around you. The ice melts fairly quickly, so you need to keep moving! Incompatible with Depth Strider.

Projectile Protection:
Reduces damage from projectiles including arrows, blaze fireballs, ghast fireballs, and tridents.

Protection:
Reduces most types of damage, except for damage from hunger and falling into the Void.

Respiration:
Helmet only. Increases the time you can breathe underwater.

Soul Speed:
Boots only. Increases your speed when walking on soul sand or soul soil; however, boots enchanted with soul speed lose durability quickly. This enchantment is available only through trading with piglins or looting bastion remnant chests (see Chapter 14 for more on bastion remnants).

Thorns:
Melee strikes by an enemy will reflect some of the damage back onto them, though your equipment will lose durability quickly.

The four main armor protection enchantments—Blast Protection, Fire Protection, Projectile Protection, and Protection—are incompatible with each other on one piece of armor. You can have different protection enchants on different pieces of armor. Protection is generally the best, as it protects against most types of damage. That said, it can be useful to have a specialty armor set geared for specific situations.

> **Challenge: Perfect Armor**
> Create a set of top-tier diamond armor. On each, place Mending, Unbreaking III, and Protection IV. On your boots, add Feather Falling IV and Depth Strider III. On your helmet, add Aqua Affinity and Respiration III. The only thing left is to upgrade your set to netherite!

SWORD ENCHANTMENTS

The three main sword attack enchantments—Bane of Arthropods, Smite, and Sharpness—are not compatible with each other.

Bane of Arthropods:
Provides additional damage when striking arthropods (such as bees, endermites, silverfish, and spiders) and gives them the Slowness IV effect.

Fire Aspect:
Will set targets struck on fire.

Sharpness:
Increases attack damage.

Smite:
Increases attack damage to undead targets, including skeletons (and variants), zombies (and variants), phantoms, and Withers.

Sweeping Edge:
Increases the damage done to mobs near the target.

Looting:
Increases the drops from mobs you kill. For example, killing a blaze could get you a maximum of one blaze rod; with Looting III, you have a chance of getting up to four.

Knockback:
Increases the distance your sword will knock (push) back a target.

Sharpness is the most desirable sword enchant, followed by Looting and Fire Aspect. If your sword is imbued with Sweeping Edge, you have to be careful that there aren't any friendly mobs or players near your target, or they'll get hurt too! A strong Knockback can remove your enemy quite a distance; keep in mind that if you knock back a skeleton, it may give them more time to recharge arrows and you less time to attack them.

BOW ENCHANTMENTS

The best bow enchantment is Power, equivalent to Sharpness for the sword, as it increases the damage you inflict.

Flame:
Sets targets struck on fire. Can also set off TNT.

Infinity:
Gives you unlimited arrow ammunition as long as you have a single arrow in your inventory. Incompatible with Mending.

Power:
Increases the damage an arrow will do.

Punch:

Increases the amount of knockback an arrow inflicts.

Infinity is a huge asset with a bow, as making new arrows can be quite tedious.

CROSSBOW ENCHANTMENTS

The crossbow is a slow but powerful weapon, and enchantments really bring it to a new level of deadliness.

Multishot:

Shoots three arrows, ten degrees apart, instead of one. (Only one arrow can be retrieved.) Incompatible with Piercing.

Quick Charge:

Lowers the time it takes to charge a bow.

Piercing:

Enables arrows to pass through multiple mobs and shields. Incompatible with Multishot.

Because Piercing requires targets to be lined up in front of each other to get the most out of it, I would recommend Multishot instead.

TRIDENT ENCHANTMENTS

The primary attack-strength enchant for tridents is Impaling; however, Loyalty is a close second, as it brings the trident back to you so you don't have to retrieve it.

Channeling:

With this enchant, when you aim and hit a target with your trident, it will be struck with lightning from above. This only works in open skies during thunderstorms. Incompatible with Riptide.

Impaling:

Increases the damage to your target when it is a natural resident of the ocean; this includes guardians, turtles, dolphins, axolotls, and squid. The drowned are not included in this, as they are categorized as undead mobs rather than ocean mobs.

Loyalty:

Returns the trident to you after it is thrown. Levels II and III lower the return time. Incompatible with Riptide.

Riptide:

When you throw a trident with Riptide, you'll be carried along with the trident, for greater distances the higher the enchant level. Riptide only works when you are standing in water or when it's raining. Incompatible with Channeling and Loyalty.

You can't always count on the weather to produce a thunderstorm and lightning, but you can use a trident with Channeling if you need a lightning bolt for a specific reason, like turning a creeper into a charged creeper.

MACE ENCHANTMENTS

You can enchant maces with fire aspect, unbreaking, mending, bane of arthropods, and smite, as well as three unique enchantments.

Breach:

Causes your target's armor to be less effective.

Density:

Increases the damage done; with more damage done when you fall for longer.

Wind Burst:

Gives a burst of Knockback, like a wind charge, throwing the target into the air.

TOOL ENCHANTMENTS

Tool enchantments are used primarily for the axe, hoe, pickaxe, and shovel.

Efficiency:

Makes a tool work more quickly; for example, it can lower the number of swings necessary to mine stone with your pickaxe. It also increases the ability of an axe to disable a shield for five seconds. (When axes strike shields, there's a chance the blow will prevent it from reducing damage.) A book enchanted with Efficiency can be applied to shears with an anvil.

Silk Touch:

Makes some blocks drop the original blocks rather than the block's drop. For example, a block of iron ore will drop the block itself rather than iron ore items. This can be especially useful for mining ores so that you can use a Fortune pickaxe on the mined blocks later to increase drops.

Some blocks and objects require you to use a Silk Touch enchanted tool on them in order to retrieve them. These include bee nests and hives, bookshelves, coral, Ender chests, glass, grass blocks, ice, mycelium, nylium, podzol, sea lanterns, and turtle eggs.

Fortune:
Increases the number of drops a tool will get from some broken blocks. Blocks affected include ore blocks as well as crops (seeds only), glowstone, gravel, leaves, melons, sea lanterns, sweet berries, and Nether vines (twisting and weeping). Not compatible with Silk Touch.

> **NOTE:**
> A BOOK ENCHANTED WITH SHARPNESS I-V CAN BE APPLIED TO AXES WITH AN ANVIL. IT'S A GOOD IDEA TO HAVE BOTH A FORTUNE PICK AND A SILK TOUCH PICK IN YOUR ARSENAL.

Fishing Rod Enchantments

Fishing can be a tedious but decent way to get some unique treasure. Having a rod with both level III enchantments is a big plus.

Luck of the Sea:
Increases the rate at which you fish better loot.

Lure:
Lowers the time spent waiting for the next catch.

Brewing

Potions grant powerful effects that you can use in battle, underwater, or in other less precarious situations. To create your own potion brewing setup, you'll need the following:

Brewing stand:
You can either craft a brewing stand from three cobblestone and one blaze rod, or trade with a cleric villager. It holds three glass bottles, or potions, at a time, and can brew three potions of the same type at a time.

Glass bottles:

These hold the potions. You can craft three glass bottles from three glass blocks.

Water source:

You'll need access to water to fill your glass bottles; while a cauldron can hold one bucket of water and fill three glass bottles, you'll likely need more to make a variety of potions. See the upcoming challenge to learn how to build an infinite water source so that you'll never run out.

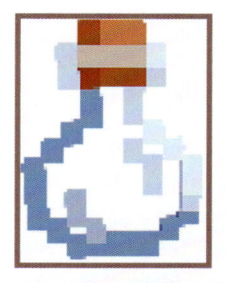

Blaze powder:

Blaze power is the fuel for the brewing stand. One blaze powder will last for twenty steps of brewing. A step consists of placing one ingredient to brew (like Nether wart or ghast tear) in the brewing stand and completing the brewing of the potions below.

Nether wart:

Nether wart is the ingredient used to make the base potion that finished potions use. For a steady supply of Nether wart, you can grow it on soul sand you've gathered in the Nether. This plant doesn't need water or light to grow.

Storage chests:

Potions don't stack (only one potion fits in one inventory slot), and require quite a few ingredients, so you'll want extra storage space in your brewery. I'd recommend starting with at least one double chest.

POTION INGREDIENTS

Before we begin brewing potions, it's crucial to know what ingredients we'll need. Each potion requires a different ingredient or two, and a few are created from other potions. Table 15-1 lists all potions, along with their ingredients and effects.

There are three levels of potions: standard, extended, and enhanced. *Extended potions* typically lengthen a potion's effects, and *enhanced potions* typically strengthen potions to make them more powerful for a shorter duration. Once a potion has

> ### Challenge: Make an Infinite Water Source
>
> The game's water mechanics are such that if you place two water sources (with a bucket, for example) with one empty block between them, a third water source will be created between them. You can pick up this central source with a bucket, and it will keep replenishing itself, as long as you don't touch the original two sources.
>
> If you place the two water source buckets diagonally to each other, they'll create two new water sources. Any of the four sources you remove with a bucket will be replenished. (This effect can be thwarted by trying to pick up all the water sources quickly.)
>
> To make an infinite water source, dig a 2x2 hole that is one block deep. In opposite corners, place two water sources. This will fill the entire pool with non-flowing water sources, and you can retrieve water from any corner continuously.

been extended, it cannot be enhanced, and vice versa. Both extended and enhanced versions require an additional step and ingredient. Brewing an extended potion requires one redstone dust; an enhanced version requires one glowstone dust.

Potions and Ingredients

Potion	Ingredient	Effect
Fire Resistance	Magma cream	Protects you from fire damage for three minutes
Harming	Potion of Healing or Poison brewed with fermented spider eye	Inflicts Damage instantly
Healing	Glistering melon	Restores some health
Infestation		Causes a mob or player to spawn silverfish when they are damaged
Invisibility	Potion of Night Vision brewed with fermented spider eye	Makes you invisible (except for armor, handheld items). Invisibility to mobs lowers at close range

MAGIC: ENCHANTING AND POTIONS

Potion	Ingredient	Effect
Leaping	Rabbit's foot	Allows you to jump almost two blocks high
Night Vision	Golden carrot	Brightens your view of the world around you
Oozing	Slime block	On death, a player or mob spawns two slimes
Poison	Spider eye	Inflicts poison damage
Regeneration	Ghast tear	Restores health
Slow Falling	Phantom membrane	Makes you fall slowly and eliminates fall damage
Slowness	Potions of Swiftness or Leaping brewed with fermented spider eye	Slows players and mobs
Strength	Blaze powder	Increases your melee damage
Swiftness	Sugar	Increases your speed
Turtle Master	Turtle shell	Slows players and mobs
Water Breathing	Pufferfish	Allows you to breathe underwater for several minutes
Weakness	Fermented spider eye	Reduces your melee damage
Weaving	Cobweb	Drops cobwebs on the death of a player or mob
Wind charged	Breeze rod	Emits a burst of wind on the death of a player or mob

Swirling colored particles will emanate from you if you've taken a potion. Also, any effects you are experiencing for more than an instant, including potion effects, are displayed as an icon in the upper right of your screen.

Some of these potions' ingredients need to be crafted beforehand. For example, glistering melon is a melon slice crafted with eight gold nuggets. Fermented spider eye is crafted with a spider eye, one sugar, and one brown mushroom. Magma cream is a drop from a magma cube and can also be crafted with one slime and blaze powder. Note that in order to get phantom membrane, you must stay awake for three in-game days and kill the phantoms that come to attack you.

Before we continue, ensure you have the necessary ingredients for the potions you'd like to create. Now, let's see how to use these ingredients to make our own potions!

THE POTION BREWING PROCESS

Once you've decided which potion(s) you're going to brew and whether you'd like a standard, extended, or enhanced version, it's time to make them! Follow the steps below.

1. Fill Glass Bottles with Water

For one set of three potions, right-click three glass bottles in your water supply to fill them.

2. Brew Three Awkward Potions

Awkward potions are the base for other potions. Right-click the brewing stand to open its interface and place three bottles of water in the bottom slots. Place blaze powder in the top leftmost slot to provide fuel for the process. Finally, place one Nether wart in the top right slot.

> YOUR BREWING INGREDIENT GOES IN THE TOP SLOT. ALL POTIONS BEGIN AS AWKWARD POTIONS, MADE WITH NETHER WART.

The bubble animation on the left means the brewing process has begun. You can close the interface and do other things while brewing. The arrow on the right will gradually fill; when it reaches the bottom, you'll hear a bubbling sound and the bottles will now hold awkward potions.

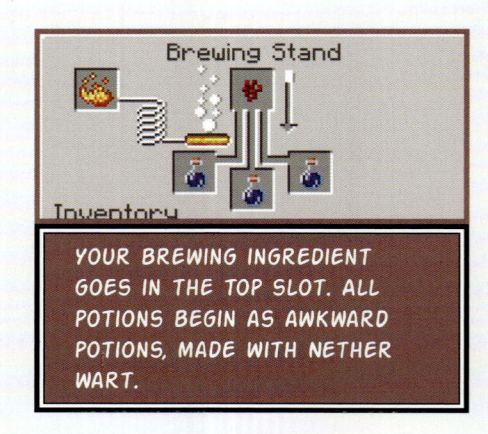

3. Brew Three Standard Potions

Keep your three awkward potions in the brewing stand, and add any ingredient listed in Table 15-1 in the top slot. For example, you'll add a pufferfish to create Potions of Water Breathing. Once the brewing process is finished, you can choose to get your potions, or continue brewing to further augment them.

The next steps for modifying your potions are optional.

4. Enhance or Extend Your Potions

To extend (lengthen the effect's duration) a potion, rebrew it with one redstone dust. To enhance (strengthen) a potion, rebrew it with one glowstone dust. Remember, not all potions have an extended or enhanced version.

5. Make Your Potion a Splash Potion

A *splash potion* is somewhat less strong (25 percent) than a regular potion, but it has the advantage of being throwable at enemies and friends. To change potions into splash potions, brew them with one gunpowder.

> TO THROW A SPLASH POTION AT YOURSELF, AIM AT THE BLOCK YOU'RE STANDING ON OR STRAIGHT UP OVERHEAD SO THAT IT WILL FALL ON YOU.

6. Make Your Splash Potion a Lingering Potion

A *lingering potion* can be thrown to leave a cloud of potion particles that stay in the area (a three-block radius) for up to thirty seconds.

To create a lingering potion, you'll brew your splash potion with a bottle of dragon's breath, which can only be collected from the End (see Chapter 16). Lingering potions have a shorter duration and less power than standard potions, but their effects can continue affecting a mob or player that stays in the cloud.

> NOTE:
> THROWING A HARMING POTION AT AN UNDEAD MOB LIKE A ZOMBIE OR SKELETON HEALS THEM. SPLASH THEM WITH A HEALING POTION INSTEAD.

7. Make Your Lingering Potion into Tipped Arrows

You can create arrows that deliver the potion's effect (without a cloud) by crafting one lingering potion with eight arrows.

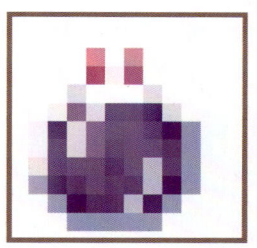

Up Next

Now that you've been inducted into the secret ways of magic, potions, and enchantments, you are ready to take on the biggest challenge of all—the Ender Dragon—and find out what lies beyond the End.

16
THE END GAME: DRAGONS AND WITHERS

As a sandbox game, Minecraft doesn't have a final goal to achieve in order to beat the game—unless you want one.

If you do, or if you're just interested in the next level of loot and adventure, you'll want to visit the End dimension and beat the Ender Dragon, the largest boss in the game. Once you've claimed the title of dragon killer, there's an even stronger boss you can create yourself. You must kill this boss to receive the Nether star, one of the rarest items in the game.

The End

The End is a separate dimension, like the Nether. At its center is an island of pale End stone with obsidian pillars. This island floats in a purple void and is populated by Endermen and the Ender Dragon. The central island is encompassed by additional End stone islands, located some thousand blocks away. These islands are home to chorus plants, End cities, Endermen, and shulkers.

There are five End biomes, all more sparse in structures

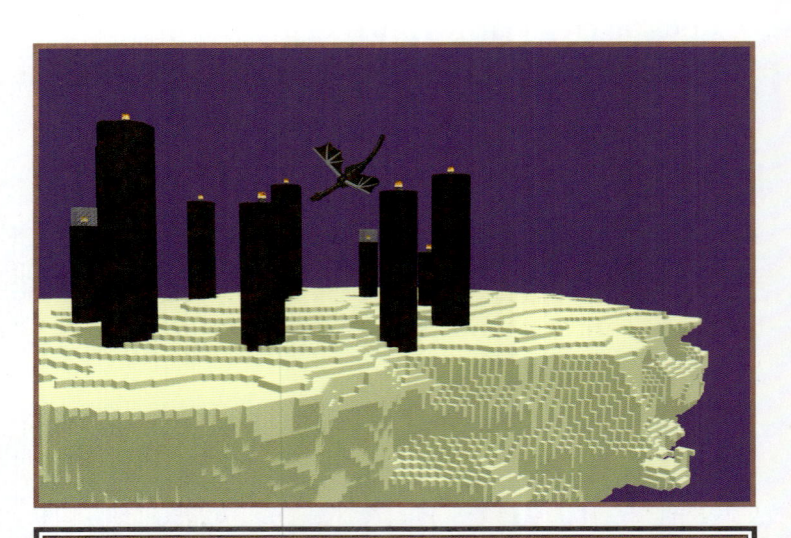

THIS CENTRAL ISLAND HAS TEN OBSIDIAN PILLARS WITH END CRYSTALS THAT HEAL THE DRAGON.

and vegetation than those in Nether and Overworld. The End biome contains the entire central island and the surrounding, empty Void that reaches to the outer islands.

The outer islands are comprised of three biomes: the End barrens, at the outer edges; the End highlands, which form raised central areas; and the End midlands, the slopes between the highlands and barrens. The smaller islands, End island biomes, dot the voids between the outer islands. Chorus trees—that bear fruit with the power of teleportation—can grow only in the End highlands biomes. End cities, which hold loot chests of valuable gold, can generate in both the End highlands and midlands biomes. Endermen spawn in all biomes, while shulkers spawn only in End cities.

Before you take on the Ender Dragon, you'll need to find and activate the End portal, which is an adventure in itself.

Getting to the End

Traveling to the End requires a bit of preparation, such as gathering supplies and locating a nearby stronghold, which will contain the End portal room.

CRAFT EYES OF ENDER

Eyes of Ender are used to locate strongholds and activate the stronghold's End portal. You can craft one Eye of Ender from an Ender pearl and one blaze powder.

The End portal uses twelve Eyes of Ender to activate, and while it often has a number of eyes already installed, it isn't uncommon to need a full twelve to repair it. You'll also need at least one Eye of Ender to find the stronghold, but the eyes can break when they fall, so it's a good idea to have some extra on hand.

You should craft at least fifteen Eyes of Ender for the journey and the portal. You can gather Ender pearls from killing Endermen and blaze rods from blazes. One blaze rod can be crafted into two blaze powders. A good place to find Endermen is in the Nether's Warped Forest Biome; for blazes, search Nether fortresses. See Chapter 14 for more on killing blazes and Endermen.

Challenge: Craft Two Ender Chests

The contents of Ender chests are shared, meaning a player can access the same goods from any Ender chests—a little like cloud storage. If you place an Ender chest in your home and add a set of armor to it, you can retrieve that set of armor anywhere by placing and opening any other Ender chest in the world. Other players can similarly only access their own Ender chest goods, regardless of who crafted the chest.

You can craft an Ender chest from eight obsidian and one Eye of Ender. Craft two Ender chests and place one in your home, keeping the other in your inventory for your journey to the End.

Once you get to the End, place your Ender chest so you can add your loot to it while exploring the End cities. Now, should you die, your goods are protected; they'll be available in your home Ender chest, as well as any Ender chest you craft or find. Ensure you carry a Silk Touch pickaxe with you, as this is the only way to pick up an Ender chest (contents will remain inside it, unlike when breaking regular chests).

Gather Battle Supplies

To be ready to face the End, you'll need to gather some supplies. The best weapons to bring for your battle with the Ender Dragon include a Sharpness sword and Power bow. You'll want to wear Protection IV diamond or netherite armor. You'll also need two pickaxes, including one with Silk Touch, to move your Ender chest. You'll want high-quality food to replenish your health, such as golden apples, golden carrots, and cooked meat. Bring a torch, which you'll use to retrieve the Ender Dragon's egg. If you want to travel to the outer End islands and back, bring extra Ender pearls (at least two). Don't forget to bring a couple of stacks of blocks to make bridges and pillar up if needed. And as with any trip, bring materials to repair or make new tools.

Be sure to bring a bucket of lava, a bed, and a chest for the stronghold and end portal room (see "The Portal Room"). The bucket of lava will prove useful for killing silverfish, as you'll see momentarily. Your chest should hold replacement armor, weapons, and more high-quality food. If you die in the End, you'll respawn back to the portal room at your bed and be ready to gear back up and reenter the fight.

Other supplies you may want to take include:

Boats:
Use these to trap Endermen in.

Ender pearls:
Throw these to travel between Outer End Islands and through the End gateway portals.

Feather Falling IV boots:
You'll likely fall, whether from an obsidian pillar or a dragon attack, but these boots can help you survive.

Glass bottles:
Use glass bottles to pick up the dragon's breath (see page 250).

Potions:
Healing, strength, and slow falling potions will be beneficial for your battle.

Carved pumpkin:
If you place a carved (sheared) pumpkin on your head in place of a helmet, Endermen will no longer be angered by you, though your view will be restricted.

Trapdoors:
You can use these to crawl through the End gateway portals (see "Exploring the Outer End Islands").

Water bucket:
Use it to create a safe landing spot or push Endermen away.

With your supplies in tow, you can move onto the next task: using an Eye of Ender to locate the nearest stronghold.

FIND A STRONGHOLD

Each world has 128 strongholds that can be located thousands of blocks away from both you and each other.

> WHEN YOU THROW THE EYE OF ENDER, IT RISES INTO THE AIR IN THE DIRECTION OF THE NEAREST STRONGHOLD.

To find the nearest stronghold, you'll need one Eye of Ender. Find an open area and throw your Eye of Ender. It will rise up to the sky (you might have to turn to see it) and float in the direction of the stronghold. After a few moments, the eye will begin to fall; it might break apart when it hits the ground, so ensure you have a couple extra Eyes of Ender on hand.

Travel in the direction the eye pointed, about 150 or 200 blocks, then throw the Eye of Ender again to check your direction. Repeat this process. When you're close to the stronghold, the direction of the Eye of Ender will change. Continue following the eye as its direction changes; when it falls, collect it and throw the eye from the location it falls on.

When you're at the stronghold, the Eye of Ender will rise and then drop straight into the ground. This is where you'll begin to dig down until you've found the stronghold. Dig a circular staircase to keep close to the Eye of Ender's last location.

Search the Stronghold

A stronghold is a large underground fortress of stone bricks and variants (including infested stone bricks) with multiple rooms, cells blocked by iron doors, stairways, and corridors. They're often partly ruined and broken by sections of caves and ravines.

Strongholds are home to plenty of skeletons, spiders, creepers, and zombies. On the bright side, you'll find loot chests in corridors, up ladders, and in libraries.

As you explore, keep an eye out for the End portal room. Its location can be almost anywhere. Every portal room will contain two pools of lava and a silverfish spawner right next to the portal.

LOCATE THE PORTAL ROOM

Once you've found the End portal room, break the silverfish spawner immediately (unless you aspire to build a silverfish spawner farm here, though I wouldn't recommend it). Remember, silverfish will multiply unless you kill them in one shot or kill them indirectly with lava—you can pillar up two blocks and drop lava on them without causing other silverfish to spawn.

THE COMPLETED END PORTAL HAS TWELVE EYES OF ENDER AND A STARRY PORTAL HAZE.

Protect the portal room by blocking it off from the rest of the stronghold and the mobs wandering around. Place your bed and right-click it to set your spawn. If you brought along replacement armor, food, and weapons, place a chest and add your belongings.

Check the End portal. Some, if not all, of the blocks will be missing a central Eye of Ender. Right-click with the Eyes of Ender in your inventory to repair them. When you place the final eye, the portal will activate. It's time to jump in!

NOTE: YOU CAN CREATE A SAFE SPACE FOR KILLING ENDERMEN BY MAKING A LEVEL ROOF THAT IS THREE BLOCKS OFF THE GROUND AND AT LEAST THREE BLOCKS WIDE AND LONG. THIS WAY YOU CAN FIT BENEATH THE ROOF, BUT ANY APPROACHING THREE-BLOCK-HIGH ENDERMAN WILL BE PREVENTED FROM GETTING TO YOU. HAVING SEVERAL OF THESE AROUND THE PILLARS CAN HELP PREVENT YOUR UNNECESSARY DEMISE!

Arriving in the End

You'll arrive in the End on an obsidian platform, which may be underground in the central island or a short distance away. You may need to bridge over to the island or dig up to the surface.

The Ender Dragon's health bar will display at the top of your screen, but your first goal is to destroy the End crystals that top the ten obsidian pillars. These crystals can heal the dragon, which is why they must be destroyed before entering battle. While avoiding the dragon and not antagonizing Endermen, shoot the crystals with your bow and arrow. To get a closer aim, you can pillar up, but this will make you more vulnerable to the dragon.

THE EXPLOSIVE END CRYSTALS ON THE TOP OF OBSIDIAN PILLARS ARE YOUR TARGET.

Several of the End crystals will be protected by a cage of iron bars. To shoot these, get close to the pillar's corner so you can aim straight up inside the cage.

DEFEATING THE ENDER DRAGON

Once you've destroyed all the End crystals, you can concentrate on the Ender Dragon and its 200 HP. Focus on shooting it in the head, as this causes the most damage.

The dragon is able to fly through blocks, ram you with its head, and use its powerful wings to throw you high in the air. It will also hurl fireballs at you, which releases a cloud of *dragon's breath*: purple particles that damage you similarly to a potion of Harming. Avoid stepping in these clouds! If you can, pick the dragon breath up by right-clicking glass bottles on the cloud. You can later use these bottles of dragon's breath to make lingering potions.

Every so often, the dragon will return to a central nest-like structure made of bedrock with a short central column. While it rests here, it can't be shot with arrows, so run up to the back of the

NOTE:
LIKE THE NETHER, CLOCKS AND COMPASSES DON'T WORK IN THE END. IF YOU TRY TO USE A BED OR RESPAWN ANCHOR, IT WILL EXPLODE. IF YOU FALL OFF AN ISLAND AND INTO THE VOID, YOU'LL DIE AND RESPAWN BACK AT THE END PORTAL ROOM.

HERE THE DRAGON'S RESTING ON A NESTLIKE STRUCTURE MADE OF BEDROCK AND LIT WITH TORCHES AS A NEARBY CRYSTAL HEALS IT WITH A GRAYISH STREAM (ON THE UPPER RIGHT).

dragon to avoid its wings and strike it with your sword; you'll likely have to jump up and down to reach it.

Make sure to have plenty of good food, potions, and golden apples to heal yourself. Keep at it, and you will eventually succeed!

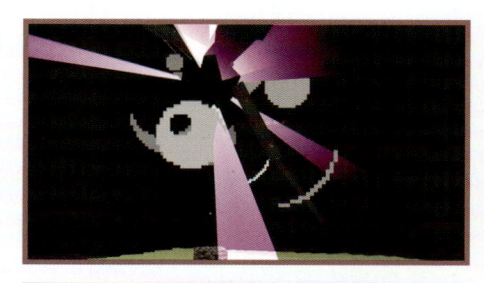

The dragon will die in a massive, colorful explosion. It drops a wealth of experience orbs—12,000 XP—and leaves behind a dragon egg on top of the central bedrock nest, which transforms into the exit portal you can take back to your spawn point. An End gateway portal leading to the outer End islands is also generated, somewhere around the edge of the main island.

The dragon egg is a decorative trophy for your hard work. However, if you try to mine it (with any tool) it will teleport somewhere within about thirty blocks. The egg is gravity-affected, so to prevent it from falling into the exit portal, cover the exit portal with blocks. Then, mine the egg and locate it after it's teleported. Leave the block it is resting on, but mine the block below that and place a torch there. Then mine the block you left between the torch and the egg. The egg will drop on the torch and convert to its item form, which you can pick up.

Once you've killed the dragon, you've officially "won" Minecraft. After you've grabbed the dragon egg, step into the exit portal. As you transport, the End poem will scroll on the screen. It's worth reading at least once, although the summary end credits are quite long. If you must, you can speed it up by holding the space bar and tapping **Ctrl**. Or you can skip the poem entirely by pressing **Esc**.

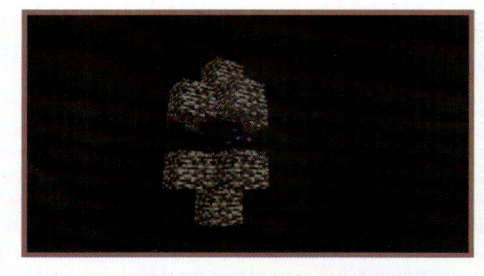

RESPAWNING THE DRAGON

If you enjoy a good dragon fight, or would like another 12,000 XP, or would like some additional gateway portals, you can respawn the dragon. To do so, first craft four end crystals from one ghast tear, one Eye of Ender, and seven glass blocks each. Place the end crystals on

THE DRAGON'S DEATH IS THE MOST SPECTACULAR EVENT IN MINECRAFT.

THE DRAGON EGG RESTS ON TOP OF THE EXIT PORTAL.

AN END GATEWAY GENERATES AT THE EDGE OF THE ISLAND IN THE AIR.

the central bedrock block on each side of the exit portal. The crystals will send beams to the tops of the obsidian pillars, replacing the original end crystals. Then, the Ender Dragon will respawn.

After you defeat the Ender Dragon again, a second End gateway portal is created. Up to twenty End gateways, circling around the central island, can be created this way, each leading to a different segment of the outer islands.

> **NOTE:**
> END CRYSTALS ARE EXTREMELY EXPLOSIVE. THEY CAN ONLY BE PLACED ON BEDROCK OR OBSIDIAN; ATTACKING OR CLICKING THEM WILL SET OFF A LARGE EXPLOSION.

Exploring the Outer End Islands

While you can return to your stronghold, I recommend remaining in the End after defeating the dragon to explore and loot the outer islands. Some of the best loot—including the Elytra—is found in the End cities.

To get to the outer islands, locate an End gateway portal. They're located around the rim of the island, a dozen or so blocks in the air. You might have to build a staircase or bridge to the gateway, and it's a good idea to make a safe platform around it while you're at it, as you'll likely come back this way. To use the portal, throw an Ender pearl through its middle. If you are low on Ender pearls, you can use a trapdoor to crawl through the space. To do this, place a trapdoor on one of the bedrock blocks that's directly above the portal block in the middle. Right-click the trapdoor to flip it up. Stand in the same block that the trapdoor is in. Now flip the trapdoor down. This will push you into a crawl mode (a swim position) and you can now fit into and through one-block-high spaces.

You'll be transported to an Outer End Island, where you'll find Endermen and chorus plants. To travel between islands, you'll need to use Ender pearls or make bridges between them, until you've mastered flying with Elytra (see "Learning to Fly").

Keep track of your gateway portal—you can record its coordinates or leave torches on your journey. The outer island gateway portal takes you back to the central island portal you left from. You might find randomly generated gateway portals on the outer islands; these will teleport you back to the main island's obsidian spawn platform.

CHORUS PLANTS, FRUIT, AND FLOWERS

Chorus plants are tall and cactus-like. At the end of each branch, a chorus flower will grow. You can mine the flowers individually to gather them; they can be planted on End stone to grow new chorus plants. You can break a chorus plant by destroying its bottom block; this will drop a random number of chorus fruit.

Chorus fruit can be eaten, which will restore 4 hunger and will randomly teleport you about eight blocks away. You can also smelt chorus fruit to create popped chorus fruit.

Popped chorus fruit is used to craft decorative, luminescent end rods (using one blaze rod and a popped chorus fruit) or purpur blocks (using four popped chorus fruit). Purpur is a decorative block, from which you can craft purpur stairs, purpur slabs, and purpur pillars.

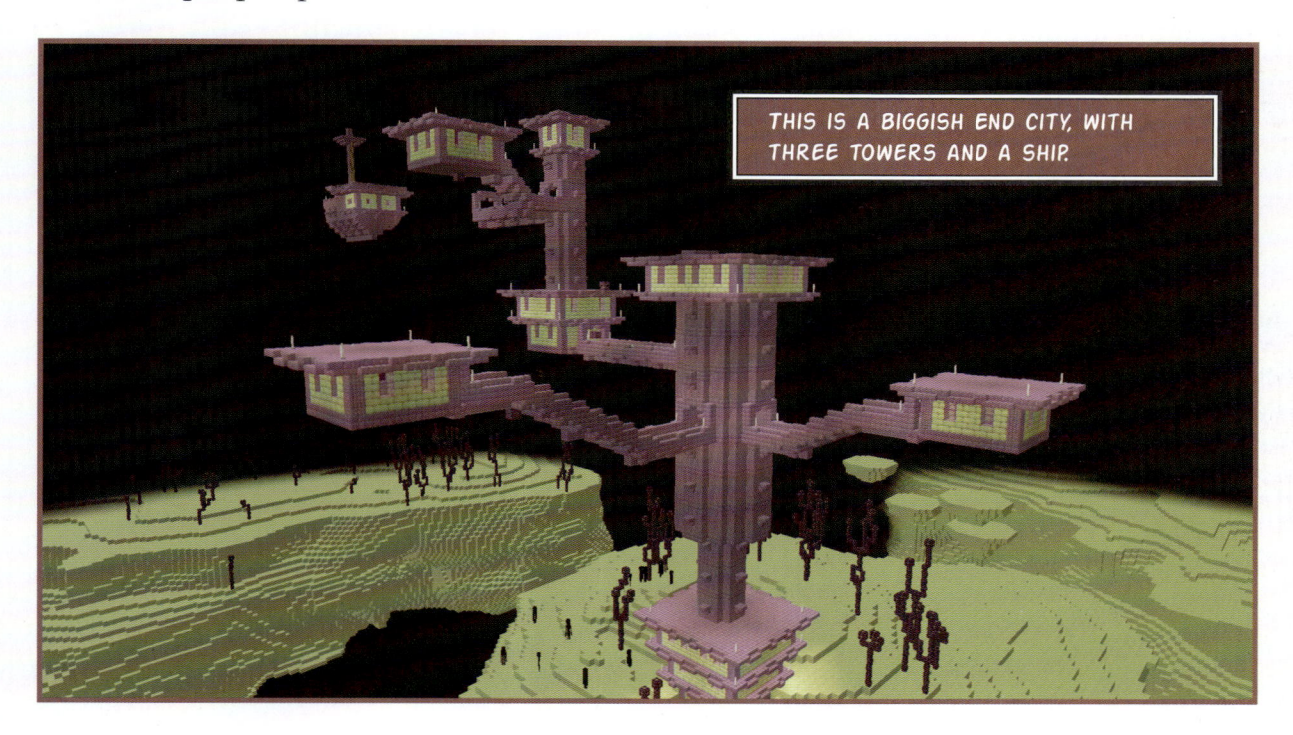

THIS IS A BIGGISH END CITY, WITH THREE TOWERS AND A SHIP.

END CITIES

A number of outer End islands will generate with *End cities*. These are branching, narrow structures of towers and connecting corridors, made of End bricks (crafted from End stone) and purpur blocks. Inside, the towers are separated into different levels and rooms; some have ladders to ascend, other have slabs to jump up.

End cities are protected by shulkers found in towers, at the top of towers, at entranceways, and at the ground level entrance. The larger towers are encircled, inside, by shulkers. The largest floors in the towers may contain two loot chests with diamond and iron gear, gold, diamonds, iron, and more. These rooms can contain one loot chest and an Ender chest instead. End cities can vary drastically in size; one may be massive with multiple towers and a ship, while another might have a single small tower.

SHULKERS

Shulkers, as described in Chapter 11, are shelled creatures that blend into their surroundings and can appear as purpur blocks. As you approach, they'll open up and fire a shulker bullet at you. The bullet inflicts 4 HP of damage and a Levitation effect, which lifts you slowly in the air for ten seconds; if you don't watch out, you might fall to your death!

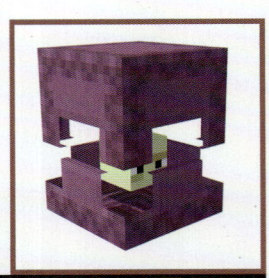

You can attack shulker bullets with a sword or defend yourself with a shield. You'll want to attack shulkers while their shells are open. They can sometimes teleport to a new location, within seventeen blocks.

SHULKER BOXES CAN BE DYED WITH ANY OF THE SIXTEEN DYES.

When you kill a shulker, it has a chance of dropping a shulker shell. You can craft the valuable shulker box from two shulker shells and a chest. Shulker boxes, like Ender chests, can be transported with their contents intact.

ELYTRA

The Elytra, wings that enable you to fly, are a primary reason to defeat the dragon and scour the outer islands. They are found in End ships, which generate in only a few of the End cities. End ships float a little ways away from a short bridge that extends out from the city, and are protected by shulkers.

Once you've cleared the ship's exterior of shulkers, go to the front of the ship. You should find a dragon's head here that you can break with any tool. Then, go to the back of the ship and walk down the stairs, where you'll find a brewing stand you can loot. Continue down the stairs to face the final shulker. To either side of the shulker is a loot chest; between these chests, hanging in an item frame, is a pair of Elytra.

YOU'VE FOUND THE GRAND TREASURE OF THE END!

After the End

Once you're back in the Overworld, there are plenty of challenges left for you to discover. The most beneficial will be learning to fly with your Elytra and creating and killing the Wither for a Nether star, one of the rarest items in the game.

LEARNING TO FLY

To use your Elytra, equip them in your chest armor slot. To start flying, you'll need to jump while you're falling. You should find a small hill or pillar to jump from in order to practice, as it can take more than a few attempts to get good at this.

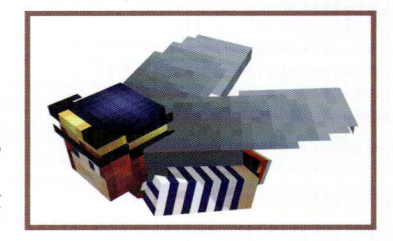

If you're able, have some firework rockets (crafted from one paper and at least one gunpowder) with you while you practice. The Elytra are like hang gliders—they don't pull you up into the sky, but let you glide along, slowly losing altitude. Right-clicking firework rockets, however, will give you the boost to get higher.

If you angle up too sharply while flying, you can stall and begin to fall. To land, descend at a shallow angle and turn as you approach your landing target to slow down. You can take quite a bit of damage from flying into the ground or cliffs, so consider wearing Feather Falling boots while learning.

DEFEATING THE WITHER

The Wither is a flying, undead, three-headed boss mob that hurls explosive wither skulls. It isn't found naturally; you have to create it in a similar way to creating an iron golem, with four soul sand blocks and three wither skeleton skulls.

Once the last wither skeleton skull is placed, the Wither comes to life—it turns blue and flashes, and its health bar appears at the top of the screen. While the health bar fills up, the Wither is invulnerable to attacks; when the bar has filled, the Wither makes a large explosion and turns black.

It is aggressive toward players and all mobs except ghasts and undead mobs and will destroy the environment with its explosive black and blue wither skulls attack. Both types of wither skulls inflict 8 HP of damage as well as the Wither II effect.

Like the Ender Dragon, the Wither is immune to potion effects except for Instant Health and Harming. It slowly regains health naturally and when it kills mobs. When the Wither kills a mob, it also leaves a wither rose in the mob's place.

When the Wither drops to half health it gains magic armor that makes it immune to arrows and tridents. When the Wither dies, it drops the rare Nether star, which you can use to create beacons.

> **NOTE:**
> WITHER SKELETONS ARE FOUND IN NETHER FORTRESSES. THERE'S A SMALL CHANCE THAT A WITHER SKELETON WILL DROP ITS SKULL UPON DEATH, SO I RECOMMEND USING A SWORD ENCHANTED WITH LOOTING III (SEE CHAPTER 16) TO KILL THEM. THIS WILL INCREASE THE LIKELIHOOD FROM 2.5 PERCENT TO 5.5 PERCENT.

> **NOTE:**
> WITHER ROSES CAN YIELD BLACK DYE. WHEN PLANTED, WITHER ROSES WILL GIVE ANY PLAYER OR MOB WHO TOUCHES IT THE WITHER EFFECT.

> BE SURE YOU'RE READY TO FIGHT WHEN YOU PLACE THE LAST WITHER SKELETON SKULL!

Challenge: Beat The Wither

Because of the destruction a Wither causes, a common tactic is to fight it underground.

Dig down to around y=0 to give plenty of overhead space between the Wither and aboveground. You'll want a solid rock blocked-off area that is free of caves. Excavate a two-block-high corridor about thirty blocks long and keep it lit with torches. The low ceilings should help keep the Wither lower to the ground, more restricted, and thus easier to fight.

At one end of the corridor, create a small, 3×3×3-block chamber for building the Wither. At the other end, dig out a space on either side of the corridor that you can hide in. Dig out a safer area a little farther away where you can place a bed and set your spawn, so you can quickly return to the fight if you die. If you have obsidian, replace the corridor floor with obsidian to help keep the ground even.

Before assembling the Wither, make sure you're stocked with supplies—armor, food, potions, a sword enchanted with Smite, and an enchanted bow or trident. You should bring high-quality foods and Strength, Healing, and Regeneration potions for yourself, as well as Healing potions to hurt the Wither. Bring a few buckets of milk to cure yourself of the wither effect.

When you're ready, assemble the Wither at the end of the corridor. Place four soul sand in a T-shape, and place three wither skeleton skulls along the top. Run to the end of the corridor and take shelter in your hideout. After the explosion, venture out to attack the Wither with your bow or trident. When you're low on health, retreat and take potions. When its health bar reaches halfway, approach the Wither and attack it with your sword. Once the battle is done, gather the dropped Nether star.

NETHER STARS AND BEACONS

Nether stars are used solely to create *beacons*. When activated, beacons give status effects to nearby players, like Regeneration or Haste.

You can craft a beacon from one Nether star, three obsidian, and five glass blocks. To activate it, you'll need to place it as the top of a pyramid of gold, diamond, emerald, iron, or netherite blocks. There are four sizes of pyramid, each with an

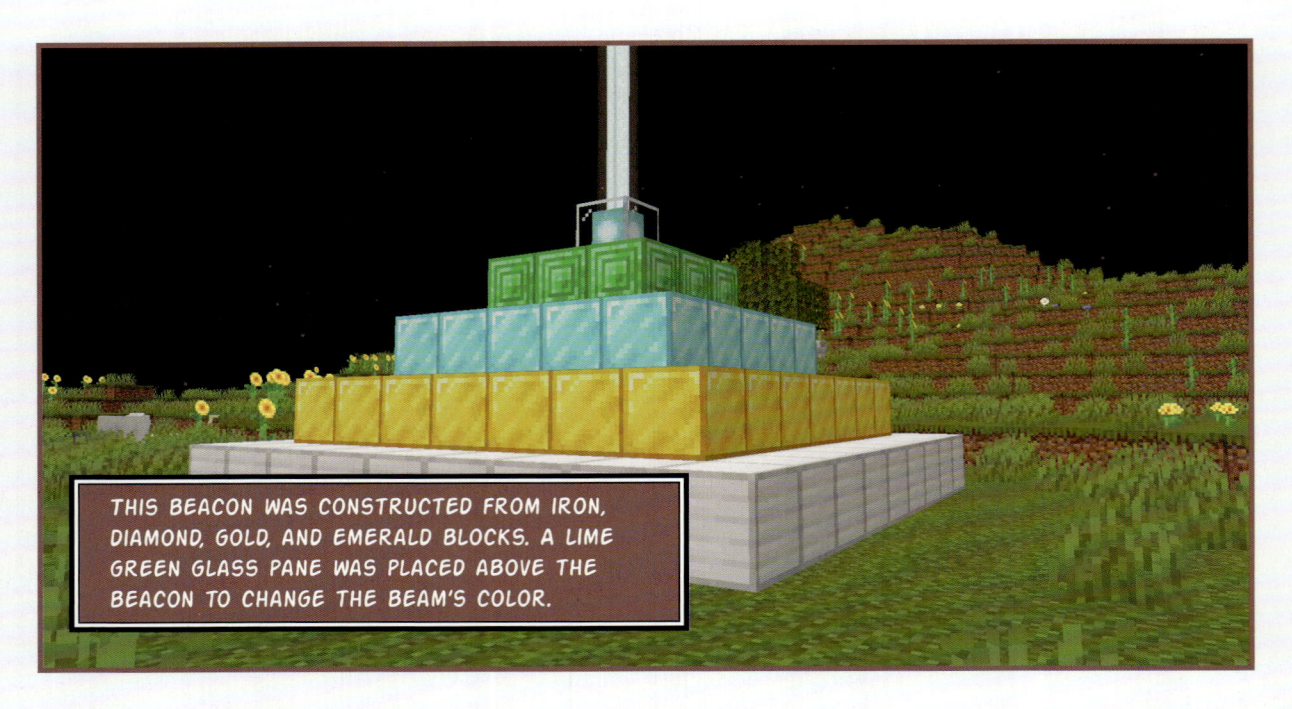

THIS BEACON WAS CONSTRUCTED FROM IRON, DIAMOND, GOLD, AND EMERALD BLOCKS. A LIME GREEN GLASS PANE WAS PLACED ABOVE THE BEACON TO CHANGE THE BEAM'S COLOR.

additional layer and status effects. The smallest has one layer of 3x3 blocks; the next adds a 5x5 layer of blocks; the third size adds a 7x7 layer; and the full pyramid adds a 9x9 layer for a total of four.

After you've constructed your pyramid, place the beacon at the top. Once activated, the beacon will emit a light beam up to the sky. To work, there can't be any obstructions between the beacon and sky, except for stained glass panes or blocks, which can change the beam's color.

Right-click the beacon to open its interface. Here you can select a primary power by clicking a button on the left. If you built a full pyramid, you can also select a secondary power of Regeneration or boost the primary power to a Level II. After making your selections, confirm your choice by placing an ingot, emerald, or diamond in the bottom slots and clicking the check mark.

If you have the smallest pyramid, you have access to Speed (moving) and Haste (mining). If your pyramid has two layers, you can also choose

Resistance (to damage) and Jump Boost. With three layers, Strength becomes available; with four, you can select Regeneration.

The horizontal range of a beacon increases with each level of pyramid, from twenty blocks at level 1 to fifty blocks at level 4.

What's Next?

Now that you've completed this book, you are a bone fide Minecraft survival gamer. But it doesn't stop there! Each year, the developers at Mojang update the game with new features and mobs, so there's always new gameplay to discover.

There are other ways to play Minecraft (see Appendix C), and there are always new vistas to see, pyramids to loot, buildings to create, and redstone contraptions to build. How about creating an automated zombified piglin farm to get masses of gold in minutes for your next challenge?

You can get inspired by finding hundreds of tutorials online to create something uniquely your own. In the meantime, keep on mining!

APPENDIX A
GAME SETTINGS

Gameplay Settings

There is a plethora of settings to adjust your gameplay, from graphics effects to the language used. Let's take a look at the various options available as you start and play the game.

LAUNCHER

When you start up Minecraft, the game launcher opens. The launcher allows you to switch between different Minecraft games (Java Edition, Windows 10, and Minecraft Dungeons) as well as different versions of Minecraft Java Edition. You can also add multiple Microsoft accounts and a custom skin. (To add a new Microsoft account, click **Settings** and then **Accounts**.)

Of most use here are two tabs that display when you click on Minecraft: Java Edition: Installations and Skins. As discussed in Chapter 2, under the **Play** tab of the launcher, you can select which version of Minecraft you want to play, including **Latest Release**, which will automatically keep your game updated to the most recent official release. You can also choose **Latest Snapshot**, which will open the latest *test version* of the game. In between official releases of game updates, Mojang releases incomplete test versions or snapshots that include features that are being worked on. In general, these are fairly stable and are a great way to play with upcoming features.

You can also create new installations with a fixed version of the game. For example, you might want to play a very old version of Minecraft, just to see what that's like. To do this, click the **Installations** tab and choose the version you want to play.

On the **Skins** screen, you can add custom skins to use for your player avatar or choose one of the default Steve or Alex skins. For more information on custom skins, see Appendix B.

TITLE SCREEN

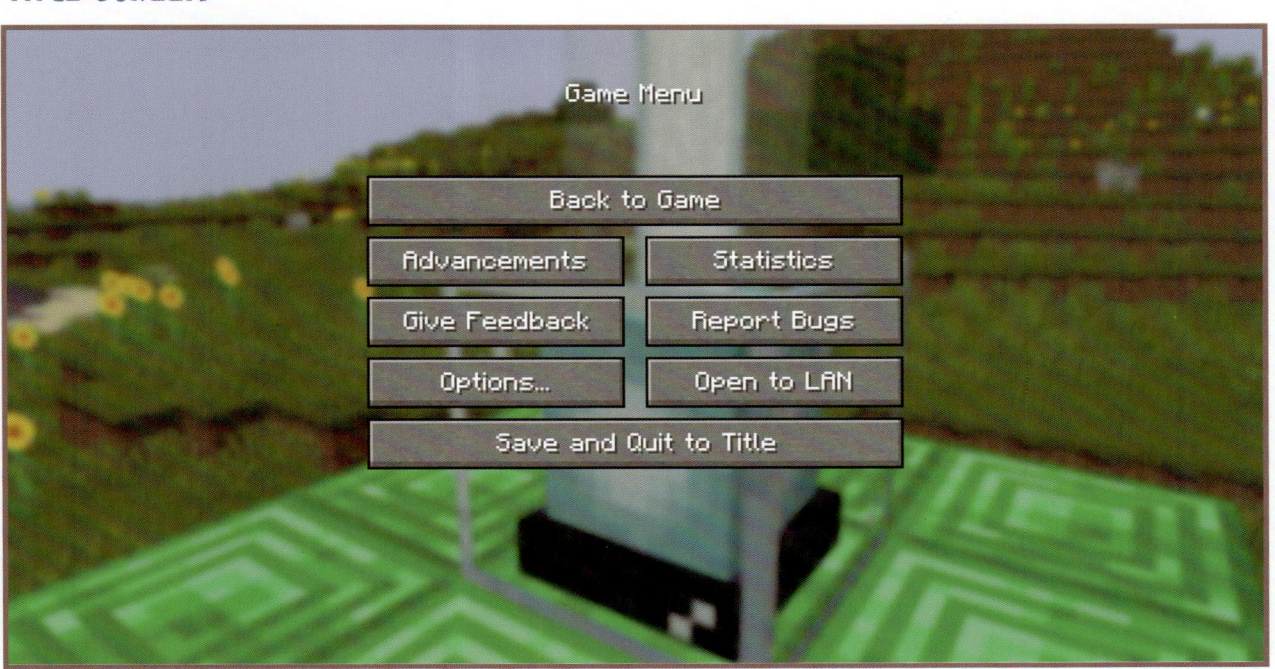

Once the game loads, you're presented with the title screen. To start your game, click **Singleplayer**, unless you are joining a server to play with others. A *server* is a computer that is built for multiple users to access. In this case, click **Multiplayer,**

and on the next screen you can add a server address (usually in the form of an IP address, like *111.11.111.1* or domain name, like *newserver.net*). You'll typically find a multiplayer server's address from the server's website or the group that operates the server. If you've purchased a *Realm* (a Minecraft service that provides a multiplayer server), you can click **Minecraft Realms** to open and connect to your realm.

The globe icon to the left of the Options button allows you to choose what language the game is in. The game's been translated into an impressive number of languages, including some pretty funny ones, like Pirate Speak and LOLCAT.

To the right of the Quit Game button is a person icon. Click this icon to see and adjust accessibility options, from *Subtitles* that will describe sounds in the game to a *Narrator* that will verbalize chat text and more. There's a link at the bottom of the accessibility screen to access the full guide to accessibility options online at http://www.minecraft.net.

OPTIONS

Click the **Options** button on the Title screen to set up your game options.

Starting from the top left of the Options screen, the options are as follows:

FOV:
This is your Field of View (FOV) in horizontal degrees. Push the slider to the left to see a zoomed-in view or to the right for increasingly wide perspectives. The standard view is **70**. Choosing a higher FOV will let you see more, but the view will be skewed and can affect your graphics rendering speed and cause lag. A lower FOV will decrease what you can see on your screen.

Online:
Here, you can select whether your name is added to notifications on multiplayer servers and whether you'll see notifications about updates and Mojang blog posts about Realms.

Skin Customization:
A custom skin can have a secondary, outer layer for your character's legs, arms, body (jacket), and head (hat). You can toggle these on and off here. If you have a cape (these are given out on rare occasions), you can toggle it to display. This screen is also where you can select which hand is your main hand.

Music and Sounds:
In this submenu, you can adjust the volume of music, overall sound, or specific categories of sound. You can also turn on subtitles.

Video Settings:
There are a wide variety of video settings available, some of which you can use to increase graphic quality or lower to improve performance.
These video settings are listed below:

> **Fullscreen Resolution:**
> Sets the resolution when you are playing in fullscreen mode. Higher resolutions make for better graphics!
>
> **Biome Blend:**
> Decides how smooth color transitions are between biomes.
>
> **Graphics:**
> Overall quality of graphics.

Render Distance:
Adjusts how far you can see, measured in 16x16 chunks. The more chunks you can see, though, the harder it can be on your graphics processor.

Chunk Builder:
Changes how chunk sections are visually updated. Threaded is the least processing intensive but may show holes in the world when breaking blocks.

Simulation Distance:
Specifies how far away entities are when the game stops animating them.

Smooth Lighting:
Selects how smooth the lighting between different light levels is.

Max Framerate:
Sets the maximum *framerate* (or *frames per second*), the rate at which a visual image, like your gameplay screen, is refreshed. Ideally, this matches your monitor's refresh rate.

To find your monitor's refresh rate on a PC, open the **Control Panel**, click **Hardware and Sound**, then click **How to Correct Monitor Flicker** (this is the refresh rate). The ensuing dialogue boxes should guide you through viewing and setting your monitor refresh rate.

On a Mac, click the apple icon at the top left of your screen. Then, click **System Preferences>Displays**. Your monitor's refresh rate should be selected on the Refresh Rate pop-up menu.

Vsync:
This limits the framerate to match your monitor's refresh rate and is helpful in preventing graphical issues with computers with older graphics cards.

View Bobbing:
Toggles whether the players view bobs side to side to simulate the experience of walking.

GUI Scale:
Sets the size of UI elements, like the chat window and your HUD.

GAME SETTINGS

Attack Indicator:

Selects the location the attack indicator displays in (by the hotbar, by the crosshair, or off).

Brightness:

Changes how bright the environment is.

Clouds:

Adjusts the quality level that clouds are rendered with, from high (3D) to normal (flat) to off (no clouds).

Fullscreen:

Toggles fullscreen on and off. If set to Off, Minecraft will run in a window instead.

Particles:

Toggles particle animations, like the swirls around a player that's taken a potion.

Mipmap Levels:

Adjusts how smoothly textures are rendered.

Entity Shadows:

Toggles shadows cast by entities.

Distortion Effects:

Changes the effects that are shown when you're affected by Nausea or in a Nether portal.

Entity Distance:

Selects how far away an entity is before you can no longer see it.

FOV Effects:

Changes how much the perspective changes your view when you are under a Speed status effect.

Autosave Indicator:

Toggles the indicator that lets you know when your game is saving. In the *vanilla* (base) game, the text *Saving World* appears on the bottom right of your screen when you pause (by pressing **Esc**).

If you're finding your game's performance to be *laggy*—or slow to respond—consider reducing Render Distance, changing Graphics to Fast, and setting Particles to Minimal. You might also want to turn off Biome Smoothing, Smooth Lighting, Mipmap Levels, and Clouds. If the problem persists, try using windowed rather than fullscreen mode.

The rest of the most relevant game options available on the Options screen are as follows:

Controls:
Under the *Controls* category, you can configure your mouse and adjust *key bindings* (what keyboard keys are used for different activities). You can also toggle whether you need to hold down a key or just tap a key to turn on sprinting and sneaking. Lastly, *Auto-jump* will turn on automatically jumping up a single block when you walk into it.

Language:
This setting enables you to select the language the game interface uses; this is the same as the title screen language settings.

Chat Settings:
These settings adjust how chat looks. By default, chat scrolls on the bottom left of your screen.

Resource Packs:
Resource packs are files that you can download and add to your game to change textures, sounds, and models. For more on resource packs, see Appendix B.

Accessibility Settings:
These are identical to the settings linked to from the title screen.

CREATE NEW WORLD

To start playing Minecraft, you first must create a world. While the default settings are great for this, you may want to create a world using built-in customization features. Some of these settings are covered in Chapter 2; we'll cover the rest here. When you open the Create New World page, there are three tabs of options.

GAME TAB

On the main Game tab, you can choose your game mode, difficulty, and whether or not to allow commands, and enter the name of your world. Allowing commands gives you access to creative commands that you wouldn't get in a survival world, including changing the gameplay mode. You can find a list of commands at the Minecraft wiki (minecraft.fandom.com/wiki/Commands).

WORLD TAB

In the World tab, you can add a string of letters or numbers to serve as the base seed for your world (this is a key used in the randomization of your world.)

World Type: World types you can choose from, besides the default, are:

- **Superflat:** A Superflat world is a completely flat world that has a top layer of grass, two layers of dirt blocks, and a bottom layer of bedrock. The top grass layer of the default Superflat world is at y= −60, which means that slimes spawn frequently. However, you can also adjust different presets for the number of layers of grass, dirt, and so on.
- **Large Biomes:** Biomes are enlarged by four times along each axis to be sixteen times larger than default biomes.
- **Amplified:** In amplified worlds, the heights are extreme and the landscape jagged.

- **Single Biome:** You can choose just one of Minecraft's biomes to use for your whole world.

Generate Structures: This allows you to prevent buildings like villages and dungeons from generating in your world. You'd most likely want to do this if you are setting up a creative world for practicing redstone.

Bonus Chest: This will spawn a single chest when you spawn, with a few tools and a little food.

More Tab

Here you can enable or disable game rules, enable experiments (gameplay features the developers are still working on), and add data packs. Game rules change miscellaneous gameplay, such as whether the weather changes, fire spreads, patrols occur, or phantoms spawn. For example, if I'm playing in a creative world, I'll usually turn weather off and stop the daylight cycle. Data packs are resources that can modify your world and gameplay. We'll take a look at them in Appendix B: Customizing Minecraft.

Game Menu

When you press **Esc** during the game, you're presented with the game menu, which gives you access to an Options menu as well as a few other relevant choices:

Advancements:

Opens up the *Advancements* interface, where you can check on your progress in your current world.

Statistics:

Lists an extensive range of statistics, from how many cake slices you've eaten to how many mobs you've killed.

Give Feedback and Report Bugs:

Both lead to Minecraft's website, where you can provide your thoughts on the game and report any technical or gameplay issues you've experienced.

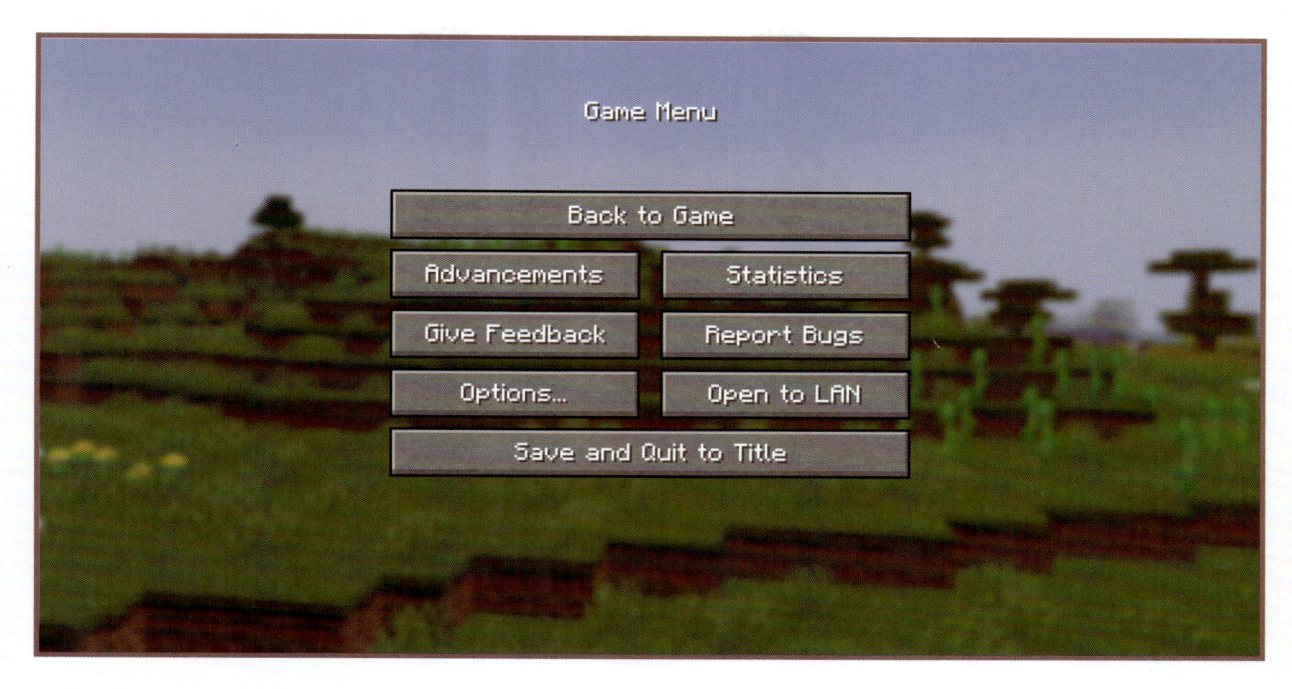

Options:

This opens a slightly different options menu where you can change your game's difficulty level; in order to do this, you must either turn cheats on or start in creative mode.

Open to LAN:

If you're familiar with setting up local area networks, you would use this setting to open up a game to allow local users to play with you. This option also allows you to change your world's game mode and whether cheats are on.

This can sometimes be a real help if you need to fix a problem. For example, say you've lost your exit portal in the End and you'll lose all your loot if you choose to die to get back to the Overworld. While you can just take the easy way and die by leaping off of the edge of an island, you can cheat your way out of this situation. Just click **Open to LAN**, change your world to **Creative**, get yourself an Ender chest, or fly to the central island. When you're back safe with your loot, save and close your world. When you reopen it, you'll be back to your regular world.

APPENDIX B
CUSTOMIZING MINECRAFT

The first way you'll likely want to customize your gameplay is to use a custom skin. Additionally, you can change how your game looks by using a resource pack that changes elements, like textures and sounds. Finally, data packs can bring in new gameplay features.

There are web sites where creators of skins, resource packs, and data packs share their creations to be downloaded by other players. Keep away from sites that ask you for personal information or money, and consider using an antivirus program that checks downloaded files. Talk with your parent or guardian about downloading an antivirus program for your computer, and ensure you do your research and find a reputable one with good reviews.

Custom Skins

To customize your skin (in the Java Edition), you first need to create or download a skin file, and then upload it. While there are many websites you can find downloadable skins, I recommend checking out The Skindex (*https://www.minecraftskins.com/*) and Miners Need Cool Shoes (https://www.needcoolshoes.com).

Both the Skindex and Miners have online skin editors that allow you to create a new skin or modify an existing one, though it's much easier to select and download an existing skin. While you are looking for a skin, take note of whether it is designed for a Steve model or Alex model. (The Alex model has thinner arms.)

To equip your skin, go to the **Skins** tab in the Minecraft launcher and click the **New Skin** button. Next, you need to choose whether the skin uses the Steve or Alex model. Click **Browse** and then locate your skin file (it should be a *.png* file) on your computer. If you have a cape option, it will show here, and you can also name your skin. Finally, click **Save & Use** to equip your character with your new skin.

Resource Packs

Resource packs (also called *texture packs*) are a way to customize the graphic and sound elements of the game without modifying the programming code. Music, sounds, 3D models, and textures can all be replaced. Creators typically publish their resource packs online, available for anyone to download and use for free. To look for resource packs, search online for *best Minecraft resource packs* and you'll get a multitude of review articles and videos about popular packs.

Resource packs come as *.zip* files. Make sure any resource pack you want to use is compatible with the version of Minecraft you play (such as 1.19). You won't need to save and quit your world after you've downloaded a resource pack *.zip* file. On the title screen, click **Options**, then **Resource Packs**. This opens the Select Resource Packs screen.

> ANY PACKS LISTED IN RED AREN'T COMPATIBLE WITH THE VERSION OF MINECRAFT YOU ARE CURRENTLY PLAYING.

The Select Resource Packs screen shows available resource packs on the left column, and the resource packs currently in use on the right.

Drag and drop your file to the left column on the Select Resource Packs screen; you'll be asked to confirm that you're adding the pack. You can also place the file yourself in the *resourcepacks* folder in the program folder. To find that folder, click **Open Pack Folder** on the Select Resources Pack screen.

To activate a resource pack, hover over its listing in the left column, and an arrow will appear to the left of the pack's name. Click the arrow. This will move the resource pack to the *Selected* column and will activate when you return to your game. To remove a pack, click its arrow in the Selected column. You can also use these arrows to order selected resource packs in priority. The resources you've given priority will be at the top of the column and will override any resources from a pack lower down in the list. For example, you might find a resource pack that just changes the way villagers sound. Moving it to the top of the list will ensure that, regardless of what other resource packs you add, the villagers will still sound how they do in that resource pack.

THE RESOURCE PACK *JOLICRAFT* CHANGES THE APPEARANCE OF VILLAGERS DRASTICALLY!

Data Packs

Data packs, like resource packs, customize Minecraft without changing the underlying code. *Data packs* change gameplay elements that the developers have allowed to be customized, including advancements, crafting recipes, biomes and dimensions, and more.

As with resource pack, you must use a data pack that's compatible with your version of Minecraft. Data packs are placed as *.zip* files in the *.minecraft/saves/(worldname)/datapacks* folder. You do not need to close your world before adding a data pack.

You can select a data pack when you're creating a world by clicking **Data Packs** on the Create New World screen, which opens the *Select Data Packs* screen. This screen operates in the same way as the Select Resource Packs screen.

To add or select a data pack for an existing world, go to the **Select World** screen and select the world. Then click **Edit**. **On the** Edit **screen, click Open World Folder**. This will open up the folder for your world (or *saves*) in your computer's file system. From here, you can open the *datapacks* folder and add data packs to it.

While the game is running, you can use the following commands to manage your data packs:

- **/datapack list** to view which data packs are available.
- **/datapack disable** to disable a pack (also reloads the world).
- **/datapack enable** to enable a pack (also reloads the world).

Ensure that any data packs you download are safe to use. In general, data packs that have been reviewed by popular magazines, or by a popular content creator, are safe. If the data pack you want to try extensively changes your world, first try it on a backup world. I highly recommend Vanilla Tweaks (https://vanillatweaks.net), which offers you the ability to pick and choose between different effects and features you'd like to try. The site gives clear steps to follow for downloading and installing. The site was created and is run by a very popular Minecraft YouTuber, xisumavoid, and his team.

APPENDIX C
BEYOND SURVIVAL: OTHER WAYS TO PLAY MINECRAFT

This book delved into the Survival single-player gameplay of Minecraft, but there are other ways to play. In this Appendix, we'll look into some of these play styles.

Creative/Maps

As discussed in Chapter 1, the Creative gameplay mode disables hostile mobs and allows you to fly around without fear of being injured. This is often a great way for the very youngest players to start out, but many players—particularly those focused on building—also play solely in Creative mode. There are several unique features available only in Creative mode, such as command blocks, that allow you to make games within games.

> NOTE:
> COMMAND BLOCKS ARE BEYOND THE SCOPE OF THIS BOOK, BUT YOU CAN FIND INFORMATION ABOUT THEM ON THE MINECRAFT WIKI (HTTPS://MINECRAFT.FANDOM.COM/WIKI/).

Players who create maps of limited worlds will use Creative mode and command blocks to make mini-games and more. You can find a variety of playable maps through the resource-rich Planet Minecraft, a long-standing community forum (https://planetminecraft.com). After you've found a map you'd like to play, you can download it and install it in your *.minecraft/saves* folder.

Modded Minecraft

There's a huge community of players that play *modded* Minecraft. Modding is the process of altering aspects of a video game through changing its code.

Mods are often combined into mod packs with a specific theme, like outer space travel, farming, or combat and looting. A mod may add new mobs, new ways to farm, or even new dimensions and biomes. Most mods within mod packs are very well made.

There are several compatibility issues to keep track of when playing a modded game, so if you're new to modded Minecraft, go to https://curseforge.com—the website of a popular modding group—and download their desktop app. The CurseForge desktop app lets you browse and install mods and mod packs. It will set up a separate instance of Minecraft for you to use with mods and mod packs so that you don't make any changes to your *vanilla* (or base) program.

Multiplayer

You don't have to play alone! There are hundreds of *servers* out there, of all types, that you can join. Servers are computers that are built to be used by multiple people over a network. You can find vanilla survival (*survival multiplayer* or *SMP*) or modded servers, or even servers with special gameplay and features.

PLAYER-MADE SERVERS

You can find smaller, informal servers—often started by people who are looking for new players to join—listed in the Reddit subreddit, r/mcservers (https://www.reddit.com/r/mcservers/). Reddit is a community discussion forum with many different topics; its subgroups are called subreddits.

In the r/mcservers subreddit, people will post their own servers and will note whether they are modded, vanilla, have specific rules, and so on. If a server has a *whitelist*, that means you must be approved before joining; you'll typically have to answer a few questions or fill out a form.

CREATE YOUR OWN SERVER

Another option for playing multiplayer is Minecraft's subscription server service, *Realms*. With Realms, you can easily create a small multiplayer server and invite your friends. To find out more about Realms, go to minecraft.net/en-us/realms, where you can find many tutorials and *FAQs (frequently asked questions articles)*.

You can also rent server space from a Minecraft hosting solution, like https://MelonCube.net, and set up a server yourself. This is more complicated than using Realms, but hosting solutions can often help you with setting up and troubleshooting a new server.

COMPETITIVE/COMMERCIAL SERVERS

In addition to vanilla and modded servers, there are a number of competitive play servers open to anyone, such as the Archon (https://thearchon.net). These servers are free to join, but are typically in the market of selling the player unnecessary cosmetic features. Keep this in mind and avoid purchasing anything online before talking with your parent or guardian.

Competitive play servers (also known as *PvP*, or *player-versus-player*) may offer one or more styles of play, including:

Anarchy:
No rules, player vs. player.

Factions:
Groups of players battle each other.

Towny:
Groups of players band together to form towns and compete or trade economically.

Roleplay:
Players take on a character in line with the server's storyline or background, such as medieval or fantasy genres.

Prison:
Players compete economically, gathering money and benefits initially by mining.

Skyblock/Economy:
Players compete economically by making crop and mob farms and selling products. In a *skyblock* server, each player is given their own floating island. (There's a mini-game version of skyblock that is PvP-oriented and quite different.)

MINI-GAME SERVERS

Mini-game servers are another type of multiplayer server that are open to all. They host a number of mini-games (many of which take less than an hour to complete) you can join as a single player. You choose in a lobby area which mini-game to play, and once enough people have joined, you're teleported to the game area to play.

A fair number of mini-games are PvP-oriented, but many are not: in build games, you compete at making small builds that represent a given word or phrase. In parkour games, you must jump and run through a tricky obstacle course, and in spleef, you break the blocks (typically snow) beneath other players' feet to hopefully make them drop down into a fiery pit of lava. In a funny hide-and-seek game, you're given the option of several blocks to disguise yourself as, and then run to hide while seekers come to hunt you. Hypixel is an extremely popular mini-game server (https://hypixel.net).

WYNNCRAFT

The Wynncraft server is a very popular, long-standing, massively multiplayer role-playing game, open to all. Log on to complete quests and level up in a giant, impressive custom map with castles, towns, dungeons and more. You can find out more and play at https://play.wynncraft.com.

Join the Community

Whether you're interested in multiplayer, consider following or joining Minecraft communities to keep tabs on updates and see how other players have designed their worlds. Following a community can inspire you with new ideas for projects and creations in your own world.

Minecraft's official Twitter (@Minecraft) and YouTube (Minecraft) accounts can keep you up to date with the game; the developers often have streams to discuss events and upcoming game features. Many of the developers have Twitter accounts where they discuss ongoing projects and engage with the community.

YouTube has Minecraft videos from hundreds if not thousands of content creators. Many of these are tutorials, but a large segment are *Let's Plays*, which follow the creator as they play their way through Minecraft. I recommend following some of the creators who play on the server Hermitcraft (https://Hermitcraft.com), like EthosLab, impulseSV, Tango Tek, FalseSymmetry, Vintage Beef, PearlescentMoon, BdoubleO100, Keralis, and Grian.

Many YouTube Minecraft creators *stream* (play live) on Twitch (a streaming service at https://twitch.com) and most have their own communities with Discord (chat) servers and multiplayer servers you can join. Joining a creator's server often costs a monthly fee of about $10 paid through https://Patreon.com. Speak with your parent or guardian before joining one of these servers.

Hopefully this list of ways to play Minecraft and join communities has given you inspiration to continue learning about the immense world(s) of creation that Minecraft has to offer!

INDEX

A

abandoned villages, 27
aboveground structures, 95–102
Absorption, 48
accessibility settings, 266
activator rails, 208
advancements, 40–41
Adventure mode, 1
AI (artificial intelligence), 142
allay, 143, 144
allium, 48
amethyst crystal blocks, 73
amethyst geodes, 73, 224
amethyst shards, 73, 113–114, 135, 193
amplified worlds, 267
Anarchy (server), 276
ancient cities, 103
ancient debris, 223
andestine, 68, 115
animal farming, 54–56
animals, ix. *See also* specific animals
   in birch forest, 78
   in plains biome, 82
anvil, 140–141, 229, 231
apples, 44. *See also* golden apples
Aqua Affinity enchantment, 233
aquifers, 68, 72–73
armadillo, 143, 144–145
armor, 7
   diamonds and, 70
   displaying your, 134
   materials for, 128–129, 133
   repairing, 140–141
   types of, 133–136
armor bar, 7

armor enchantments, 233–234
armorer, 178
armor slots, 9, 133
attack indicator, 265
Attack Indicator setting, 265
Auto-jump, 4, 266
automatic iron door, 194
autosave indicator, 265
Avomance, 212
awkward potions, 242
axe, viii, 137
axolotls, 72, 143, 145
azalea tree/bushes, 91, 92
azure bluet, 48

B

baby villagers, 175–176
baby zombies, 171, 185
badges, of professional villager, 178
badlands, 77
Bad Omen effect, 108, 166, 186
Bad Omen Effect, 185
baked potato, 44, 46
bamboo, 81
Bane of Arthropods enchantment, 234
banner patterns, 182–183
banners, 124
basalt, 224
basalt deltas, in Nether, 214–215
bastion remnants, 220, 222–223
bats, 72, 143, 145
battle(s)/battle supplies, x, 137, 246–247, 250–251, 257
Bdouble0100, 277
beach biome, 77–78

beacons, 257–259
bed(s), 25
    crafting a, 20
    in the End, 250
    gathering wood and wool to make, 20
    for mining, 62
    in Nether, 214
    in villages, 27
beef, raw, 44
bees, 58–59, 154, 155–156
beetroot, 45, 50
beetroot soup, 43, 46
berries, 45
Biome Blend setting, 263
biomes, 75, 76–94
    cave, 68, 88–91
    End dimension, 244–245
    enlarging, 267
    land, 77–85
    mountainous, 86–88
    in Nether, 214–216
    ocean, 91–94
Biome Smoothing Lighting, 266
birch forest biome, 78
black dye, 119
blackstone, 224
Blast Protection enchantment, 233
blaze powder, 239, 241
blaze powders, 245
blaze rods, 216, 221, 245
blazes, 161, 163
blocks, breaking and placing, viii. See also specific blocks
blue dye, 120
blue ice, 93
blue orchid, 49
boats, ix, 140, 247
Bonus Chest, 268
booby traps, 98
book and quill, 118
bookshelf, chiseled, 122

bookshelves, 230
boots, dyeing, 135
bottle o' enchanting, 118
bow and arrow, 38, 129–130
bow enchantments, 235–236
branch mines, 62–63
Breach enchantment, 237
bread, 44
breaking blocks, viii
breeze rod, 241
breezes, 163
brewing potions. See potions
brewing stand, x, 97, 179, 238, 239, 242
bricks, 112. See also specific types of bricks
bridge (bastion type), 220, 222
bridges, 218, 219, 252
brightness setting, 4, 265
brown dye, 60, 119
brush, 138
bucket of milk. See milk, bucket of
bucket of water, 70–71, 139, 140, 147, 151, 211
buffs, 48
build(ing), ix
    an iron golem, 158
    a campfire, 47
    a roller coaster, 208
    a shelter, 30–37
    with stairs, 36
building blocks, types of, 112–114
buried treasure, 104
buried treasure map, 110, 111
butchers, 178–179
buttons, 191

C

cactus/cacti, 59, 77
cake, 45
calcite, 68
calibrated skulk sensor, 193
camels, 143, 145

campfire, building a, 47
candles, 122
carpets, 117
carrot on a stick, 138
carrots, 44, 46, 50
cartographer villager, 102, 109, 179
cartography table, 122, 179
cats, 143, 146, 175
cauldrons, 181, 239
cave openings, 65
caves/caving, 65–67, 88–91
    biomes, 67, 88–91
    Deep Dark caves, 88–90
    dripstone caves, 90–91
    finding your way in, 66
    lush caves, 91
    types of, 66–67
cave spiders, 105, 154, 156
cave spider spawners, 105, 106, 156
chainmail armor, 128, 135, 178
chains, 124
challenges
    automatic iron door, 194
    bartering with piglins, 223
    beating the Wither, 257
    bee wizadry, 59
    biome discovery, 94
    bow mastery, 130
    breeding a company of llamas, 159
    building a campfire, 47
    building an iron golem, 158
    building with stairs, 36
    build your own roller coaster, 208
    caving mastery, 73
    crafting two ender chests, 246
    crafting with the recipe book, 18
    creating a diamond armor, 234
    creating tunes, 202
    creating your own zoo, 151
    critical hits, 131
    crop mastery, 53
    curing a zombie villager, 97
    dyeing boots, 135
    finding a Nether fortress and bastion, 219
    fishing, 47
    flower finesse, 80
    four-way intersection, 206
    furnace upgrade, 201
    gathering blaze rods, 221
    horse breeding, 149
    husbandry expert, 57
    inventory management, 17
    lush foliage finesse, 92
    making a new village, 175
    making an infinite water source, 240
    map mastery, 125
    meet the phantoms, 26
    mending trades, 232
    mountaineering, 65
    ocean looting spree, 111
    record collector, 164
    riding a pig, 138
    sign skills, 127
    spawn slimes, 169
    suspicious stew, 50
    tree mastery, 85
    using TNT, 133
    village security, 184
    wool wizadry, 117
Channeling enchantment, 236
charcoal, 25
charged creepers, 76
chat box, 7
chat settings, 266
cheats on, 2, 269
cheese (connected) caves, 66
cherry groves, 86
chest minecart, 204, 207, 208
chestplates, 133, 134
chests
    about, 29–30

INDEX

furnace upgrade using, 201
   for sugar cane farm, 209
   to travel to the End, 246–247
   in village houses, 27
chicken, cooked, 43
chicken farm, 54–56
chicken, raw, 45
chickens, 21–22, 143, 146
chiseled bookshelf, 122
chiseled stone, 115
chorus fruit, 253
chorus plants, 253
chorus trees, 245
Chunk Builder setting, 264
classic farm, 51–53
clay, 71. *See also* terracotta
clay blocks, 112
clerics, 179
clocks, 118
   comparator clock, 196–199
   in the End, 250
   in Nether, 214
cloud layers, 75
clouds setting, 265, 266
coal, 22, 61, 62, 68
cobblestone, 32, 33, 37, 62, 68, 105, 201
cobwebs, 27, 241
cocoa beans, 60
cocoa pods, 81
cod, 143
   cooked, 44
   raw, 45
cold ocean, 93
commercial servers, 276
comparator, 195–196, 203
comparator clock, 196–199
compasses, 118–119
   in the End, 250
   in Nether, 214
concrete, 113
concrete powder, 113

conduit, 122–123
Conduit Power, 122–123
containers, 193
contraptions. *See* redstone contraptions
controls, 4, 11–12, 266
cookie(s), 45
cooking food, 46–47
copper, 22, 61
copper blocks, 58, 69, 113
copper bulb, 203
copper ingot, 69, 123, 135, 139, 193
copper ore, 69, 72, 91
coral reefs, 94
cornflower, 49
cows, 21–22, 146
cracked stone, 116
craft(ing), ix, 10
   a bed, 20
   a bow and arrow, 38
   a chicken farm, 54–56
   a crafting table, 14–17
   food, 43–46
   a golden apple, 48
   with the recipe book, 18
   stone tools, 18–19
   suspicious stew, 48–49
   wooden pickaxe, 17–18
crafter (crafting table), 203
crafting grid, 9, 17, 140
crafting output slot, 9
crafting recipes, 46
crafting table, ix, 14–15, 62, 203
Create New World, 4, 6, 266–267
Creative mode, 1, 274
creepers, 101–102, 161, 163–164
crimson fores, in Nether, 215
critical hit, 131
crop farming, 50–53
crossbow enchantments, 236
crossbows, 40, 130
crying obsidian, 99, 224, 227

INDEX

Curse of Binding enchantment, 233
Curse of Vanishing enchantment, 232
cursor, 7, 8
custom skins, 4, 261, 263, 270
cut copper, 113
cut stone, 116
cyan dye, 120

D

damage points, 154
dandelion, 49
dark forest biomes, 78
data packs, 268, 272–273
daylight sensor, 192
death
    digging and, 63
    of the Ender dragon, 250–251
    of player, xiii
debuffs, 48. See also potions
Debug screen, 13, 14, 61, 104, 169
decorated armor, 134–135
decorative blocks, 124–127
Deep Dark biome, 88–90
deepslate, 61, 67, 68, 115, 116
Density enchantment, 237
Depth Strider enchantment, 233
desert/desert biomes, 28, 59, 74, 79
deserted island, 28
desert pyramids, 79, 95–96
desert wells, 79, 96–97
detector rail, 208
diamond armor, 133
diamond pickaxe, 70
diamonds, 61, 70, 111
diamond trim, 135
difficulty levels, 2
diorite, 68, 115
dirt, 72
Discord, 277
dispenser, 98, 120, 198, 199
distortion effects setting, 265

dolphins, 154, 156
donkeys, 87, 143, 146–147
doors, 33, 37, 109, 194. See also trapdoors
double chest, 30, 201, 209, 239
dragon. See Ender Dragon
dragon egg, 251
dragon's breath, 250
dripleaf plants, 91, 92
dripstone caves, 68, 90–91
dropper, 200
drops
    hostile mobs, 161–163
    neutral mobs, 154–155
    passive mobs, 142, 143–144
the drowned, 110, 130, 161, 172, 236
dungeons, 105, 108
durability, 129
dye(s)/dyeing, 117, 119–120, 135

E

Easy difficulty, 2, 42–43, 154, 186
Efficiency enchantment, 237
eggs, 133
elder guardians, 109, 110, 114, 152, 161, 164
Elytra, xi, 75, 120, 252, 254, 255
emeralds, 39, 62, 70, 104, 111, 135, 153
emergency escapes, 26–27
enchanted golden apples, 48
enchant(s)/enchantments, x, 229–238
    armor, 233–234
    bow, 235–236
    crossbow, 236
    fishing rod, 238
    general, 232
    levels of, 231–232
    mace, 237
    sword, 234–235
    tool, 237–238
    trident, 236–237
    using an anvil, 231
    using an enchanting table, 230

enchanting table, 229, 230
End barrens, 245
End cities, 252, 253–254
end crystals, 251–252
End crystals, 250, 251–252
End dimension, 2, 75, 106, 165, 167, 244–259
    arriving in, 249–252
    biomes of, 244–245
    exploring outer islands of, 252–254
    preparing to travel to, 245–249
Ender chests, 246
Ender Dragon, 161, 165, 187, 244, 246, 250–252
Endermen, 155, 157, 214, 215, 216, 244, 245, 247, 252
endermites, 161, 165
Ender pearls, 246, 247, 252
End highlands, 245
End midlands, 245
End poem, 251
End stone islands, 244
enhanced potions, 239–240
entity distance setting, 265
entity shadows setting, 265
EthosLab, 277
evokers, 101–102, 161, 166, 170, 187
experience bar, 8
experience level, 7
experience points (XP), xii, xiii, 140, 141
extended potions, 239–240
Eyes of Ender, 245, 246, 249

F

Factions (server), 276
falling sand, 79
FalseSymmetry, 277
farm animals, 21, 57, 142
farmers, 180
farming
    animal, 54–56

cactus, 59
cocoa beans, 60
crop, 50–53
honey, 58–59
sugar cane, 58
trees, 57
vines, 60
Feather Falling boots, 247, 256
Feather Falling enchantment, 233
Feather Falling IV, 234, 247
fence(s), 36, 37, 54–55
fermented spider eye, 240, 241
Fire Aspect enchantment, 150, 234
fire charges, 132
Fire Protection enchantment, 233, 234
Fire Resistance potion, 48, 160, 240
firework rockets, 120, 130, 255
fireworks, 120
firework star, 120
first day
    goals of, 6–7
    saving your world spawn, 13–14
    tasks of, 14–26
fish(ing), 46, 47, 93–94, 147
fisherman, 173, 180
fishing rod, 47, 137
fishing rod enchantments, 238
Flame enchantment, 235
fletcher, 180
fletching table, 180
flint and steel, 138, 216, 218
flower garden, growing a, 80
flower pots, 125
flowers
    in birch forest, 78
    in forest biome, 80
    suspicious stew, 48–49
fly, learning to, 255–256
food
    cooking, 46–47
    fishing for, 47

INDEX

gold-encrusted, 48
hunger and, 42–43
neutral mobs, 154–155
of passive mobs, 143–144
sources/hunger value of, 43–46
suspicious stew, 48–50
toxic, 50
for your first day, 20–21
forest biome, 80
fortresses, Nether, 216, 219–220
Fortune enchantment, 238
fossils, 74
four-way intersection, 206
FOV (Field of View), 263
FOV Effects, 265
foxes, 87, 155, 157
froglights, 147
frogs, 84, 143, 147
front door, 33
Frost Walker enchantment, 233
frozen ocean, 93
frozen peaks, 86
frozen river biome, 82
full day, duration of, 6
Fullscreen Resolution, 263
fullscreen setting, 265
functional blocks, 122–124
functional items, 117–122
furnace upgrade, 201

G

Game Menu, 268–269
game mode
 about, 1–2
 choosing under Game tab, 267
 switching, 2, 269
game options, 4, 262–266
gameplay settings, 260–269
game rules, 268
Game Tab, 267
generated structures
 about, 95
 aboveground structures, 95–102
 underground structures, 102–109
 underwater structures, 109–111
ghasts, 161, 166, 214–215, 256
ghast tear, 239, 241, 251
gilded blackstone, 225
glass blocks, 59, 113–114, 209, 212, 239, 251, 257
glass bottles, 59, 239, 242, 247
glazed terracotta, 116
glistering melon, 180, 240, 241
glow berries, 45, 76, 91, 92
glow lichen, 72
glow squid, 72, 127, 143, 152
glowstone, 214, 216, 225, 227
glowstone dust, 120, 130, 225, 240, 242
goats, 86, 87, 155, 157–158
gold, 62, 70, 111, 128
gold bell, 175, 184, 187
golden apples, 48, 97, 172, 178, 246, 251
golden carrots, 48, 148, 180, 241, 246
golden desert rabbits, 79
gold ingots, 48, 70, 135, 160, 192, 207, 217, 223, 225
gold ore, 70, 77. *See also* Nether gold ore
granite, 68, 72, 115, 181
Graphics setting, 263
gravel, 38, 63, 72, 79. *See also* suspicious gravel
gray dye, 119
green dye, 59, 77, 120
green-robed villagers, 175
Grian, 277
grindstone, 140, 183–184, 231
groves, 87
guardians, 109, 110, 114, 152, 161, 165
GUI Scale, 264
gunpowder, 71, 120, 132, 243

H

hand, main, 9
Hardcore mode, 1, 187
Hard difficulty, 2, 8, 43, 154, 160
Harming potion, 171, 240, 243, 250, 256
Haste effect, 122, 257, 258
hay bales, 27, 46–47, 148, 155, 159
heads-up display (HUD), 7–9, 134, 148, 149
Healing potion, 240, 243, 257
health bar, 7, 8, 171, 256
heart of the sea, 123
Hermitcraft, 277
Hero of the Village status, 178, 187
hidey-hole, 24, 25, 30
hitbox, 7, 8
hoe, 137
hoglins, 161, 165–166, 213, 215, 220, 227
hoglin stables (bastion type), 220
honey, 58–59, 156
honey bottle, 43, 50
honeycomb, 58–59, 69, 113, 122, 127, 138
hopper minecarts, 204, 207, 208, 209, 212
hoppers, 200, 201, 209–210
horses, 136, 143, 147–149
hostile mobs, 2, 25, 26, 142, 161–172
    disabling, 274
    light level and, 76
    in woodland mansions, 101–102
hotbar/hotbar inventory, 7, 8, 9, 10, 17, 19, 224
housing unit (bastion type), 220
hunger bar/levels, xi, 2, 7, 8, 22, 42, 50
Hunger effects, 50, 172
hunger values, 43–46
husks, 79, 162, 171–172

I

ice spikes biome, 83
ice, types of, 93
icy area, 28

igloos, 83, 85, 96–97
Impaling enchantment, 236
impulseSV, 277
Infestation potion, 240
infested stone bricks, 68, 86, 168, 248
Infinity enchantment, 235
inhospitable starts, 28
ink sacs, 47, 118, 142, 152
Installations tab, 261
Instant Health potion, 256
intersection, four-way, 206
inventory management, 17
inventory screen, 9–10
inventory slot(s), 9, 10
Invisibility potion, 240
iron door, 194
iron golem, 27, 155, 158, 166, 175, 176, 185, 186
iron/iron ingots, 22, 32, 47, 50, 62, 69, 118, 124, 128, 135, 140, 158, 178, 181, 186, 192, 194, 200, 204, 205, 208, 231
iron ore, 69, 72
islands, of the End, 244
item frames, 125

J

Jack o'Lanterns, 123, 152, 158, 169
jagged peaks, 87
Java Editions, 260, 261, 270
job site block, 173, 174, 175, 176, 177
Johnny (name tag), 166
jukebox, 123
Jump Boost, 50, 259
jump control, 11
jump-sprint control, 11
jungle biome, 81
jungle pyramid, 97–98
junk (fishing), 47

K

kelp, dried, 46

Keralis, 277
Knockback, 230, 235, 237

L

lagging responses, 266
land biomes, 77–85
language, 266
LANs (local area networks), 269
lanterns, 32, 37, 228
lapis lazuli, 62, 69, 135, 136, 229, 230
large biomes, 267
launcher screen, 3, 260–261
lava, 62, 63, 64, 68, 70, 213, 246
lava bucket, 133, 223
leads, 139
leaf blocks, 15
Leaping potion, 151, 241
leather boots/armor, 87–88, 135
leatherworker, 181
lecterns, 181, 203
leggings, 103, 133, 134
Let's Plays, 277
levers, 189, 191
Levitation effect, 167
librarians, 178, 181, 232
light, 66, 76
light blue dye, 120
light gray dye, 119
lightning, 76, 237
lightning rod, 123, 193
lily of the valley, 49
lily pads, 84
lime dye, 119
lingering potions, 130, 243
llamas, 39, 155, 158–159
lodestone, 225
LogicalGeekBoy, 212
loom, 182
loot(ing), x, 95, 96, 104, 108, 110, 111, 222, 254
loot chests, 97, 98–99, 100, 101, 105, 220

Looting enchantment, 235
Loyalty enchantment, 236
Luck of the Sea enchantment, 238
lukewarm ocean, 93
luminescent end rods, 253
Lure enchantment, 238
lush caves, 68, 91, 92

M

mace, 131–132
mace enchantments, 237
magenta dye, 120
magma blocks, 73, 92, 99, 110
magma cream, 240, 241
magma cubes, 147, 162, 166, 214, 222
main hand, 9
main inventory, 9
main menu, 4, 5
mangrove swamp, 84
map mastery challenge, 125
maps, 104, 121–122, 179, 214
masons, 181–182
Max Framerate, 264
meadows, 87
meat, 22, 23, 25
melon farm, 53
melons, 81
melon slice, 45
Mending books, 232
Mending enchantment, 232
Microsoft account, 260
milk, bucket of, 50, 59, 105, 110, 153, 185, 257
milk, from cows, 57, 146
milk, from goats, 157
minecarts, 105, 204–205, 206, 207, 208
Minecraft community, 277
Minecraft launcher screen, 3
Minecraft Live, xiii
Miners Need Cool Shoes, 270
mineshafts, 105–106

mines/mining
   nighttime, 25
   ore levels, 61–62
   resources in, 67–72
   rules for, 63
   setting up a branch, 62–65
   stone, 18–20
mini-game servers, 276–277
mining, 61–65
Mining Fatigue, 110
Mipmap Levels, 265, 266
mob farms, 105, 114
mob heads, 125–126
mobs, vii
   categories of, 142
   ocean monument and, 109
   on ravine walls, 65–66
   starter house, 37
   thunderstorms/lightning and, 76
   transporting with rails and minecarts, 204–208
   in trial chambers, 108
mob spawner block, 105
modded Minecraft, 274–275
modding community, xiii
Mojang, xiii
monsters, xii, 25–26, 105
moon, 76
mooshroom, 81, 143, 149
More Tab, 268
moss/moss blocks, 91, 92, 152
mossy stone bricks/cobblestone, 60, 105, 115
mountaineering, 65
mountainous biomes, 86–88
mountain peaks biome, 86–87
mud blocks, 84–85
mud bricks, 84
mules, 143, 147, 150
Multiplayer, 261, 275–277
Multishot (crossbow enchantment), 236

mushroom field shore, 81
mushrooms/mushroom fields biome, 78, 81–82, 215. *See also* mooshroom
mushroom stew, 44, 46, 48, 217
music, adjusting volume of, 263
musical notes, 202–203
music discs, 103, 123, 164
music settings, 263
mutton, cooked, 43
mutton, raw, 45
mycelium, 81

N

name tags, 141, 161
Nausea effects, 50
Nether, 2, 75, 99, 213–228
   biomes of, 214–216
   entering, 216–218
   landscape of, 213
   resources and blocks in, 223–228
   supplies to bring to, 217
   unique characteristics of, 213–214
Nether fortresses, 216, 219–220
Nether gold ore, 159, 214, 225
netherite, 223–224
netherite armor, 70, 246
netherite ingots, 135, 183, 223–224
Nether portals, 216–218
Nether quartz, 135, 181, 196, 201, 214, 216, 226
netherrack, 99
Netherrack, 226
Nether stars, 255, 256, 257
Nether wart, 179, 215, 216, 220, 226, 239, 242
Nether wart blocks, 226
Nether wastes biome, 214
neutral mobs, 142, 154–161
new world, creating a, 266–267
nighttime, xii, 24–26
Night Vision effect, 122–123
Night Vision potion, 241

nitwits, 175, 176
noodle caves, 66
Normal difficulty, 2, 42, 186
note blocks, 144, 202–203
notifications, 263. *See also* advancements
nylium, 215–216, 226–227

O
oak trees, 83
observers, 201, 209, 212
obsidian, 70–71, 99, 216
ocean monument, 109–110
ocean/ocean biomes, 28, 75, 91–94
ocean ruins, 110
ocelots, 81, 143, 150, 164
off hand, 9, 187
old-growth giant spruce taiga, 85
old-growth pine taiga, 85
Online setting, 263
Oozing potion, 241
open world, vii
Open World Folder, 273
open world, meaning of, vii
Options, 4, 262–266
orange dye, 119
ores, 61–62
ore veins, 72
Outer End Island, 252
Overworld, 75, 126
   cave biomes, 88–91
   generated structures in. *See* generated structures
   land biomes, 77–85
   mobs in. *See* mobs
   mountainous biomes, 86–88
   ocean biomes, 91–94
   villagers of. *See* villagers
   villages of. *See* villages
Overworld portal, 217
oxeye daisy, 49
oxygen level/bar, 7, 8, 28

P
packed ice, 93
paintings, 126
pandas, 81, 155, 159
parrots, 81, 143, 150
particles setting, 265
passive mobs, 142–153
Peaceful difficulty, 2
PearlescentMoon, 277
phantom membrane, 241
phantoms, 26, 162, 166–167
pickaxe, viii, 136–137
   crafting a wooden, 17–18
   diamond, 70
   iron, 69
   materials, 136–137
   for mining, 67–68
   stone, 69
Piercing (crossbow enchantment), 236
piglin brutes, 162, 167, 222–223
piglins, 155, 159–160, 214
   bartering with, 223
   looting chests and, 222
   in Nether, 215, 222
pigs, 21, 139, 143, 150
pillager outposts, 21, 82, 83, 85, 86, 98–99
pillager patrols, 40
pillager raids, 185–186
pillagers, 21, 162
pillar up, 26–27
pink dye, 120
pistons, 200, 209, 211–212
plains, 31, 82
planks, 15–16, 17–18, 32–33, 116
player-made servers, 275
Play tab, 4
Poison effects, 50, 59
poisonous potatoes, 50
Poison potion, 154, 171, 241
polar bear, 155, 160
polished stone, 115

INDEX

popped chorus fruit, 253
poppy, 49
popularity raking, in villages, 176
porkchop, cooked, 43
porkchop, raw, 44
portal room, End, 249
portals
   the End, 245
   exit, after defeating the Ender dragon, 251
   gateway, on the outer end islands, 252
   loosing your exit, 269
   Nether, 216–218
   outer island gateway, 252
   Overworld, 217
   ruined, 99–100, 216
   solutions to lost and damaged, 218
potatoes, 46, 50
potions, x, 216, 238–243
   brewing process for, 242–243
   to bring to the End, 247
   enhancing or extending, 242
   ingredients, 240–241
   levels of, 239–240
   supplies for making, 238–239
potion stand, 97
powder snow, 87–88
Power bow, 246
powered rails, 207, 209, 210
Power enchantment, 235
pressure plates, 191–192
prismarine, 114, 123
Prison (server), 276
professional villagers, 175
professions, villager, 178–184
Projectile Protection enchantment, 233
propagules, 84
Protection enchantment, 233
Protection IV diamond, 246
pufferfish, 50, 143, 241
pumpkin farm, 53

pumpkin pie, 43
pumpkins, 83, 247
Punch enchantment, 236
purple dye, 120
purpur blocks, 253

Q

quartz, 226. *See also* Nether quartz
Quick Charge (crossbow enchantment), 236

R

rabbit, cooked, 44
rabbit foot, 151
rabbit hide, 151
rabbit, raw, 44
rabbits, 87, 144, 150–151
rabbit's foot, 241
rabbit stew, 43, 46
raids, 185–187
rails, 205–208, 209
rain(ing), 47
ravager, 162, 167, 186
ravines, 23, 65
raw meat, 22, 23, 25, 44, 45
raw porkchops, 150
Realms, 275
recipe book, 9
Recipe book, 10
recovery compass, 103
red dye, 119
red Nether bricks, 219, 226
red sandstone, 77, 115, 116
redstone, xi, 62, 69, 103. *See also* minecarts
   basics of, 188–190
   devices, 199–203
   power components, 190–193
   transmission components, 195–196
   tutorial creators, 212
redstone block, 191
redstone contraptions, 188, 189, 203
   automatic iron door, 194

INDEX

simple comparator clock, 196–199
   three parts of, 189
   trip wire, 98
redstone devices, 199–203
redstone dust, 69, 135, 195
   brewing with, 240, 242
   note blocks crafted from, 202–203
   observer crafted from, 201
   for simple comparator clock, 196–199
   for sugar cane farm, 209
redstone ticks, 189, 203
redstone torch, 189–190, 196
Regeneration, 48
Regeneration potion, 241, 257
Render Distance, 264, 266
repeater, 195
Resistance, 48
resource packs, 266, 271–272
resources
   for caving, 65
   in mines and caves, 67–72
   for mining, 62
   in Nether, 223–228
   for starter home, 31–32
   storage for, 29–30
resources, gathering, 20–24
respawn anchor, 227
respawning, xiii, 38–39
   the Ender dragon, 251–252
   if you die in the End, 247
Respiration enchantment, 234
Riptide enchantment, 237
river biome, 82
Roleplay (server), 276
roller coaster, 208
rotten flesh, 50, 161
ruined portals, 99–100, 216
rules, for mining, 63

S

saddles, 139, 148
salmon, 43, 45, 144
sand, 63, 71, 79
sandbox game, Minecraft as a, vii
sandstone, 71, 79, 115, 116
saturation points, 42
savanna biome, 82–83
scaffolding, 124
screaming goats, 157–158
screenshots, of spawn location, 13–14
sculk blocks, 88
sculk catalysts, 90
sculk sensors, 89, 193
sculk shriekers, 89–90
sculk veins, 88
sea lanterns, 110, 112, 123
Select World screen, 4, 6, 273
servers, 261, 275–277
settings, 4
shapeless recipes, 15
Sharpness enchantment, 234, 235
Sharpness sword, 246
shears, 138
sheep, 20, 21–22, 87, 144, 151
shelter, building a, 30–37
shepherds, 182–183
shield, 131
shipwrecks, 23, 111
shovel, 71, 137
shroomlights, 215
shulker box, 167, 254
shulkers, 162, 167, 245, 254
signs, 126–127
Silk Touch, 73, 114
Silk Touch-enchanted pickaxe, 225, 226
Silk Touch enchantment, 237–238
silverfish, 68, 162, 168
simple comparator clock, 196
Simulation Distance setting, 264
Single Biome, 268
Singleplayer, 4, 261
skeletons, 2, 80, 101–102, 162, 164, 168, 215

INDEX

skeleton skulls, Wither, 256
skeleton trap horse, 168
skin customization. *See* custom skins
Skin Customization setting, 263
The Skindex, 270
skins, 3, 270
Skins tab, 4, 261
Skyblock/Economy (server), 276
slabs, 114–116
sleep(ing), xii, 24–25
slimeballs, 169
slime block, 241
slime chunks, 169
slime mobs, 83–84, 162, 168
slimes, 168, 169
Slow Falling potion, 241
Slowness IV effect, 234
Slowness potion, 130, 154, 171, 241
Smite enchantment, 234
smithing table, 135, 183
smithing templates, 134, 135
smooth basalt, 68
Smooth Lighting setting, 264, 266
smooth stone, 115
sneak control, 11
sniffer, 144, 151–152
snifflet, 152
snowballs, 133
snow golem, 144, 152
snowy area, 28
snowy beach, 78
snowy plains biome, 83
snowy slopes biome, 87
snowy taiga biome, 85
soul lantern, 228
soul sand, 227
soul sand valley, in Nether, 215
soul soil, 227–228
Soul Speed enchantment, 234
sounds, adjusting volume of, 263
sound settings, 263

spaghetti caves, 66
spawn(s) and spawning. *See also* respawning; world spawn
    hostile mobs, 161–163
    neutral mobs, 154–155
    passive mobs, 143–144
    slimes, 169
    into your world, 6–7
spawn location, recording, 13–14
specialty armor, 135
Spectator mode, 1–2
spectral arrows, 130
spider eyes, 50, 241
spider jockey, 168
spiders, xii, 2, 155, 160
splash potions, 132, 243
sponge blocks, 109
sprint control, 11
sprint knockback, 129
spyglass, 139
squid, 144, 152
stable, 149
stairs/staircases, 34, 36, 62–64, 114, 115
starter home, 30–37
status effects, 48–49, 50
steak, 43
steel. *See* flint and steel
stews, 46
sticky pistons, 200
stone
    infested, 68
    mining, 18–20, 68
    for a shelter, 30
    starter home built with, 32–35
    types of, 115–116
    for weapons, armor, and tools, 128
stonecutter, 181–182
stone pickaxe, 17, 69
stone pressure plates, 191
stone shore biome, 77–78
stone tools, 18–20

INDEX

stony peaks biome, 87–88
storage, 29–31
storage chests, 239
stray, 162
streaming service, 277
Strength potion, 241, 257
strider, 144, 153
stripped log blocks, 117
stripped wood blocks, 117
strongholds, 106, 247–249
subtitles, 7, 8, 263
sugar cane, 23, 58, 84
sugar cane farm, 209–212
sun, 76
Superflat world, 267
Survival Mode, 1
suspicious gravel, 106–107, 134, 138
suspicious stew, 48–50
swamp hut, 100
swampland biome, 83–85
sweeping attack, 129
Sweeping Edge enchantment, 235
sweet berries, 45
Swift Sneak, 103
Switfness potion, 241
sword enchantments, 234–235
swords, 21, 129

T

taiga biome, 85
Tango Tek, 277
target block, 203
terracotta, 77, 116
texture (resource) packs, 271–272
Thorns enchantment, 234
thunderstorms, 76, 168
tipped arrows, 130, 243
title screen, 261
TNT, 95, 110, 132, 133
TNT minecart, 205, 208
tool enchantments, 237–238

tools
    materials for, 128–129
    repairing, 140–141
    stone, 18–19
    types of, 136–140
    using, 12
toolsmith, 183
torches, 22, 24, 32, 37
    caving and, 66
    for mining, 63
    redstone, 190–191
Towny (server), 276
toxic food, 50
trade/trading, x, 177–184, 232
trail ruins, 106–107
trapdoors, 164, 186, 247, 252
trapped chest, 192
traps, 98, 186
treasure (fishing), 47
treasure chest, 111, 156, 222
treasure room (bastion type), 222
tree mastery challenge, 85
trees
    in birch forest, 78
    in cherry groves, 86
    chopping down on first day, 22
    in dark forest, 78
    on deserted island, 28
    farming, 57
    in forest biome, 80
    leaving half-broken, 15
    mangrove, in mangrove swamp, 84
    pillar up next to a, 27
    punching, 15
    in swampland biome, 83–84
    in taiga biome, 85
    wood and, 116
trial chambers, 107–109
Trial Omen effect, 108
trial spawners, 108
trident enchantments, 236–237

tridents, 130
trim, for armor, 134–135
trip wire hook, 98, 192
tropical fish, 46, 93, 94, 144, 147
tuff, 68, 72, 108
tulip, 49
tunes, creating, 202
turtle, 144, 153
Turtle Master potion, 241
turtle shell helmet, 135
Twitch, 277
Twitter, 277

U

Unbreaking enchantment, 232, 237
underground features, 72–74
underground lakes, 72–73
underground structures, 102–109
underwater
    armor enhancements and, 233, 234
        conduit placed, 122–123
        Hunger Bar, 7
underwater structures, 109–111
unemployed villagers, 175, 176
user interface, 7–9
utility mob, 152

V

Vanishing, Curse of, 232
vexes, 162, 170, 187
Video Settings, 4, 263–264
View Bobbing, 264
villagers, 166
    curing a zombified, 178
    daily schedules, 176
    four main types of, 175
    mating, 176
    professions of, 178–184
    trading with, 177–178
    types of, 101–102

villages
    abandoned, 27
    about, 21, 100–101
    under attack, 185–187
    looting, 27
    making a new, 175
    popularity ranking in, 176
    residents of, 175–176
    security of, 184
    size of, 174
    structures of, 173–174
vindicators, 101–102, 162, 166, 186
vines, 60, 81, 83, 91, 92, 138
Vintage Beef, 277
Void, 75, 245
Vsync setting, 264

W

walk control, 11
wandering traders, x, 39–40, 144, 153, 166
wardens, 88, 90, 103, 162, 170
warm oceans, 94
Warped Forest, in Nether, 215–216, 245
warped fungus on a stick, 153
WASD keys, 11, 28, 148
water, 96, 213. *See also* bucket of water
Water Breathing, 123, 241, 242
water bucket, 52, 247. *See also* bucket of water
waterlogged caves, 72–73
water source, for brewing, 239
Weakness potion, 97, 130, 171, 172, 178, 179, 241
weapons, 12
    to battle the Ender Dragon, 246
    materials for, 128–129
    repairing, 140–141
    types of, 129–133
    using, 12
weaponsmith, 183–184

INDEX

weather, 76, 213
Weaving potion, 241
weighted pressure plates, 192
wheat, 27, 44, 45, 50, 143, 144, 155
white dye, 119
Wind Burst enchantment, 237
Wind charged potion, 241
windows, 36
windswept forest, 88
windswept hills, 88
windswept savanna, 83
witches, 76, 100, 162, 171
witch huts, 84, 100
Wither II effect, 256
wither rose, 49, 119, 256
wither skeletons, 126, 162, 167, 171, 219, 220, 255, 256
wither skeleton skulls, 256, 257
Wither, the, 2, 162, 171, 187, 256–257
wolf armor, 136
wolves, 80, 85, 87, 151, 155, 160–161
wood, 116–117
    gathering, 14–15
    growing trees for, 57
    making a bed with, 20
    for mining, 62
    for a shelter, 30
    for weapons, armor, and tools, 128
wood blocks, 117
wooden pickaxe, 17–18
woodland mansions, 78, 95, 101–102, 166

wood pressure plates, 191–192
wool, 20, 89, 117, 138, 166, 182
world spawn, xiii
    first-day tasks in, 14–26
    inhospitable starts in, 28
    protecting area of, 38–39
    saving your, 13–14
    setting up, 2–6
    spawning into your, 6–7
World tab, 267
World Types, 267
Wynncraft server, 277

X

xisumavoid (YouTuber), 273
XP levels, 229, 230

Y

yellow dye, 119
YouTube, 277

Z

zoglins, 163, 166
Zombie Doctor, 97
zombies, xii, 2, 125, 153, 163, 171–172. *See also* baby zombies
zombie sieges, 185
zombie villagers, 2, 27, 97, 163, 172, 176, 178
zombified piglins, 76, 150, 155, 160, 214, 215, 219
zoo, creating a, 151

ALSO AVAILABLE FROM MEGAN MILLER

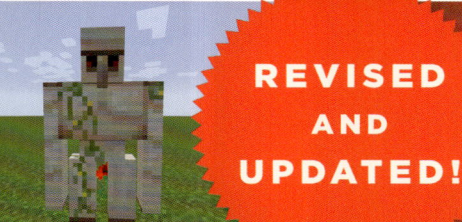

REVISED AND UPDATED!

The Ultimate Unofficial
ENCYCLOPEDIA
FOR
MINECRAFTERS

AN A–Z BOOK OF TIPS AND TRICKS THE OFFICIAL GUIDES DON'T TEACH YOU

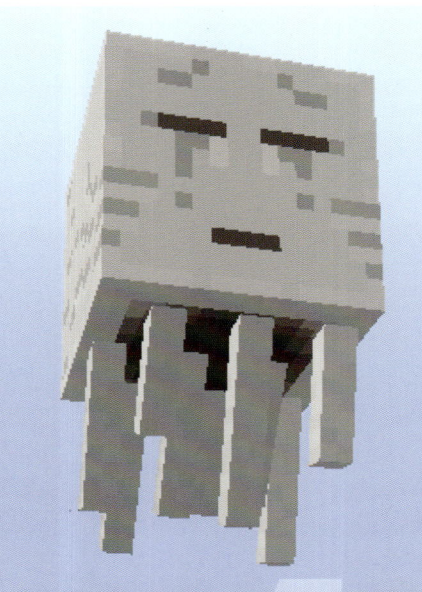

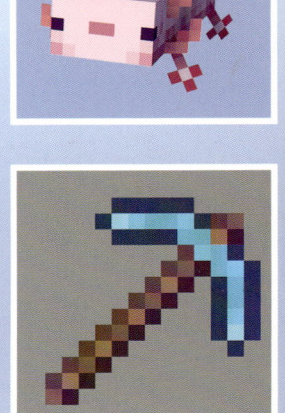

MEGAN MILLER

NEW YORK TIMES BESTSELLING AUTHOR